Smallmouth Fly Fishing

The Best Techniques, Flies, and Destinations

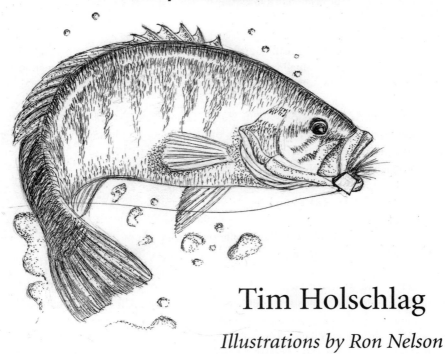

Tim Holschlag

Illustrations by Ron Nelson

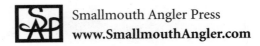
Smallmouth Angler Press
www.SmallmouthAngler.com

*To all who share a passion
for the mighty smallie.
May your casts land true
and each fishing day be
better than the last.*

Illustrations by Ron Nelson, at Nelson Wildlife Studio (nelsonwildlife.com)
Front cover and internal design and composition by Dorie McClelland at Spring Book Design (springbookdesign.com), and Lyn Verthein
Back cover design by Image Design 1 (info@imagedn1.com)
All photos by Tim Holschlag, Lyn Verthein, and Bruce Ingram
Cover photo: Tim Holschlag with a 20-incher

To order copies of this book, and other smallmouth fishing products, please visit us online at www.**SmallmouthAngler.com**

ATTENTION CLUBS AND SHOPS:
Quantity discounts are available on bulk purchases of this book for educational use, gifts, or premiums for increasing club memberships, magazine subscriptions, etc. Special books or book excerpts can also be created to fit specific needs. For information please contact Smallmouth Angler, 2309 Grand St. NE, Minneapolis, MN 55418, phone 612-781-3912

ISBN-13: 978-0-9763876-0-2
ISBN-10: 0-9763876-0-3
LCCN 2005906923
Manufactured in the United States of America
11 10 09 08 07   2 3 4 5 6 7 8
First Edition
Second printing, 2007

Praise for *Smallmouth Fly Fishing*

(a sample of nearly 200 endorsements so far . . .)

"Tim Holschlag is a renowned smallmouth angler, and this is one of the most comprehensive books on fly-fishing for smallmouth to come out in some time."
—*Fly Fisherman* magazine

"This thick volume is crammed full of information on every aspect of fishing for smallmouths. Even if you've been chasing these fish for decades, Holschlag provides enough new information to make your fishing much more successful and rewarding."
—*American Angler* magazine

"A fine and complete book, loaded with practical info fly rodders need to chase my favorite fish, the smallmouth."—Lefty Kreh

"Key to the content of this book is Holschlag's vast experience with smallmouth bass. He has explored waters all over the United States and has fished more than 250 streams and 100 lakes."
—*Eastern Fly Fishing* magazine

"A must-read for every angler in pursuit of smallmouth." —Ron Schara, 'Backroads' Host, The Outdoor Life Network

"Cutting-edge presentations. How to catch smallies in any size water. Targeting big bronzebacks. It's all here, brilliantly written in a 'no nonsense' fashion."
—Ed Story, *Feather-Craft Fly Fishing*

"Nobody knows smallmouth bass like Tim Holschlag. Tim turns the sport of fly fishing for smallies inside out and enables the reader to fish smart and understand the biology and behavior of the species."
—Tom Helgeson, editor, *Midwest Fly Fishing*

"Mr. Smallmouth's latest treatise, *Smallmouth Fly Fishing*, is a hit! "Tim Holschlag's immense on-the-water knowledge comes through time and again on these pages. . . . Anyone with even a smidgen of interest in pursuing smallmouth bass on the fly rod should buy and thoroughly read this book."
—*Bronzeback News*

"Holschlag's smallmouth passion has inspired him to write books. The new book is devoted to the art of fly fishing for smallies, and he expertly covers the topics, ranging from the right gear to the right fly to the right place."
—*Minneapolis Star Tribune*

"Successful strategies—smallmouth bass fishing guru Tim Holschlag spells them out in his new book, *Smallmouth Fly Fishing*."—Dave Carlson, host of "Northland Adventures"

"Tim 'Mr. Smallmouth' Holschlag takes only fishing vacations, and he just returned from fishing six rivers in five days, catching 17-inch-plus smallmouth in every river. *Smallmouth Fly Fishing* is filled with this same passion for smallmouth and his secrets for catching them."
—*St. Paul Pioneer Press*

"Tim Holschlag knows bronzebacks better than anyone. The real value of this book is the tips and tricks that Holschlag shares. And then there are the flies, all proven producers and some of the very best around. *Smallmouth Fly Fishing* really is three books in one, and will make you one with the smallmouth."
—Fisherman's Corner, Hunt the North.com

More Praise for *Smallmouth Fly Fishing*

"*Smallmouth Fly Fishing* should be required reading for any smallmouth enthusiast. It is the standard I will be grading other fishing books on for quite some time."
—Steve Winters, President,
Wisconsin Smallmouth Alliance

"Really three volumes packed into one convenient package, with modern and innovative techniques. No doubt about it, a very helpful book for fly-fishers of all levels of experience. I especially liked the guidance on how to hook up with a porkster bronze-back." —Troy Winebarger,
Georgia River Fishing.com

"*Smallmouth Fly Fishing* covers 40 years of pursuing smallies. I've re-read some chapters three times."
—Steve White, president,
Missouri Smallmouth Alliance

"A Masterpiece!! What a tremendous accomplishment, just fantastic!"
—Pikemasters, Inc.

"I love the book. Truly a terrific work, with countless bits of information I had never thought about."
—Larry Gavin, *Midwest Fly Fishing*

"The definitive book on smallies, *Smallmouth Fly Fishing.*"
—Bob Mitchell's Fly Shop

"Holschlag's fly selection is innovative and you can tell by his choices that he is a fisherman, not just a fly tyer. . . . The Crayfish Hop technique alone will really increase the number of bass caught during a day. . . This is a book every bass angler should have."
—Forth Worth Fly Fishers

"A great read, with lots of good information."
—Twin Tiers Fly Club, Corning, NY

"Absolutely fabulous, the best small-mouth fly book to date."
—Bob Long Jr.,
Fishing instructor
for the City of Chicago

"Your new book is great! You really covered everything."
—Brian Shumaker,
Susquehanna River Guides, PA

"The most complete book on small-mouth bass fishing I've ever read."
—Bob Geibe, Master fly tier, Lititz, PA

"The Destinations section alone is worth the price of the book."
—Tom Bentley, Huntington, WV

"I found a wealth of general information about smallmouth fishing that's extremely helpful no matter what kind of tackle you use."
—Brad Albin, Nashville, TN

"Very comprehensive but at the same time easy to follow. I have been a fly fisherman for 40 years, and am enjoying the book immensely. The section on flies makes the book for me a good buy."
—Richard Mallard, Bloomington, IN

"I loved this book. It has it all! The tremendous color photos are worth the price of the book alone."
—Jim Bennett, River Falls, WI

"*Smallmouth Fly Fishing* sets a new standard for warmwater fly fishing books."
—Craig Reindeau, Cumming, GA

"*Smallmouth Fly Fishing* is qualitatively different than all other bass books, it's so much better."
—David Brameld, Leavenworth, WA

(Continued in the back of the book)

Contents

Part I
Smallmouth Fly Fishing Techniques

Part II

Flies for Smallmouth

Part III

100 Top Smallmouth Destinations

List of Instructional Visuals

Acknowledgments

In a sense I've been working on this book for 40 years, because *Smallmouth Fly Fishing* is an encapsulation of over 4 decades of learning about and pursuing small-mouth. Over that time, countless people have contributed to my knowledge of the species.

I would like to acknowledge the hundreds of anglers I've guided over the years. Getting so many people with varying skill levels to catch smallies is truly the best laboratory to test what techniques work (or don't). Those who have taken my Smallmouth Schools and attended my seminars also deserve a big "thank you." Addressing anglers' questions and problems, and seeing what teaching methods work best has been very helpful.

There are also dozens of warmwater fly tiers who have directly or indirectly contributed to this book. Creative and generous folks from all parts of the continent have sent me new patterns, offered tying tips, and shared their ideas and thoughts on fly design. A special thanks goes to two good friends, Dan Johnson and Jay Bunke. As the primary tiers for Smallmouth Angler.Com, they are valued sources of ideas on fly development and design.

I'm also grateful to the many smallmouth fans thought North America who have shared their local waters with me, in my travels doing book research, on assignment for magazines or just fishing for fun. And the dozens of Smallmouth Alliance members I've come to know over the years are hard-working conservationists and skilled anglers from whom I have learned much.

Numerous fisheries professionals from many different state, federal or provincial agencies have also helped me immeasurably over the years. I've had a long-standing interest in aquatic biology, and sincerely appreciate the dozens of smallmouth-savvy fishery department managers and research biologists who have shared their data and insights with me.

My fellow outdoor writers who write about smallmouth have been another important source for this book. A number of them have directly contributed with photos, flies and destination information. Greg Breining's input and editing assistance has been especially helpful.

Finally, I want to acknowledge artist and illustrator Ron Nelson for his excellent drawings throughout this book. And most of all my wife, Lyn, my co-pilot in steering this prodigious project to completion.

Please see the "List of Contributors" in Appendix B for other individuals who have contributed to this book.

Introduction

After over 4 decades of smallmouth angling and nearly 20 years as a fishing writer, I finally decided to put everything I've learned about smallmouth fly fishing into one big book. Of course, I quickly realized it would take several volumes to tell everything, so I've tried to distill it down to just the most pertinent information, yet still cover every aspect of this multifaceted sport.

This new book is designed to be the place to go for up-to-date, scientifically based information on any and all smallmouth issues. There are 15 chapters of how-to material covering rivers and lakes, on-foot and watercraft fishing. Following that, Part 2 is an entire section devoted to fly patterns for smallmouth, featuring 40 favorite flies, plus chapters on how to create, judge and classify smallmouth flies. And Part 3 contains descriptions of 100 premier smallmouth fly fishing destinations spread across the entire continent.

An awful lot in just one book, to be sure, but why such a big effort? In the past decade, there has been a veritable explosion of interest in fly fishing for smallies. Trout anglers, spin anglers taking up fly fishing, even those brand-new to fishing—all these and many other folks are increasingly interested in smallmouth on the fly. However, a single source of solid information has been lacking. There have been a few other books written in the past dozen years covering some of the same topics, but these are either outdated or have a narrow, parochial focus. And previous smallmouth fly fishing books (or generic "bass" books) generally didn't have sound biological underpinnings like the strong scientific background many trout books incorporate.

There is a vast amount to know and learn about smallmouth fly fishing, and more being discovered every day. I've tried to include as much of this wealth of information as possible in one volume. But don't assume this is some dry academic treatise. As a longtime magazine writer, seminar speaker, on-the-water instructor and guide, I know how important it is to impart knowledge in a clear and lively way. The book's numerous illustrations, photos, charts and smaller subsections help make the material easy to digest.

I also hope this book transmits some of the special appeal that smallies on the fly rod have for me. Fishing is so much more than just catching fish, and angling for bronzebacks is immensely enjoyable on many different levels. Difficult as it is to share this experience on paper, I've tried, in both the text and numerous photos, to capture the beauty and allure of smallmouth fishing.

Tim Holschlag

About the Author

Tim Holschlag's 1990 book, *Stream Smallmouth Fishing,* was widely acclaimed as the classic work on small water smallmouthing. A big reason for the book's popularity is the depth of experience that Tim draws from. He's been pursuing smallies for over 40 years, and has explored and fished more smallmouth water than virtually any other angler—250 different smallmouth streams and well over 100 lakes.

For the past 20 years, Holschlag's lifelong passion has also been his occupation. A full-time writer, guide and angling instructor, he has authored hundreds of magazine articles for publications such as *American Angler, Eastern Fly Fishing, Midwest Fly Fishing, Fly Fishing Quarterly* and *Bassmaster.* He guides for smallmouth on numerous Upper Midwest rivers, streams, and lakes. Every summer his popular Stream Smallmouth Schools teach a wide assortment of anglers the finer points of the sport.

During the winter seminar season, Tim Holschlag is a popular speaker, bringing his passion and expertise to many more smallmouth fans. He also designs and markets a line of innovative and effective smallmouth flies. An active smallmouth conservationist, Holschlag is also the co-founder of The Smallmouth Alliance and has received the Federation of Fly Fishers national Henshall award for warmwater conservation.

To contact Tim Holschlag, to read his current writings, or for more information on his books, speaking, schools, trips, flies, and other smallmouth-related products go to Smallmouth Angler.com.

Part I

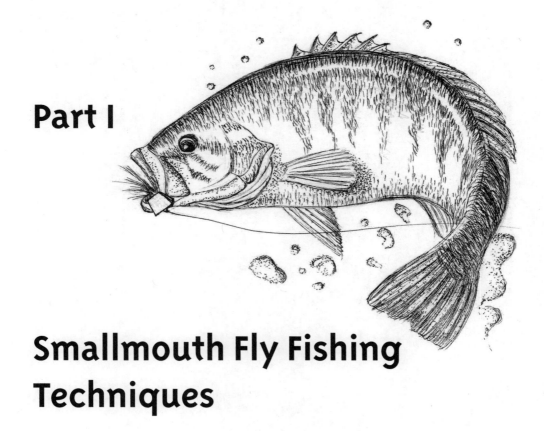

Smallmouth Fly Fishing Techniques

Scenic uncrowded waters, shallow hard-fighting fish! Tim Holschlag displays why he's passionate about smallmouth.

1

Why Smallmouth Fly Fishing?

Four decades separate me from that first smallmouth. I was only ten, and the fish barely 10 inches, but it's still a vivid image. So bold and powerful, yet so beautifully colored and proportioned. Life since then has brought many challenges and adventures but, surprisingly, catching that little fish was one of the milestones. It has led me down hundreds of streams, along countless miles of lake shore—to so many great places, over so much time—always and everywhere seeking smallmouth.

A lifelong passion for *Micropterus dolomieui* is one of the easier obsessions to explain. After all, this fish has a heck of a lot going for it. That little ten-incher pulled plenty, and when I started catching 15-inch beauties I was stunned. Such spectacular jumps, such incredible power and stamina. Thousands of smallies later, I'm still impressed.

Barreling downstream, then just as quickly upriver, staging a spectacular leap, then another, followed by more finger-burning runs back and forth across the flow. Classic smallmouth battles like this thrill and excite me like few other occurrences in the piscatory world. Sure, trout and largemouth bass can put a nice bend in the rod, but the never-give-up smallmouth will pull a comparable-sized bigmouth or brown inside-out.

Of course, I'm not the only guy to be awed by the smallmouth's amazing power. Well over a century ago, a core of American fly fishers were already singing the praises of "small mouthed bass" or "black bass," as they called them. The legendary 19th-century angler, James Henshall, lauded the species' sporting characteristics in his famous *Book of the Black Bass.* "Inch for inch and pound for pound, the gamest fish that swims," Dr. Henshall so aptly put it.

In more recent times, every angler I've seen has been wowed by the smallie's punch. As a longtime guide and angling instructor, I've put a passel of folks onto smallmouth. Even the most jaded international fly fishers (you know, guys who fish salmon in Alaska, trout in New Zealand and bonefish in Belize) get positively energized when three pounds of bronze power charges off with their fly. They invariably compare smallmouth to the hardest-fighting saltwater species.

In fact, I've seen more than a few guys who are certain (when they hook their first smallmouth) that the surging fish on the line weighs at least 5 pounds. When they finally see a fish barely 2 pounds appear near the boat they'll swear that a lunker has somehow managed a boatside hand-off of the fly to the more modest specimen in the net.

Big Smallmouth

The chances of catching a big smallmouth are better than they have been in decades. Undoubtedly, improving water quality has benefited some populations, and perhaps a warming climate has, too. But catch-and-release is the primary reason so many more 18-inch smallmouths are showing up on the line. Forty years ago, in all but the most remote or inaccessible waters, many 14-inchers ended up in skillets. Today, all the harping about catch-and-release by fishing writers like me has finally paid off. A large and growing recycling movement, both mandated and voluntary, means more smallies can once again attain their biological potential.

I know of many waters where 17-inchers were rare catches 20 and 30 years ago. These were the exceptional fish you felt fortunate to hook once or twice a season. Today, in these same waters, 3-pounders are almost everyday catches. And your chances of catching a bona fide 20-inch, 4-pound smallmouth are better than ever. Even the true giants of the smallmouth world, the 5-pounders, are no longer just the stuff of my clients' imaginations. Every season I weigh a few at 5 pounds, and many of the top destinations listed in this book have increasing numbers of these giants. Indeed, "the good ol' days" of smallmouth fishing may be right now.

Great Waters

The adaptable smallmouth swims across an increasingly large chunk of North America. The 200-plus rivers and the hundreds of lakes where I've fished them may be a lot more water than the average smallmouth fan has tried, but it's just a trickle in the available flow.

Almost every state and most provinces have populations of bronzebacks. This includes rivers from near the Mexican border all the way north into British Columbia. In a huge swath of the middle and eastern US and Canada the smallmouth is extremely widespread. The species lives in some remote waters, but it also

So many great places to fish! Beautiful, smallmouth-filled waters, like this Michigan river, are common across the bronzeback's range.

thrives in hundreds of close-to-home streams. Even many large urban centers like Washington, Chicago, Philadelphia, St Louis and Minneapolis have fishable populations of bronzebacks within their city limits or very nearby. So today's smallmouth fans have the best of both worlds: there are plenty of distant exotic waters to savor, plus a bounty of angling right outside our door.

Smallmouth waters are some of the most enjoyable and satisfying places to spend time. Even in agricultural or urbanized areas, smallmouth waterways are often soothingly quiet and scenic. Wade a small New York stream, and you won't believe you're in one of the most populous states in the nation. Float an Iowa river with its spectacular limestone bluffs, and you'll never know you're in one of the most agricultural parts of the country. Best of all, many of these twisting ribbons of water are little fished by today's lake-oriented boat anglers or trout-focused fly rodders. On any of hundreds of smallmouth waterways, you can quickly escape the crowds that fill many lakes and trout streams. Hike or float a few yards from the bridge and it's only you, the moving water and the creatures that live in and around it.

And I can't fail to mention another attribute of our warmwater rivers—species diversity. Smallmouth share their environment with many other fine fish. A few purists may groan if they hook a rock bass, pickerel, pike, carp or other species while smallmouth fishing, but not me. I love these bonus catches. Hooking one of these fish between smallmouth adds an extra measure of fun and excitement to the day.

Why Fly Fishing?

Sure, you can catch smallmouth on other types of tackle. But why? Fly fishing is such a uniquely satisfying way to angle. For centuries, both Old and New World anglers have known how well this method works for trout. And with the modern advances in tackle and techniques, the fly rod and smallmouth go equally well together.

Living in shallow environments that are easily accessible to fly anglers, the aggressive bronzeback is ready and willing to take a well-presented offering. Just as salt-rodders have discovered that redfish, bonefish, tarpon and such are fly-catchable, sweetwater anglers are discovering how enjoyable and productive fly fishing for smallmouth can be.

In fact, I've seen plenty of days when the long rod in skilled hands beat absolutely every other method. For example, surface smallmouthing is about the most enjoyable fishing on earth, plus it's an extremely effective technique. And it's nearly always more productive with fly tackle. A competent fly angler laying out casts with speed and accuracy, picking the fly off the surface and quickly delivering it again, is a study in grace and efficiency, and something that no spin fisher or bait caster can match.

Besides hundreds of streams, fly fishers can find big smallmouth in the shallows of thousands of lakes.

Even subsurface fly fishing techniques are often superior to comparable spin methods. Using the current to an advantage and employing a strike indicator, the fly angler can work a fly effectively along the bottom for long distances, all the while detecting even the lightest takes.

Fly fishing's inherent strengths translate into consistent success for a growing cadre of savvy smallmouth anglers. We may not catch hordes of bronzebacks during the toughest times, but most days we see plenty of fish on the line, and some of us are catching 'em all year long. Naturally, you need to adapt to changing conditions and seasons, but fly fishing surely produces—often both in quantity and quality.

However, hooking fish is only part of the equation, sometimes only a small part. Some of my best days on the water have been when only a few fish showed themselves. Maybe the water was too cold or too dirty, or the fish just too darn finicky. But great satisfaction came from having the rod in my hands, the line in my fingers, laying out casts, working the fly, feeling the water. Few other activities offer as much tactile and cerebral pleasure as does fly fishing. On days when the bite is slow, I really enjoy improving my skills, perfecting techniques and perhaps learning something new about the conditions I encounter. If I catch a fish or two, this just adds to an already excellent day.

Over the decades, many noted writers have tried to convey the joy and satisfaction they felt when spending time on a trout stream with fly rod in hand. I believe most who try smallmouth fly fishing will develop those same intense feelings. And why not? The smallmouth is an extraordinary creature, its environments are wondrous places and the act of fly fishing is remarkable. The synergy of the three makes for a truly unrivaled experience. Welcome aboard!

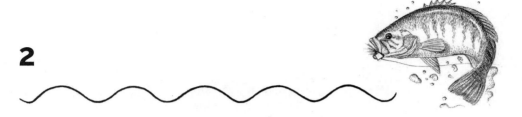

2

Understanding Smallmouth

It happened again this October. Driving by one of my favorite streams I saw a fly fisher near the road. He was throwing 50-foot casts with nice tight loops, and seemed to be enjoying the experience. But I couldn't help myself; I had to ask him about the fishing. When he said he was out for smallmouth, I hated to break the bad news. There were no smallies in this stream now. They had left a couple weeks ago, migrating to their winter hibernacula, in an impoundment 40 miles downstream.

Understanding smallmouth biology is more than an academic endeavor. It's made me a better angler, and it can do the same for you. In fact, gaining greater insights into the species' biology is as vital as learning good fly presentation skills. This is especially true because of the many misunderstandings about smallmouth that circulate among fly anglers. So let's get right to the facts:

1. Smallmouth Aren't Stout Trout!

There is a widespread assumption among trout-oriented fly rodders that stream smallmouth are a lot like trout. And even some fly fishing writers continue to promote this myth by suggesting trout tactics for smallmouth fishing. In fact, brown trout and smallmouth bass come from two distinctly different families of fishes. The physiology of these two species is extremely dissimilar, including their temperature requirements, reproductive needs, and their habitat and food preferences. They even respond quite differently to stimuli in their environment, with smallmouth displaying a level of boldness and curiosity far greater than trout do. In biologist's lingo, smallmouth are "opportunistic piscavores"—bold and aggressive fish-eating fish, which consume what's most available or easiest to capture.

SMALL STREAM HABITAT

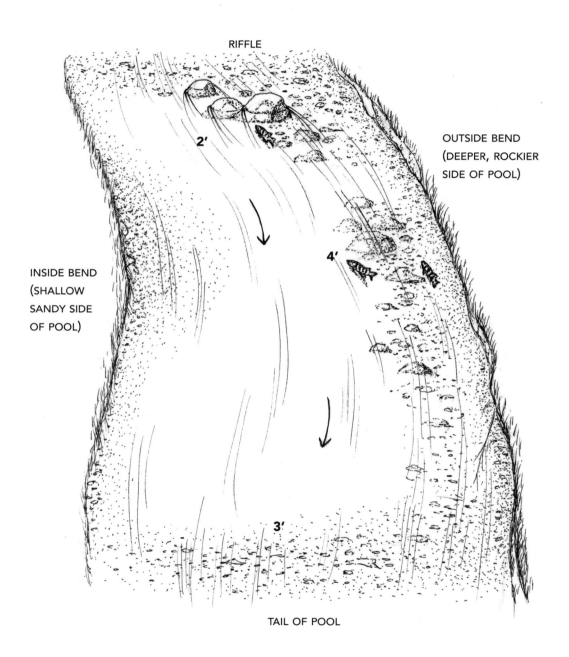

RIFFLE

2'

OUTSIDE BEND
(DEEPER, ROCKIER
SIDE OF POOL)

INSIDE BEND
(SHALLOW
SANDY SIDE
OF POOL)

4'

3'

TAIL OF POOL

Fish gravitiate towards rocky portions of the stream to hunt crayfish and
minnows. Smallmouth can live in a wide variety of waters, but populations
are highest where rocky substrates are available.

It may be fair to say that because the trout and smallmouth's life strategies are so dissimilar, even their "psychologies" are different. The trout, spending much of its life feeding on tiny, drifting insects in a crystalline environment, is often able to scrutinize these minuscule food sources before it eats them. Keying in on just one abundant bug keeps the trout from inadvertently ingesting flotsam. (In other words, it's sticking with a proven food source.) And because the soft-rayed, sleek trout in its shallow, clear habitat is very vulnerable to predation, it survives by being extra cautious (shy).

In contrast, the typical smallmouth is often pursuing large, fast-moving prey in a relatively low-visibility environment. The crayfish and minnows it eats would be long gone if the smallmouth took time to carefully examine them. Most of the time, teeny bugs drifting quietly through the water column arouse little interest among smallmouth. And as a top-line predator in its larger sizes, this fish boldly seeks out and investigates possible food sources. Therefore, trout tactics such as "matching the hatch," dead drifting, using tiny flies and delicate presentations are seldom the best approach for smallmouth.

Knowing Smallmouth

The better you understand the smallmouth bass for what it actually is, the more effectively you can fish for this species. Beyond this utilitarian approach, a more academic study of the bronzeback and its life cycle is also quite worthwhile. Personally, I've had a long and abiding interest in all things smallmouth. Reading fisheries studies, pondering scientific data and discussing the species with biologists is fascinating to me, no matter where it leads. The more I learn, the more I want to know. And the more I know, the more I respect the species and the more meaningful my fishing experiences become.

There is a growing body of scientific knowledge available about smallmouth, as state and provincial fishery departments devote more time to studying the species. I've made an effort in this book to be scientifically grounded, but every facet of smallmouth biology can't be incorporated into a single volume. If you have further interest in this complex species, I encourage you to delve deeper into the scientific literature. Joining the American Fisheries Society and reading its various journals is one good way to start. And of course, visiting Smallmouth Angler.Com for discussions of current biological questions and issues will be helpful, too.

2. Smallmouth, the "Plastic Bass"

Another notable fallacy still circulating is the idea that smallmouth occupy a relatively narrow ecological niche. Some still believe that smallies are just fish of clean streams and clear, cool lakes.

In fact, smallmouth bass have become one of North America's most widespread sportfish, perhaps second only to largemouth bass. Certainly, smallies thrive in hundreds of streams of moderate size, clarity and gradient. These are the classic rocky riffle-pool-riffle waterways that many fly anglers know and love, and envision when they dream of fishing. However, Micropterus dolomieui has adapted to an enormous variety of other habitats, too.

Some smallmouth live in huge, industrialized rivers like the St Lawrence, Mississippi and Columbia. And as human activity has impacted many waterways, smallies have learned to survive in rivers with only minimal visibility. Illinois' Rock and Fox rivers are exceptionally turbid and algae stained. Yet smallmouth hold their own in these and many other farmbelt waters. The fish also does well in Wisconsin pasture streams so tiny one can almost jump over them in a single bound. Smallmouth prosper (perhaps because they're so tough to catch) in absolutely crystalline creeks of West Virginia and Tennessee. Even in the hot and

Not every metropolitan area offers downtown smallmouthing like this one does, but most cities have good fishing within easy driving distance.

The Great Lakes encompass millions of acres and hold outsized smallmouth. Some can even be caught by the wading angler.

harsh west Texas desert, introduced smallmouth are going well in the forbidding Devils River. Transplanted bronzebacks also swim among the vineyards of northern California and in dozens of other western waterways, including some right in Montana's trout country.

Stillwater environments are also home to millions of this species. Eastern water supply reservoirs nestled among millions of people hold smallmouth. So do thousands of wilderness lakes from New Brunswick to Manitoba. Even some minuscule Missouri farm ponds hold lunker smallies, ditto for wind-swept, high plains reservoirs in the Dakotas. In fact, smallmouth often do well in a wide variety of lakes, especially if competitors, like largemouth and walleyes, aren't abundant.

Even the largest, coldest sweetwater sea on the planet, Lake Superior, has excellent bronzeback populations in select bays. And Superior isn't the only place the species has adapted to extremely sterile environments. There are lakes in northern Michigan where smallies survive solely on invertebrates, and where neither crayfish nor other fish species are present.

Smallmouth are truly a plastic species, adjusting to fit so many environments. What does this mean for us? First, there are a lot more interesting and unusual places to pursue smallmouth than you probably imagined. Second, you should vary your fishing strategies and tactics based on the widely different habitats and conditions the species finds itself in. Smallmouth can be very cautious and secretive, or aggressive and bold. Some have a narrow home range, others have a large territory. It all depends on the environment they live in.

Part 3 of this book provides descriptions of 100 excellent smallmouth destinations across the country. If you're willing to travel, you can find the type of angling that suits your fancy. In the remainder of this chapter, I'll focus on several other often-misunderstood biological issues that have big impacts on angling.

3) Smallies Like It Hot

The old myth that smallmouth prefer cool water is still a troublemaker. A decade ago it was even worse. Back then, all sorts of trout-oriented fly fishers were under the erroneous assumption that smallies, like trout, didn't feed much in warm water. When doing smallmouth seminars, I'd continually run into folks who said they quit fishing in mid-summer when "the water got too warm." (Yikes! Quitting smallmouthing just as the peak of the season arrives!) Thankfully, this notion isn't as widespread as it once was, but it's still prevalent among a core of fly anglers.

Here's how the cool water confusion got started and why it continues to circulate: In the early '50s, cursory observations of smallmouth in a Tennessee lake led some fisheries personnel to believe the species always and everywhere prefers deeper (cooler) water. The reasons the smallies in that lake were found in deeper (cooler) water was more a matter of competition with largemouth bass, rather than temperature. Nevertheless, the cool water idea quickly got published in fishing books and magazines. This started a vicious cycle of writers unquestioningly repeating what previous writers had said. Hence, the fallacy that "smallies prefer 65-degree water." (And let me come clean about outdoor writing: simply repeating what others have written is all too common in my field. Since the pay is low, many of my fellow scribes feel they cannot afford to spend time doing independent research on a topic.)

Fortunately, fisheries biologists aren't as poorly paid. They did more research and discredited the cool water notion over a quarter-century ago. And most non-fly-fishing writers and anglers have also discounted the myth.

So what about fly rodders? There are two reasons some fly guys are still confused about water temps. Not surprisingly, one reason is our sport's powerful trout tradition, which leads some to view things through trout-colored glasses (Trout like/need cool water, so by golly, smallmouth must, too).

The other reason the cool water idea still has support is because for some folks it seems to be true! They fish in the spring when water temps are in the 60s and smallmouth are spawning. Though the smallies don't feed during reproduction, they are guarding their nests and strike aggressively. Another situation where the cool water myth sometimes gets reinforced is on streams that get extremely clear during mid- and late summer. On these waters daytime smallmouthing can be challenging. Larger fish in ultra-clear water may become spooky and hard to fool during midday, or become semi-nocturnal. While on hundreds of lower-visibility rivers the warmest water temps means the best fishing of the year, in some clear waters the warm-water period is tough. The issue is actually clarity, rather than temperature. But a fly angler who has already heard of the smallie's "cool water nature" is likely to think this experience shows it's true.

Okay, enough background. Here's the real deal on temperatures: Like most of their sunfish kin (largemouth, bluegills, rock bass, etc.) smallmouth do best in warm water. Sure, smallies are hardy fish who can survive in frigid Canadian lakes, but offer them 70 degrees and they'll grow a lot faster than in a 60-degree environment. Give them 80 degrees and they'll do better yet. Heck, give 'em bathtub temps of 85 degrees and they'll be in hog heaven—growing quickly to porkster size. In a number of power plant discharge reservoirs where smallies have been introduced, the water is in the 80s much of the year. Without largemouth, the smallmouth do incredibly well there, and these hot-water habitats offer some of the best angling around for big bronze.

And consider this: forty years of personal temperature records clearly show that some of my very best smallmouthing occurs when stream temps reach the 80s! That's thousands of fish my clients and I caught in 80-plus-degree water, including some of the very biggest fish of the year.

For instance, back in the late 1980s, a two-year drought and heat wave gripped much of the country. Rivers flowed at historic low levels and record high temperatures. Cities implemented water bans, farmers got federal aid and trout anglers cried. Me? I fished my buns off—in dozens of streams across four states. And mostly when water temperatures were 83 to 87 degrees. During these two years of drought the fishing was the best I've ever seen. Big fish, small fish, lots of fish. On a big river I landed a personal record of 81 smallies in just 5 hours of wading, and in dinky creeks 35-fish afternoons were common. Because they're cold-blooded animals, the smallies' metabolism rose through the roof during this hotwater period. They were rapidly digesting food and, of course, eating ravenously.

And the good times didn't end when this hotwater period was over. Because low flows and high temps are so good for smallmouth spawning, the record reproduction from the drought years filled the rivers with fish. Two enormous "baby booms" were produced, which dominated the catch for nearly a decade. Smallies like it hot; I do too, and so should you.

4. Traveling Bronze

Yet another old cliché which turns out to be false in many instances is that smallmouth are homebodies. This notion arose decades ago, when Missouri found that their stream smallmouth moved very little over the course of a year. Since other states at that time didn't have the inclination or budget to study their smallmouth, many biologists assumed that all riverine smallmouth were homebodies.

Boy, has radio telemetry blown this belief out of the water! When northern states like Wisconsin started tracking their smallies with tiny transmitters, they discovered that the fish move enormous distances each season. They've found that every fall the fish move many miles (sometimes over 50) to downstream wintering pools, often completely evacuating headwater streams by mid-September. These wintering pools are completely slack and often deep, too. Smallmouth gather in these "hibernacula" to conserve energy. Northern winters are long, river temps are barely above freezing and fish are nearly dormant. Finding areas completely free of current (and current's drain on the fish's energy reserves) is essential for overwinter survival.

In the spring, the now hormonally-primed smallmouth charge back upstream, often traveling even greater distances than they did in the fall, on their way to

Tracking smallies using radio telemetry, as this fisheries biologist is doing, has uncovered many secrets of smallmouth movements.

spawning habitat, perhaps up a feeder creek. Then after spawning, the fish move yet again, this time to summer feeding areas. So, far from being "homebodies," many riverine smallies have 3 distinct seasonal movements. They act more like steelhead or salmon than like some of their stay-at-home cousins in southern climes.

Even on rivers without fall migrations, spring spawning movements can still be extensive. Tagged smallies have been found to travel 20 miles up tributaries to spawn. The male will remain in the tributary for several weeks, until parenting duties are complete, then he heads back downstream to his summer feeding habitat. Naturally, on any water where smallies are travelers, this has enormous implications for where you should fish at various times of the year.

I've had a long-standing fascination with smallmouth movements, and here's what I've found: Extensive fall movements seem to occur mostly in Canada and rivers across the northern tier of states (Maine, New Hampshire, Vermont, New York, Michigan, Wisconsin, Minnesota and the Dakotas). Migrations often start when water dips into the upper 50s. But fish may not migrate in every river in these regions; instead, waterways that are relatively shallow and faster flowing are likely to see the biggest movements.

5. What's for Dinner?

It used to seem so simple. Find out what they're eating and they were as good as caught. At least that's how a lot of fly anglers approached smallmouthing 15 years ago. Fortunately, in recent years many warmwater aficionados have moved away from this dogma and are using flies of every size, shape and color.

Smallmouth eat many things, but crayfish account for much of their diet during the summer months.

So does it really matter what the smallies are eating? Yes and no. Sometimes just knowing the season, water temperature, depth, clarity and fish activity levels will be enough to catch smallmouth. In other situations, forage will influence where the fish will be, which retrieve to use, plus fly size and color. And this sort of complexity is precisely why angling is so enjoyable. Various factors influence how well the fish will bite, and the interplay between the factors continuously changes. Challenging to figure out, and oh-so satisfying when you do.

Okay, here's what smallies eat: whatever's the easiest to catch and most nutritious. That's crayfish in many waters. But even in crayfish-rich locales, small fish make up a big part of the smallmouth's diet during the cold water periods of spring and fall when crayfish are not very available. Various minnow species, shiners, chubs, sculpins, perch, etc. are all consumed if readily available. And increasingly, in some lakes that are very clear due to water-filtering zebra mussels, smallmouth are pursuing pelagic (open water) species such as smelt, shad and ciscoes. Hellgrammites, because they are such huge insects (almost like small crayfish) are also significant forage in the waters where they are numerous. Even small insects, which seldom constitute a major food source, are eaten where there are heavy caddis or mayfly hatches. Insect-eating is most common where smallmouth numbers are very high or larger forage is scarce.

6. It's a Matter of Clarity.

Water clarity is unquestionably a major factor in angling. Either too much or too little clarity can greatly influence technique and fly pattern choices, and limit or enhance success. Many know this, but far fewer realize it's not just the actual clarity of the water. **Relative visibility** is often more important. If a turbid river usually offers barely a foot of visibility and it improves to 2 feet, fishing may become fantastic. Conversely, if a river with normally 5 feet of visibility declines to just 2 feet,

This little creek fishes best when visibility is about 30 inches. On this ideal day, this angler caught 5 smallies over 17 inches.

the smallies may close up like clams. The same clarity in each river, yet two entirely different responses. Tricky, huh? It demonstrates how much fish react to the existing visibility relative to what it was previously. So it's important to know what the normal clarity of a particular river is before you fish it, and which direction it's going (clearer or cloudier).

"Dirty" water isn't all the same either. Many river neophytes assume that visibility (and fish behavior) is the same in every type of off-colored water. In fact, there's a lot of difference between the clarity of "muddy" water (with silt suspension), brown algae-stained water and dark bog-stained water. Extremely muddy (silty) water is very hard to see in and is usually a temporary condition. Smallies can react by going into a very reduced feeding mode. On the other hand, algae- and bog-stain in waters is more or less permanent during the summer, plus fish can see much better in these types of water. Therefore, they seldom stop feeding solely due to heavily stained water. (The "Difficult Water Conditions" chapter covers "dirty" water techniques in detail.)

7. Crack o' Dawn or High Noon?

Many anglers who only fish clear-flowing rivers in woodland watersheds assume that early morning angling is better than midday. But on some bronzeback waters this isn't true. On streams with high nutrient loads (like those that drain agricultural or urban land) the fish feed very little before 8:00 or 9:00 AM, because of low morning temperatures combined with low oxygen levels or low visibility. So hitting the water early is a waste of time on these streams.

Why low oxygen in the morning? With so much organic material in the water, oxygen levels slowly decline during the night as this material decomposes. On some small agricultural streams where oxygen has been monitored, levels can be as low as 3 parts per million (ppm) by morning. Then as the sun rises and photosynthesis kicks in, oxygen levels jump back up to 8 or 10 ppm. While levels are low, the smallies are suffering from a mild form of oxygen deprivation and aren't interested in feeding. Fortunately, it seems only a minority of rivers experience this human-caused condition.

On other rivers, fishing improves during the midday period because of warming water and increased visibility. On some cool, low-visibility rivers I've guided on, this is such a common occurrence I call it the "high-noon frenzy." Especially earlier in the summer, river temps can be a brisk 67 degrees at 9:00 AM and a relatively balmy 71 by 1:00 PM, promoting a much better bite.

8. No Kissing Cousins

I make a big deal about smallies not being like trout. But what about being similar to their big-mouthed cousin? No question, smallmouth share some common characteristics with largemouth bass, such as similar spawning strategies. However, these two species' differences are also extensive. Perhaps the most notable distinction is the habitats each prefers, and the fact that largemouth do very well in extremely warm water. While the mid- to upper 80s seems to be about the upper temperature limit for smallies, bigmouth thrive in water well into the 90s. This is why Cuba, Mexico and Florida are Meccas for largemouth, but not smallmouth.

Both species can live in weedy environments, but largemouth do much better in dense vegetation, and they outcompete smallmouth in these environments. Conversely, in very rocky lakes, smallmouth seem to outcompete largemouth. This may be because smallies are more adept at hunting crayfish among rocks, and largemouth are better at catching minnows in weeds. As a rule, largemouth also do poorly in rivers that have significant current. Smallmouth, of course, flourish in moving water.

There are places (such as large lakes and rivers with diverse habitats) where both bass species comfortably coexist in their respective niches. But in many places, one or the other rules. Bigmouths dominate weed-choked lakes and ponds; smallies reign in rocky streams and lakes. To me, it's no contest— we smallmouth fans got the best part of the bargain.

8 THINGS TO KNOW ABOUT SMALLMOUTH

1. THEY'RE NOT LIKE TROUT
The two species are very different and require different strategies

2. ADAPTABLE SPECIES
More widespread and adaptable than most realize

3. THEY LIKE IT HOT
They do well in warm water, grow fastest in 80-plus-degree water.

4. THEY MOVE A LOT
In some waters smallmouth travel many miles annually

5. VERSATILE FEEDERS
They eat whatever is easiest to capture and most nutritious, seldom insects

6. CLARITY IS KEY
Water clarity is one of the most important angling factors

7. ACTIVE AT MIDDAY
Temperature, clarity and oxygen levels can all cause a hot midday bite

8. NOT LARGEMOUTH
Smallmouth predominate in rivers and rocky, clear lakes

3

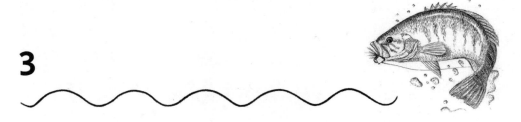

Gearing Up

You see them more and more on smallmouth waters—fly anglers enthusiastically pursuing bronzebacks. Some are having great success, but others are not. One reason is that they don't have the right tools for the job. They may not have the right rod for smallmouthing, the line isn't loading it properly, or maybe they haven't mastered the casting required for bass flies.

So how do you choose the right tools (rod, reel, line and leader) for this endeavor? It mostly depends on the *type of waters you intend to fish* and *your casting ability*. And frankly, your attitude will go a long way in determining both your casting ability and overall angling expertise.

The attitude a person brings to any pursuit has a major influence on how much enjoyment and success they'll derive from it. This is particularly true for smallmouth fly fishing. One of the great attractions of this sport is the fact that it's so challenging and multi-faceted. One can spend a lifetime learning new skills and improving on old ones.

Unfortunately, experienced fly fishers who are smallmouth neophytes don't always see it that way. Because they already have considerable skills in other areas of fly fishing, they sometimes harbor an attitude that they already know almost everything worth knowing. And they don't realize how different casting for smallies is from trout casting. Occasionally, guys with this know-it-all attitude take my smallmouth schools. Inevitably, it limits their ability to embrace the new skills and casting techniques that smallmouthing requires.

Beginning fly fishers can get waylaid by another hang-up: some view learning to cast as an onerous chore. This attitude leads some folks to never invest the time necessary to become adequate casters; hence they get frustrated, catch few fish and may retire the rod to the closet. The wise alternative is to approach fly casting as an

Big flies are often best for big fish. Casting a large fly requires solid casting skills.

exciting new skill to learn, and an enjoyable part of the sport. Anyone can master it, but everyone must also make a concerted effort to learn to cast. Those who do so are richly rewarded.

Casting Competence

So what kind of casting expertise does it take to catch smallies? Thankfully, it's a somewhat flexible requirement. If you stick to wind-protected small streams and smaller flies, it won't be hard to get proficient with the 40-foot casts that will put you on fish. If you want to do well on large rivers and lakes, it will require more effort learning to throw those 50-footers in a 15-mph wind.

Fly casting for smallmouth is actually quite challenging. Big water small-mouthing is more akin to salt water casting than trout fishing; big water flies are often hefty, winds are common and you need to make a lot of casts per day. Even for small stream smallmouth, you'll still be casting much larger flies longer distances than is required for creek trout fishing (making delicate presentations with a size 16 Adams bears little resemblance to driving out a big popper).

While plenty of trout fans love dabbling dry flies or nymphs a few feet beyond their rod tip, I much prefer laying out substantial casts. Feeling the power as the line loads the rod, seeing the popper rocket 55 feet and settle next to a boulder, then watching a formidable fish engulf the fly—for me, this is fishing at its finest.

Practice is Key

Of course, it requires expertise and stamina to throw a bass fly all day. And no matter what your accomplishments or skills in other endeavors, no matter what expensive tackle you buy, no one can fly cast without practice. I've seen a Fortune 500 CEO who had the very best gear, but couldn't cast worth a darn. And I've seen a 14-year-old equipped with only a budget rod become an outstanding caster by the time he was 15. The difference between the two was the CEO's unwillingness to practice and the kid's burning desire to cast every chance he got.

Of course, taking casting lessons is an excellent idea, so is studying a good casting video. But this isn't enough. The only way to become really handy with a fly rod is to get out there and cast it—a lot. If you're a beginner or used to throwing only tiny trout flies, make a commitment to doing three 40-minute sessions a week for two months.

After a few sessions, start practicing with flies similar to ones used in small-mouth fishing. A cork or foam popper and 1/50th-ounce Clouser Minnow (both with the hooks snipped off) are good. In a park or large lawn, carefully mark off 30, 40 and 50 feet. Start at 30 feet, and as you get better progress to the longer

DOING THE DOUBLE HAUL

The double haul is often essential for smallmouth fishing

1) Start by grabbing the line in front of you.

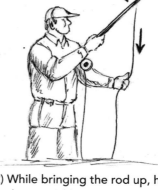

2) While bringing the rod up, haul line down quickly.

3) When the rod has stopped, your line hand should have pulled the line down to your hip.

4) While the rod is drifting back during the pause, feed the line through the guides.

5) After the backcast has straightened out, start the forward cast and haul the line down forcefully.

6) After completing the forward cast, release the line for shooting.

distances. And learn to cast both flies, since their different weights and bulk require slightly different casting strokes.

Developing Line Speed

Your goal (at least initially) isn't pinpoint accuracy, delicate presentations, roll casting or other fancy moves. Instead, an effective smallmouth angler needs to quickly deliver the fly with a minimum of false casting and often into a substantial wind. This means learning to haul well enough so your line speed is sufficient to "shoot" the line. Being able to shoot even 10 feet of line on the forward cast will enable a person to deliver the fly to the target with just one or two backcasts. The single haul as well as the double haul aren't particularly difficult. But they are best learned with the help of a good video or a warmwater- or saltwater-oriented casting instructor who understands the necessity of fast line speed.

Will you be an expert caster after two dozen sessions on the grass? Not likely. But I'll guarantee you'll be much better than before you started, and your actual fishing time will be infinitely more productive and enjoyable. And anytime your commitment to practice wavers, consider the alternative: I've seen dozens of guys who, instead of practicing regularly, attempt to become proficient fly fishers simply by fishing a few times a season. After years, most are still poor casters. They remain frustrated fly fishers because they wouldn't make that relatively small initial investment in practice time. Don't make the same mistake.

Rods and Reels

Small sheltered creeks, canoe-sized streams, wide windy rivers, protected lakeshores and windswept reefs far from land. These are vastly different physical environments, yet they're all places people pursue smallies. And of course, no single rod will be perfect for all of these situations, just as there's no one outfit for all types of trout fishing. In fact, the right rod is often more important for smallmouthing than it is for trouting. Trout purists may howl at this statement, but consider the facts.

Most trout creeks are wind-sheltered and small, the flies used are small and casts are short. Sure, the perfect combination of rod, line and leader might allow you to finesse a few more fish, but a trout-savvy angler will do okay with a wide variety of outfits. On the other hand, casting a bulky fly 50 feet all day on a large wind-blown river is truly demanding. Choose the wrong rod or line for these challenging conditions, and you drastically limit your casting distance, hook-setting ability and number of fish caught.

Rod Recommendations

A broad range of rods, from delicate 4-weights to 9-weight muscle-sticks, can be effectively used for smallmouth. (See the Rod Chart) Most people won't need the extremely low or high-end weights. But if you intend to fish different types of water (like big rivers and small creeks) you could use a couple different rods—perhaps a 6-weight and an 8-weight. Actually, the 6 and 8-weight combo has become quite popular with warmwater fly fishers in recent years. The 6-weight is used for bronzebacks on small and mid-sized streams and maybe other warmwater species, such as bluegills or white bass. The significantly heavier 8-weight is the tool for big-water bronze, plus largemouth or pike. Of course, the 8-weight stick is also great for various salt water species and steelhead.

There are some occasions for the lightest and heaviest rods. I often use a 5-weight and sometimes a 4 for the smallest waters. These light, whippy wands are fine for short-range casting and allow even 10-inch fish to provide a battle royale. But these light rods won't easily throw large flies, they can't punch through much wind and hook-setting is difficult unless your hooks are kept extremely sharp. The beginning fly caster should never start out with a 4 or 5-weight for smallmouth; these are rods to consider once you have become an accomplished angler.

Nine-weight rods are equally specialized. They are not needed for most situations. But if a person is going to do a lot of lake angling, where winds are stiff, the fish are big and largemouth or pike are also common, then a 9-wt has its place. When I'm fishing waters where big pike and lunker smallmouth are mixed together, I'll sometimes throw large flies for both using a 9-weight. Offshore fishing on big lakes is another situation where I might pack a 9-weight. If the morning breeze turns into an afternoon gale, I'll pull out the heavy rod so I can keep fishing.

Rod Length

A rod's line rating is critical, but it's not the only component to pay attention to. Rod length is also important, and generally longer is better. Nowadays, 9-foot rods are common for warmwater fishing, but going up to a 9½-footer seldom hurts and makes both casting and hook-setting easier.

Rod Action

The "action," or "flex," is the most critical component next to the rod's line weight rating. It's also the most confusing, since there are really two different aspects to flex and different manufacturers may use different ratings to describe their rods. A rod's "power" or "stiffness" is one aspect. It is how much the rod bends during a cast. Stiffness is often rated medium, medium-stiff, stiff and extra-stiff. The stiffer

	BEGINNINER INTERMEDIATE CASTER	ADVANCED CASTER
SMALL STREAMS	6 WT	4 WT / 5 WT
MID-SIZED RIVERS	6 WT / 7 WT	6 WT
BIG RIVERS SMALLER LAKES PROTECTED LAKES	8 WT	7 WT / 8 WT
BIG WATER OPEN WATER WINDY CONDITIONS	9 WT	8 WT / 9 WT

the rod, the higher the line speed and the easier it is to cast in wind, but the greater the arm strength and casting ability it requires. For most situations and for most casters, a rod rated medium-stiff is the best. For an advanced caster intending to throw long distances or into strong winds, a stiff rod might be better.

The other aspect of flex is a rod's "taper" (where it bends) and is commonly called its "action." (The slower the action the farther towards the butt the rod bends.) Action is often rated slow, moderate, medium-fast, fast or extra-fast. Slow and moderate-action rods develop large line loops and slow speed; they're best for creek trouting (small flies, short distances and no wind). The medium-fast rating is the best for beginning and intermediate warmwater casters. Some advanced casters prefer fast or extra-fast-action rods for their ability to develop quick line speeds.

Be very honest with yourself when buying a rod. The majority of fly fishers aren't hot-shot casters with perfect techniques that allow them to make the best use of a fast-action rod. For most folks, a medium-fast action rod will be much easier to use.

The All-Purpose Rod?

What if a person wants to fish different types of water, but can only afford one good rod? That's simple—get a 7-weight, 9½ foot, medium-stiff, medium-fast-action good quality rod. Seven-weights may be out of style right now, but they're still the best all-purpose smallmouth rods available. Over the course of a year, I probably use a 7-weight more than any other type of rod.

Rod Price

Some of the very cheapest rods are wretched. They are exceedingly difficult to cast any distance and even expert casters will quickly tire out trying to use them. They're inexpensive, but still aren't worth the money. At the other end of the spectrum are some excellent smallmouth rods made by manufacturers such as Sage, Loomis and Thomas & Thomas. I've used their products for years and regard them as first-rate. However, too many of these high-end rods are prohibitively expensive, soaring to well over 500 dollars for a multi-piece model.

Recently, several companies have been striving to produce high quality rods at more reasonable prices. New models are coming out all the time, and some manufacturers are even starting to consider the warmwater angler in their designs. Don't hesitate to check out these new mid-priced products, some are nearly as good as the more expensive models.

The Reel Deal

What about reels for smallies? Fly industry honchos groan when I say this, but it's true: a bass reel is primarily a place to store line when you're not using it. A fancy reel with a super-smooth drag (and mega price tag) just isn't needed. The bass clan, no matter their size, make strong, but very short runs. That's one reason I seldom play smallmouth off the reel. When I'm fishing from a boat, I may not even reel up my loose line for hours, but leave it on the deck or in the stripping basket where it's instantly ready for another cast.

When I'm guiding, I often caution my less-experienced clients not to attempt to play a fish off the reel. The real danger of trying to "get the fish on the reel" is that you can loose the fish by inadvertently giving it slack while you're busy cranking up the loose line.

Rather than an expensive drag system, a more-helpful feature is a large arbor. Line won't coil as tightly on the spool and you'll be able to crank line back unto a large-arbored reel much faster. If money is no object, get one of those beautiful 500-dollar models. If you want to save your cash for more important tackle items, get a well-built large-arbored reel for a quarter the price of the expensive model with the super-slick drag.

Lines for Smallmouth

Proper Line Weight

Next to your rod, the second most important part of your tackle ensemble is the line. A simple trick that makes casting much easier (especially with hefty flies) is to use line that's heavier than the rod's rating. For 35- to 50-foot distances, most rod models load and cast much better with a heavier line. For guiding, I always overload all my rods by at least one line weight (i.e., an 8 line for a 7-wt rod). For casting extra-heavy flies short distances, a floating line two weights heavier than the rod is even better, especially for beginning casters.

I can't emphasize this enough. *Using too light a line will dramatically hinder your casting.* Using the "right" line weight on your rod may allow you to deliver a tiny dry fly with delicacy, but you'll struggle to drive a bulky popper 50 feet in the wind. With *floating line,* you'll often cast much better with a line heavier than what your rod is rated for. An exception to this is sink-tip lines; with most sink-tips, use the one rated the same as your rod. Of course, the best way to find out what casts the best for the rods you own and the type of fishing you do is to actually try different lines.

A strike indicator (visible on the right) is essential when using a floating line and a with-the-current retrieve.

Floating Lines

Though manufacturers now offer a dizzying array of different fly lines, the old reliable bass bug taper is still one of the best tapers for floating lines. Sure, some of the new lines with specialized tapers are nice for unusual conditions, but for most warmwater angling, a bass bug taper or its equivalent is hard to beat. It has plenty of weight up front to really load the rod and drive out a heavy fly. Just make sure it's good quality. Today's high-grade lines are pricey, but they cast well, float well, are long-lasting and worth the money. However, even the most expensive line will get dirty and will cast much better if you regularly clean and dress it. For river fishing, it's best to clean and relubricate the line every outing.

Sinking Lines

If you just use topwaters or confine your fishing to shallow streams, you'll never need a sinking line. However, for certain situations full-sink or sink-tip lines are invaluable. An obvious settings that requires a sinking line is the deep water of lakes. Because this is a rather specialized type of fly fishing, there is a detailed discussion of full-sinking lines to the "Lake Fishing: Open Water Methods" chapter. A sink-tip line is much more versatile; it's good for mid-depths and sometimes for stiff current.

Sink-tip lines come in a variety of weights (sink rates) and lengths. A heavy (fast sinking) tip can be used to get down 8 or 9 feet in still water or to cut through 6 or 7 feet of moving water. A lighter (slower sinking) tip can be used to keep a very lightweight fly in the middle of the water column while retrieving it against the current. You can also get down using a floating line and a weighted fly. But it's often easier to cast a light fly on a sink-tip than to cast a heavy fly on a floating line.

If you intend to fish in a variety of river situations and perhaps also lakes, I recommend two different sink-tips: for getting down quickly, go with a heavy tip such as Scientific Anglers Ultra 3 Wet Tip, Type IV. With a 13-foot fast-sinking tip, this line allows you to get down quickly and stay there, even in moderate current. For shallower settings, bring along a shorter, slower sinking quick-change sink tip that can be easily attached to and detached from to your floating line.

Quick-Change Sink Tips

If you want to change from floating to sinking lines several times a day, consider a removable sink-tip (sometimes called a "mini-head"). Often manufactured in 4- or 5-foot lengths, these sink-tips are quickly attached with a loop connection. You can also make your own removable sink-tips. Starting with a 30-foot fast-sinking shooting head, cut it into various lengths and then put loops on both ends. Depending on how fast you want it to sink, a mini-tip can range from 6 inches to 6 feet long. With tips in 3 or 4 different lengths you can cover a wide range of depths/sink rates. Another big advantage of these removable sink tips is that you don't need extra reel spools for them. Coiled, they store in leader wallets or plastic bags.

Leaders—The Top and Bottom System

The desire for delicate dry fly presentations in some fly fishing has made leaders seem overly complicated. Luckily, leaders for warmwater fly fishing are pretty straightforward. My simple, 2-leader system will work for 98% of the smallmouth fishing situations you'll encounter.

Surface Fishing Leaders

For surface fishing, use a rather heavy tapered leader that has enough power and stiffness so it straightens out (turns over) even in the wind and with a heavy fly. Commercial tapered monofiliment leaders 9 feet long with a "bass bug taper" and a tippet strength of around 10-lb test (1X) work well. Only when using very small topwaters or when fishing ultra-clear water might you want to step down to a lighter leader, perhaps one with a 2X or 3X tippet.

Furled (woven) nylon leaders are also excellent for surface fishing. They turn over flies extremely well and seldom kink or tangle. They cost more than standard tapered leaders, but the ones I've used seem to last nearly forever and only require you to add more tippet material occasionally.

Want to make your own topwater leaders? That's easy, too! Just use the three-by-three formula. The butt section is 3 feet of .020 diameter (about 25-lb test) monofilament line, the middle section is 3 feet of .015 diameter mono, and the tippet is 3 to 4 feet of about .010 diameter (10-lb test). Don't use fluorocarbon line for surface leaders because it will sink and reduce the topwater's action.

Subsurface Leaders:

A straight (untapered) section of fluorocarbon for subsurface fishing is the other half of my 2-leader system. Untapered lengths of fluorocarbon ranging from 6- to 10-lb test will cover the vast majority of subsurface situations you'll encounter. The intent of subsurface fishing is to break the surface film and cut through the current to get the fly down quickly. The smaller the diameter of the leader, the better this is accomplished; thick butt sections aren't wanted. Fluorocarbon line is best because it's more abrasion-resistant and sinks better than monofilament.

When using a floating line and weighted fly, my rule of thumb for leader length is 2 1/2 times the water depth. Hence, a 10-foot leader for water 4 feet deep. To probe 5-foot depths I'll use a 12-foot leader. Leader diameter varies with fishing conditions. For clear water with few snags, a 6-lb leader is best; for extra-snaggy conditions and big fish, a section of 10-lb test is the way to go.

Favorite Knots

By using loop-to-loop connections you can quickly change from a tapered leader for topwatering to an untapered one for bottom-bouncing. In fact, a good loop knot is indispensable for smallmouthing. My favorite is a simplified Rapala Loop (see illustration). Another version of this is called the Non-Slip Loop. This loop knot is fine for connecting the leader to the line. It's a knot that can't slip, is fast and easy to tie and has good strength. To put a loop on the end of your fly line, you can buy pre-made loops, but those you make yourself are stronger. Simply double the end of the line on itself and secure it with heavy fly-tying thread and cement.

The simplified Rapala Loop is especially good for connecting flies to the leader. Another loop knot, the Surgeon's Loop, isn't as useful because it requires you to pull the fly through the loop twice (tough with a large fly). It also uses up a lot more leader material.

RAPALA LOOP KNOT

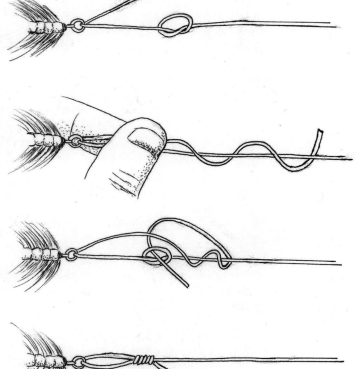

1) Tie an overhand knot 4 inches from the end of the leader (do not tighten). Run the tag end (free end) through the hook eye.

2) Press the overhand knot and tag end between thumb and index finger, then wrap the tag end around the standing part of the leader above the over-hand knot.

3) Now run the tag end back into the loop created in front of the hook eye, then into the overhand knot.

4) Moisten the knot and tighten. Trim off excess.

However, I do use the Surgeon's Knot. Really only a double overhand knot using both sections of leader material, the common Surgeon's Knot is exceedingly simple. It works well for adding new tippet material to an existing leader and also for building an entire tapered leader. While its strength may not be 100% like some more complicated knots, I like the Surgeon's quick simplicity. A similar and equally easy knot is the Orvis Tippet Knot (see illustration). The Ovis Knot is best for attaching light tippets (6-lb test or less) because of its superior strength with small-diameter leaders.

For all knots, always wet them (spit is good) before tightening. And retie— often!! Carefully retie your tippet-to-leader knot and tippet-to-fly knot after landing a big fish or two, or after fishing a few hours, or a weak knot can ruin your day.

ORVIS TIPPET KNOT

1) Overlap 4 inches of both ends and form a loop.

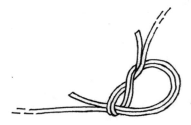

2) Tuck the tippet section and the end of the leader through the loop from behind to create a figure 8.

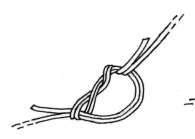

3) Make another wrap with the tippet section and the end of the leader to create an improved figure 8.

4) Moisten the knot and tighten it by pulling all 4 ends. Trim the tag ends

Other Gadgets and Gear

A fly angler can easily collect scads of nifty little gadgets. But there are really only 4 essential year-round items—nippers, forceps, hook hone and strike indicators. I prefer hard Styrofoam strike indicators. In the spring and fall, a thermometer is another necessity, and if you want to know how big those lunkers are, pack a tape measure, too. I also carry a multi-tooled pocket knife, but I've always toted one of those, so I don't regard it solely as a fly fishing item.

Some anglers like to carry most of their gadgets on the outside of their vest or around their neck on a lanyard. I think too many loose items catch on brush or on the line. On the outside of my vest, I have only a nipper on a retractor; everything else I stow in pockets.

Breathable chest waders are preferred by many smallmouth anglers, but some like to wet-wade during the summer. A fishing vest is also preferred by most folks, but others opt for a waist pack.

How Much to Spend?

Of course, companies also offer all sorts of expensive clothing items for fly fishing, and a person can spend richly on fancy pants, hats, shirts, even fly fishing socks. However, these products certainly aren't required for enjoyable and productive fishing; a good rod and reel, appropriate line, nippers, forceps, hook hone, indicators and a few good flies are the only truly essential items. Don't worry about image while you're on stream. In all my years of smallmouthing, I've never seen a fish that cared what I was wearing.

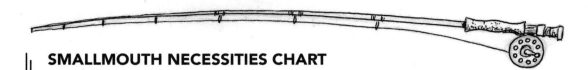

SMALLMOUTH NECESSITIES CHART

CASTING ABILITY: Small Streams—35 feet with no wind
Big Rivers/Lakes—45 to 50 feet in 15-mph wind

ROD(S): General Purpose—6 to 8-weight
Specialized—Down to 4-weight, up to 9-weight

REEL(S): Large arbor most important feature, drag secondary
Extra spool

LINES: General Purpose—Bass bug taper floating, one weight over
rod rating
Secondary—Intermediate-rate sink-tip

LEADERS: Topwater—Bass bug taper monofilament, 8- to 10-lb tippet,
9 feet long,
Subsurface—Untapered fluorocarbon, 6- to 10-lb test,
9 to 12 feet long

SMALL TOOLS: Essential—Nippers, forceps, hook hone
Fall and Spring—Thermometer
Optional—Tape measure

STRIKE INDICATORS: Two sizes, peg-on hard Styrofoam type

CARRYING GEAR: Multi-Pocket Vest—Best for lots of gear
Waist-Pack—Hot weather option

WADING: Breathable Chest Waders—Most versatile
Wet Wading—Warm water, hot weather option
Hip Boots—Creek fishing option

Note: For rod recommendations, see the Rod Chart earlier in this chapter. For more information on waders, boots, and vests, see the "On-Foot Smallmouth" chapter.

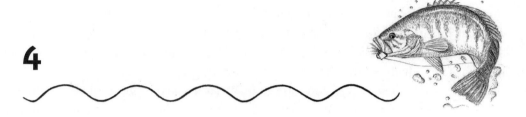

4

Anatomy of a Smallmouth Stream

The changing currents, swirling eddies, quiet pools, and chattering riffles that make river water so beautiful can also make river habitat confusing for the angler. In this chapter, I'll briefly describe the most important components of a river and explain how and when smallmouth use each area. (Many river features have several names, so I try to use the most widely accepted terms.)

If you haven't done much river fishing before, you'll find that moving water is a different world with plenty of new elements to understand. And even trout anglers already familiar with the features of a stream can benefit from this chapter, because smallmouth sometimes utilize habitat differently than trout do.

River Substrates

Substrate simply means the river bottom, and most river substrates fall into four general types: silt/sand, gravel, rubble, or boulders. Of course, each of these bottom materials, and combinations of them, have specific meaning for both smallmouth and angler.

Silt/Sand

Silt/Sand is the small stuff river anglers hate. This soft material is not only hard to wade in, but silt, especially, is destructive to riverine ecosystems. Extra-fine particles of loamy soils suspend in the water column for extended periods, creating the coffee-with-cream look that anglers dread. This silt-laden water greatly reduces visibility for the fish and limits photosynthesis. And when it finally does settle to the bottom, silt smothers the rocky substrates that support much of a stream's invertebrate production. Sadly, silt in our rivers has become common in agricultural areas. And while many silty waters still support limited numbers of smallmouth, generally the more silt, the lower the density of all species.

Sandy substrates are also common in many rivers, stemming from both natural and human-caused erosion. Shifting sand bottoms allow very little food production, so are poor fish producers. However, areas of a river with hard sand can hold fair to good numbers of smallmouth. If large logs are mired in the sand, the smallies (and minnows and invertebrates) can use the wood cover as a partial substitute for rocks. As a rule, a river collects more sand the farther it flows. So while a large river may be mostly sand in its lower sections, its middle and upper reaches generally contain less sand and better smallmouth habitat.

Gravel

Gravel is important for a healthy stream. It's often defined as anything larger than course sand and smaller than fist-sized rock. While gravel will shift during high water episodes, much of the time it stays put, allowing the production of aquatic life. Gravel is also the prime spawning substrate for smallmouth. In a few places, some individual fish spawn on flat rocks or hard sand. But in most rivers and lakes gravel is essential for reproduction.

Rubble

On many rivers, rubble makes up the majority of good smallmouth habitat. Rubble (sometimes called cobble) is about 3 inches to a foot in diameter (fist to football-sized rock). It supports a multitude of minnows, crayfish and smaller invertebrates. It is also large enough to offer the smallmouth some current protection and small ambush sites. If I were assigned to create the ideal smallmouth stream, I'd give it about 75% rubble, and make the remainder gravel and boulders.

Boulders

Smallies seem to love boulders, so lots of guys go Ga-Ga over 'em, assuming the more of them in a river the better the fishing. Well, it's true that big rocks, especially those over 18 inches in diameter, make good current buffers and ambush sites for smallmouth. Mid-channel boulders, especially, act as fish cover. On faster-flowing waterways, large boulders may be the prime locations where fish escape strong flows.

However, rivers that are primarily boulders or have lots of slab rock don't produce much forage, so have low fish densities. And plenty of superb smallmouth streams across the continent have very few big rocks; in these waters the fish get along just fine with wood, rubble and smaller substrates.

Where big rocks are common, resist the temptation to cast only to above-the-surface boulders. On most rivers, obvious rocks get pounded by anglers. Furthermore, on sandy rivers the eddy downstream of a big rock often collects so much sand that it isn't a prime smallmouth location. On these rivers, deep water boulders (at least a couple feet below the surface) and wood cover invariably hold more big fish.

Understanding River Current

Here's where stream anatomy gets really interesting. I've been fishing moving water for decades, but the complexities and effects of river current still amaze and fascinate me.

Fishing classic smallmouth habitat—a riffle tumbling into a small pool with a distinct current break.

ANATOMY OF A STREAM

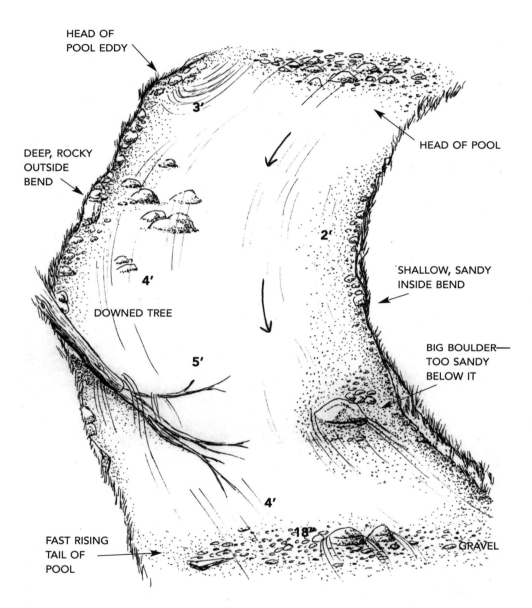

HEAD OF
POOL EDDY

3'

HEAD OF POOL

DEEP, ROCKY
OUTSIDE
BEND

2'

SHALLOW, SANDY
INSIDE BEND

4'

DOWNED TREE

BIG BOULDER—
TOO SANDY
BELOW IT

5'

4'

18"

GRAVEL

FAST RISING
TAIL OF
POOL

Common stream features. At different times, smallmouth use the head and tail of the pool and all the areas on the left.

Gradient

A river's gradient is simply how many feet it drops per mile. Gradients between 4 and 7 feet per mile seem to suit smallmouth best. Waterways with less fall than this are often regarded as low-gradient or "slow-flowing," and those with more are considered high-gradient or "fast-flowing."

However, numerous western and mid-south mountain rivers have high gradients overall, but still offer great smallmouthing. In these cases, most of the drop occurs in just a few sets of rapids or waterfalls and long stretches of the river have only moderate, smallmouth-friendly gradients. So when trying to determine if a river supports smallies (or where in the river they might be), observe it from as many locations as possible.

Riffles

Riffle, pool, riffle, pool, riffle, ad infinitum—the ideal smallmouth stream would be an endless series of shallow, rocky, fast-water riffles and deep, hard-bottom slow-flowing pools. Percentage-wise, it would be around 75% pool habitat and 25% riffle water. Of course, few real-life waterways are arranged exactly so, but almost all good smallmouth rivers have a significant amount of riffles.

Sometimes described as the food larders of a stream, riffles are indeed full of aquatic life. When doing forage assessments for my stream smallmouth schools, riffles are where we routinely find high concentrations of minnow species, hordes of crayfish and a plethora of aquatic insects. So even though smallies may not venture as far into shallow riffles as bug-eating trout do, riffles are as critical for the biological health of warmwater rivers as they are for coldwater streams. And as most smallie fans know, the species loves to feed at the head-of-pool area just downstream of a riffle.

Runs

A run is essentially a transition between a riffle and a pool. Runs (also called glides) are faster-flowing than pools, slower than rapids and deeper than riffles. Runs are abundant on some rivers and uncommon on others. How much smallmouth bass actually use runs also varies from river to river. On waterways that have numerous rocky runs but pools which are quite silty or sandy, smallmouth regularly do much of their feeding in the runs. Conversely, in rivers where pool substrates are mostly rock and gravel, fish use runs during low light periods and from the mid-summer through the early fall period. And on almost all rivers, runs are prime locations in early fall for minnow-eating smallies.

Big rivers, if they aren't sandy or silty, can produce lots of big smallies like this one.

Boulder Fields

Boulder fields or "rock gardens" (as paddlers often call them) are a riffle/run hybrid. They are most common on large rivers with low banks and extremely rocky bottoms. In this situation, the river is unable to scour a deep channel, so it spreads out and creates wide, shallow flats with dozens of emerging boulders. Besides being picturesque, boulder fields offer a huge array of fish holding locations in the form of small eddies, pockets and current breaks.

Rapids

Rapids are another fast-water hangout for bronzebacks. They're created where the gradient is steep, the channel narrows and the bottom is heavily rock, forcing the river to rush through a constricted channel that it can't scour any deeper. The main difference between a riffle and a rapids is that the rapids has more gradient.

If numerous large boulders create eddies and pockets of calmer water in the whitewater, plenty of smallies will use them, so fishing rapids can be highly productive. But use extra caution when wading or float fishing in fast water. A wading staff is helpful if you're on foot; if you're floating, wear your life jacket and secure the gear in a waterproof bag.

Outside and Inside Bends

On rivers that carry significant amounts of sand or silt, understanding the outside and inside bend concept is essential. It's simply the hydrology of current speed. As the river winds around a bend, slower-flowing water near the inside (shorter) bank gets filled with fine-particle substrates, while faster-flowing water near the outside bank keeps it scoured out. Thus, the outer side of the bend may be 4 feet deep with cobble substrate and the inner side sandy and just 10 inches deep. One side holds fish and the other obviously doesn't. But it isn't so obvious on low-visibility rivers; many times, I've seen inexperienced river anglers fruitlessly flailing away at inside bends. Don't make the same mistake.

River Pools

Like people, pools come in a variety shapes. Pools below waterfalls and dams (also called "plunge pools") can be scoured out to extreme depths—even 25 feet. In contrast, most pools in slower-flowing water are only a few feet deep, often in the 3- to 7-foot range. Some pools are very short, perhaps only a few yards long, while other pools extend hundreds of yards. But they all serve as essential resting, sanctuary and feeding habitat for smallmouth. In fact, a major factor limiting the number of large smallmouths in a given section of stream is the lack of deeper pools. I've seen many shallow sections of smaller streams where few pools exceed 3 feet deep and few fish surpass a foot. But if those pools were around 5 feet deep, that part of the river would have big smallies. If those pools also had wood or boulder cover, the number of smallies over 15 inches could be truly impressive.

On larger rivers, smallmouth also hold in other areas of the waterway besides pools. But in small streams, smallies may spend almost all of their time in pools, because all other areas in the stream are so shallow. On these smaller waters the value of adequate pool habitat can't be overstated.

Head, Middle and Tail

Because pools are so important to both the fish and the fisher, it pays to understand their different components. Many pools have well-defined "head," "middle" and "tail" sections. The upper or "head-of-pool" area is a prime location for actively feeding fish of all species. And on some rivers, the head-of-pool area holds virtually every smallmouth. On extra-low-fertility rivers (rivers with very low alkalinity, most often dark-stained from bog or marsh drainage) food sources are extremely limited. Therefore, smallmouth gather where that forage is concentrated—at the head of the pool. In these waters, a great-looking pool can be a hundred yards long, but all the fish will be in the upper 15 feet of it.

The mid-pool area, while not necessarily in the exact middle of a pool, often holds the deepest and slackest water, and is used by the fish as a resting or sanctuary zone. What old-time river anglers call a "hole" is the very deepest mid-pool area.

On larger streams and rivers where pools commonly exceed 100 feet in length, the lower end or "tail-of-pool" area often holds feeding fish. As the pool shallows out, the current velocity increases, which creates and maintains a rocky food-producing shelf. Especially when the river drops to summer velocities, smallmouth and other species regularly use the tails of pools. In this situation, don't fail to fish the tail.

Flats

The most confusing and ill-defined pool feature is the flat. Some fishing writers like to call virtually every shallow tail-of-pool area and inside bend, no matter how tiny, a flat. But most of us use the term more sparingly. Many streams are too small to have flats worthy of the name. On big rivers, extensive inside bend areas 2 to 3 feet deep qualify as flats. If these areas are gravel-bottomed rather than silty, smallies will often hunt on these flats during mornings and evenings. Flats with weed beds can be particularly productive.

RIFFLE/POOL SIDE VIEW

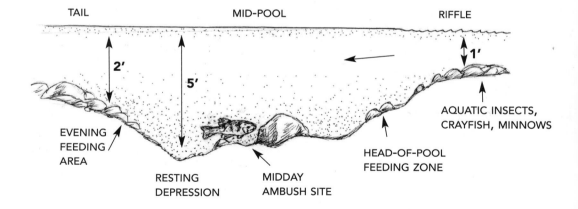

Other Fish-Holding Features

Eddies

Look for bronze where the river flows backwards. Bank eddies are often the primary fish-holding locations in outside bends and on stretches of river where most of the current is moderate to fast-flowing. Eddies are actually water going upstream, so they're easy to recognize by observing the surface current. They range from mini-eddies of barely a square foot to ones larger than a living room.

An eddy is created when large rocks rise above the surface, where the bank juts out, or where an island blocks the current, causing some water to flow back upstream to fill the void. The bigger the obstacle in the channel and the faster the downstream flow, the larger the eddy will be and the faster its reverse flow. Conversely, where the downstream current is slow, eddies will have almost slack water. In extra-large eddies, the inside (bank side) of the eddy may have sand deposits and not hold many fish, at least not active ones. The feeding fish will be closer to the outside of the eddy, in or near the current break.

Current Breaks

Current breaks (or "seams"), where two different currents meet, are prime locations for both smallmouth and trout. This mixing of separate currents creates a narrow strip of water, probably only a few inches wide, where the flow is reduced, allowing fish to easily position themselves in the seam. This puts the fish in a good position to grab anything that's swept towards them. You'll find current breaks in lots of places, but especially on the edges of eddies, downstream of boulders and where two channels merge.

Bulges

Most folks don't know it, but the current immediately upstream of a boulder may be slower than the current only inches away. When the river flow meets a large, blunt boulder or log, the water will "bulge" just above the obstruction, slowing as it's pushed slightly upstream. Bulges are seldom large and not easy to see, but active smallmouth regularly use them as feeding stations. While several fish may be in the eddy downstream of the boulder, one aggressive (and often large) fish will position itself in the upstream bulge to be first in line for feeding. So make sure your fly covers the bulge as well as the eddy.

Riprap

Riprap is simply material like boulders, concrete or bricks artificially placed along outside bends to stabilize stream banks and prevent erosion. On many rivers in urban areas, riprapped banks are common. Chunks of concrete dumped over the side of a steep eroding bank may not be aesthetically pleasing, but they do attract smallmouth—often lots of 'em. Especially on sections of rivers where most of the natural rock substrates have been dredged or silted over, riprap may be one of the few places left that supports smallies. The best riprap for smallies is mixed-sized chunks in moderate current.

Undercuts

Undercuts, where dirt banks have been eroded below the water line, are most common on small streams. Trout, even big ones, are notorious for tucking into tiny cuts; smallmouth like larger undercuts. Unless the undercut is at least about 6 inches deep and a foot and a half long, it won't attract smallies. By far the best bronzeback-holders are those that extend well under a tree's root system. The roots are easy to snag on, but if you thoroughly fish these underwater caverns with a snag-guard equipped subsurface fly you'll often be rewarded with big smallmouth.

There you have it—the key river features that any smallmouth-seeker ought to know. Take the time to understand basic stream anatomy, but remember that every waterway is unique. Each river has a distinct personality, and getting to know it well is one of the true joys of smallmouthing.

5

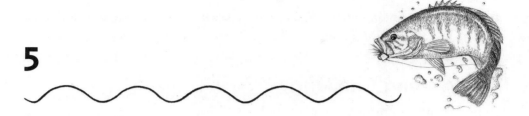

On-Foot Smallmouth

Fly fishing the way it was meant to be. That's how plenty of folks regard on-foot smallmouthing. And it is truly simplified angling; there's no need for pricey watercraft, no need to organize a shuttle, you don't even have to round up a trip partner. With just a rod, some flies and a sturdy set of legs you can head out and fish. For many, this simplicity is the ultimate way to angle.

On-foot smallmouthing has a lot more going for it than just the fishing. Standing in a stream on a quiet summer evening can be an almost mystical experience. Hearing the soft murmur of a rocky riffle, feeling the power of the flow against your legs, watching the water slip downstream as you rhythmically cast—this soothes the soul and puts the body in touch with the natural world like few other outdoor activities. And many of my most memorable wildlife viewing experiences have been while I'm quietly standing in or easing along a stream. I've had plenty of engaging on-stream encounters with deer, otters, beavers, coyotes, armadillos, herons and other critters.

Wade fishing has utilitarian value well beyond the enjoyment and relaxation it offers. In our increasingly sedentary society, flab and lack of exercise have become major health concerns. So I'm happy when I feel thoroughly tired after a full day on stream, because regular wade fishing is such a great way to keep fit. I've rarely visited a gym, yet I'm still fly-rod thin. Can I attribute my sleek physique at least partly to all those marvelous miles hiking up and down streams? I think so, and you could, too.

Of course, not every smallmouth destination is on-foot friendly, but competent wade fishers still have an immense amount of water to enjoy. Many mid-sized rivers comfortably accommodate the on-foot as well as the float angler. Even some of the very largest smallmouth rivers and lakes have shallow sections that are eminently wadable. And hundreds of intimate creeks are the exclusive domain of the wader. This tallies to thousands of miles of fishable water.

The Wading Challenge

Every year in my Stream Smallmouth Schools, I teach dozens of people to fish on foot, but only some become committed wade anglers. Why? 'Cause wading is a challenge. Anyone who wades knows that walking in water, especially in rivers, is a lot tougher than on land. The uneven river bottom may be covered with slippery rocks and unseen obstacles, while changing currents try to throw you off balance. If you're new to wading, don't be discouraged if you feel awkward and exhausted the first time. The next day will seem easier, and over time you'll develop a skill you can be truly proud of, because only the fit can master it.

Fitness is essential for on-foot smallmouthing, because of the need to cover water—lots of it. Because of what they eat, smallmouth densities are often much lower than trout numbers. Even in a small creek there can be over 1,000 trout per mile, while that same amount of water will seldom support more than 300 smallies per mile. And most of these will be small. So on smaller streams, you'll need to cover a mile or two of water a day—wading along, getting in position, casting, then moving again as soon as the bite at that spot dries up.

For me, the wading challenge is part of what makes smallmouth angling so rewarding. I love to work water never seen by those who hover within 100 yards of the bridge. I consider it a compliment when buddies complain they can't keep up with me. How about you?

Just a rod and reel, some flies and sturdy legs are all the on-foot fisher needs to enjoy quiet, scenic streams and high-jumping smallmouth.

Carefully and cautiously working bank eddies is a productive technique for the on-foot angler.

The Sneak Technique

It's hard to overemphasize the need for careful and cautious approaches while wading. Especially when you're coming at the targets from an upstream position, it's easy to send silt and sound down to the fish. There are several ways to minimize alarming the quarry when wading. One is to walk on the bank whenever possible. This eliminates wading sounds or kicking up debris, plus it is often easier than wading. And if the water is clear, hunker down to lower your silhouette and sneak into casting position. Smallies in small, clear waters can be extremely spooky. Your shadow, towering silhouette and bank vibrations can all spook the fish, so work to minimize these alarm bells.

When you must wade, choose your route carefully. Try to avoid slogging through silty flats. If you inadvertently stir up debris, just stand in place for several minutes to allow the material to pass downstream and let the fish resume feeding. To minimize loud splashing sounds that can also scare fish, do the "wader's shuffle" as you approach a casting position. Slowly and quietly slide your feet along the bottom rather than high-stepping. The goal is to get close enough for accurate casts, but not so tight you spook 'em; 40 to 45 feet is the usual distance.

If you can't get within casting range of a choice downstream target, feed out slack line and allow the current to carry the fly to the fish. Sometimes this works. On occasion, I've only been able to wade within 80 feet of a spot, so after stretching out a 65-foot cast, I let the fly drift the rest of the way. Working a fly on an 80-foot line is interesting, and hooking a 17-incher that far away is hair-raising.

The Top Down/Bottom Up Approach

Want to "double your smallmouth, double your fun?" You scour the same water two entirely different ways, first using topwaters and then with bottom bouncers. I call it "Top Down/Bottom Up" fishing.

Start by heading down river armed with an appropriate surface fly. Fishing your topwater against the current, you can hook the most active fish in the most enjoyable way. When you've reached your downstream limit, it's time to "hop" your way back upstream to the car with a subsurface fly. Switch your leader as well as your fly; instead of a tapered topwater leader, change to a long, untapered one.

Even if the topwaters produced plenty of fish, there are likely still more smallies that wouldn't strike on the surface. These can often be tempted by the Crayfish Hop or another with-the-current technique. In the course of the day, you give the fish two appealing presentations, probably catch some on both techniques and end up right where you started. Like I said, Top Down/Bottom Up fishing is great.

Wading Gear

Waders and Boots

The official image of the on-foot fly fisher is always a person in chest waders. But that's only one wading option for the smallmouth angler. I grew up in hip boots on shallow streams and still wear hippers quite often. They are easy to get on and off, extremely comfortable and adequate for many small streams. I do lots of brush-busting, so I like the heavy-duty latex variety for their durability, and I rarely get too hot in hip boots. If you're going to do a lot of creeking around, a quality pair of hip boots is a good choice.

Naturally, if you want to dry-wade in bigger and deeper waters, chest waders are the ticket. Good quality breathable waders are pricey, but if you're careful they will last a long while and they're much more comfortable than non-breathable varieties. One situation where the non-breathables are fine is in cold water. If you plan to wade only during spring and fall, a less expensive, but warmer pair of neoprene waders is the way to go.

The smallie fan's third option is wet wading. Just about everywhere, summer streams warm into the 70s or 80s. When the air is hot and the water is bath temperature, wet wading is the most comfortable way to fish. But, don't try to get by with just shorts and sandals. Unless you have rhino hide, your legs will get scratched up, and open-toed sandals are a recipe for bruised feet. Instead, wade in a pair of thin, fast-drying synthetic long pants and some ankle-high wading boots with good grip. Watersport shoes with an enclosed toe and quick-draining foot can also work well. No matter what your footwear, get felt soles if the stream's rocks are smooth and slippery. If substrates are more gravely and you're going to do a lot of stream bank hiking, get longer-lasting lug soles.

Packing the Gear

For on-foot fishing, I much prefer a traditional multi-pocket vest for carrying flies and gear. A vest allows me to bring additional items like extra reels, a camera, even a rain jacket or lunch. However, some find a vest too hot or uncomfortable and like to squeeze everything into a waist pack. A good compromise may be to use a vest during spring and fall, and switch to a waist pack during the heat of summer.

Wet-wading and carrying only limited gear in a waist pack and on a lanyard is a good way to travel light and stay cool.

Vest Contents

A favorite part of my Smallmouth Schools is the vest contents exhibit. If you unpack all the pockets of my vest, here's what you'll find:

TIM'S VEST CONTENTS

Box of 20 Topwaters
Box of 30 Subsurface Flies
Box of Specialty and Hot Patterns
Fluorocarbon (6, 8, 10 lb test)
Tapered Leaders
Mono Tippet (8, 10 lb test)
Steel Leaders (for Pike, Muskie)
Extra Line Spool (Sink-Tip Line)
Line Dressing and Cleaning Cloth
Strike Indicators (3 sizes)
Small Split Shot

Thermometer
Nippers
Forceps
Hook Hone
Insect Repellent
Sunscreen
Band-Aids
Multi-Tool Pocket Knife
Small Camera
Orange and Snickers Bars
Water Bottle

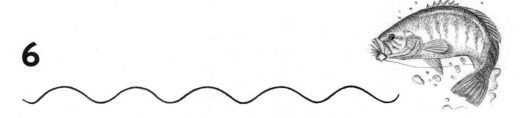

6

Subsurface Smallmouthing

It's true, sometimes just about any technique will catch smallies. When water conditions are optimum and the stream is filled with hungry nine-inchers, plenty of methods will snare a fish or three. But if you want to catch more than the occasional specimen, if you want to score when conditions aren't so favorable, and if you want to consistently fool the big boys, then mastering the best techniques is essential.

The Crayfish Hop

Here's what I've long told my smallmouth school students: "If you only learn one fishing technique, make sure it's the Crayfish Hop." This is equally apt advice for everyone reading this book. Certainly the Hop is superb during the summer crayfish season, but it's also deadly in the spring and fall. In fact, when I positively, absolutely gotta produce bronzebacks, this is my go-to method.

As its name implies, the Crayfish Hop represents the motion of a crayfish—a fleeing crayfish. And therein lies its secret. While "matching the hatch" with a perfect imitation often catches trout, "matching the motion" is the key to catching smallmouth. Here's why:

Why So Good

Smallies eat lots of crayfish. In fact, in many waters these crunchy crustaceans account for over 75% of the fish's diet during the summer. But the crayfish is no fool; when it sees a smallmouth approaching it tries to escape with a backwards hopping motion. Millennia of genetic programming cause the smallmouth to instantly notice and key in on this motion. This "triggering characteristic" is the most prominent feature of the prey (the crayfish), which causes instant recognition in the brain of the predator (the smallmouth).

By exaggerating this triggering characteristic we can create a "supernormal stimulus" (in scientific lingo) with our fly. Which, in fact, causes the fish to focus on our offering sooner than it would on a natural crayfish! And this motion (and sometimes color) often triggers fish into striking even when crayfish numbers are low! A pretty neat trick, eh? Here's how to do the Hop.

THE CRAYFISH HOP—SIDE VIEW

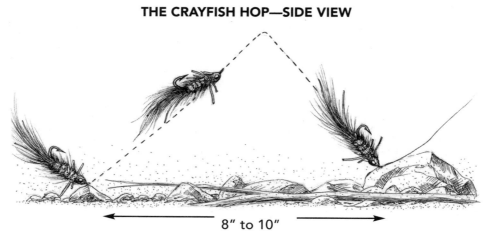

8" to 10"

The Crayfish Hop retrieve exaggerates the motion of a fleeing crayfish, a powerful stimulus for smallmouth.

Doing the Hop

First, start with a "weight-forward" fly. (Part 2 of this book covers fly patterns in detail; in this chapter I'll just briefly discuss fly types to use for specific techniques.) A fly tied with barbell metal eyes will sink head-first, quickly reach bottom and produce the best up-and-down motion. Attached to an untapered leader and a floating line with a strike indicator, a weight-forward fly can be hopped enticingly along the bottom. The idea is to work the fly with-the-current through likely pools, eddies and current breaks. Use a pull-and-pause retrieve, just slightly faster than the current, yet slow enough to allow the fly to stay near bottom. The indicator is essential and allows you to detect the often light strikes of big smallmouth.

As testimony to the Crayfish Hop's consistency, I've seen it produce day after day, on the tiniest streams and the largest rivers. It's one of the very best techniques when rivers are high and turbid, but it also pays off when waterways are low and clear. The Hop creates the fly action that fish, especially big ones, like. And it keeps your fly near bottom in the prime strike zone, tempting even sluggish fish.

Another attribute of this fine technique is its ability to also entice other river-ine species. There really isn't any better way to catch walleyes, channel catfish and freshwater drum on the fly rod. And I've done exactly that, hundreds of times. When you hook five pounds of hard-charging catfish, you'll wish for a heavier rod and be happy you can do the Hop.

Chuck and Strip?

To do the Hop successfully, knowing when you're in the strike zone is essential. "Chuck and Strip" isn't the name of a topless steak house. It's the technique too many guys employ when they're fishing subsurface flies. They chuck out a fly and absentmindedly strip it in, with little clue to how deep it is or how it's performing in the current. This isn't the way to consistently catch fish. Instead, you should know where in the water column your fly needs to be and keep it there. Often this is right on bottom. Certainly smaller bronze are often aggressive and charge 10 feet to nail a shallow-running fly, but the bigger ones can be maddenly selective. You can pelt a four-foot-deep pool with dozens of casts, your fly passing midway through the water column. Your offering is only 2 feet off bottom, every fish can obviously see it, yet all you catch are small fry. Then you use a fly that reaches bot-tom, and suddenly you're in business, hooking larger fish than you imagined were in the pool. I've seen this scenario play out countless times.

Thus, the weight of your fly is just as important as the pattern. You want to use enough weight so the fly will make contact with the bottom, but not so much that it plummets like a stone. For 3-foot deep, slower-current water, 1/50th-ounce eyes are fine. In 5 feet of water, 1/36th-ounce eyes are better.

A variety of patterns tied "weight-forward" are good for the Crayfish Hop, especially those with plenty of tail animation. Some of these are the Holschlag Hackle Fly, Clouser Minnow, Hare Leech, and HiTail Craw. However, many anatomically correct "crayfish imitations" (so beautiful in a fly box, but stiff and lifeless in the water) are only mediocre producers.

Leaders and Strike Indicators

A fluorocarbon leader is best for subsurface fishing because it's heavier than water, but an untapered thin-diameter mono leader is fine, too. Either should test out at about 8 lbs of strength (2X or 3X diameter). When the water is extremely clear, a 6-lb (4X) leader will increase strikes, but is only practical if fish aren't large and bot-tom substrates aren't snaggy. Leader length should be about 2 1/2 times the water depth (e.g., a10-foot leader for 4 feet of water, a 12-footer for 5 feet).

Next you need a strike indicator large enough to be clearly seen at 35 feet (about the size of your little fingernail or larger). A strike indicator this size isn't buoyant enough to float a 1/50th-ounce fly; it acts solely as a device to detect light strikes. I prefer hard Styrofoam peg-on indicators in bright orange. Whatever type you use, put it right at the leader/line junction. And don't try to get by with too short a leader when using this method, or the indicator will be pulled so far below the surface it won't be visible.

The Hopping Retrieve

Once you're properly rigged, it's time to work on the retrieve. Cast several feet past the targeted area and allow the fly to sink almost to the bottom. Bring the fly back with a pull-and-pause retrieve, letting it momentarily tick bottom on the pause. If the current is very slow, simply pull the fly forward a foot or so with a short line strip. When the current is a little stronger, 6- to 12-inch twitches of the rod tip will hop the fly nicely.

As the illustration shows, the idea is to use the small belly that develops in the line to help pull the fly downstream in short, measured distances. I know, I know. Some preach that you should never allow a belly to develop in the line and never animate the fly with the rod tip. Nuts.

Often a line belly is inevitable during river smallmouthing, and we must learn how to deal with it. And sometimes (such as doing the Crayfish Hop) a belly can be used to our advantage! Once you get the hang of it, you'll find that maintaining that small belly is the best way to precisely control the retrieve speed. As for animating the fly with the rod tip, it's often the best way to impart the proper action to the fly.

Striking and Hooking

The reason some writers caution so strongly against belly in the line and rod tip use is because they worry these practices always lead to poor hook-setting or not detecting the strike at all. Not necessarily. The key is your strike indicator. I know that a multitude of warmwater fly fishers seldom use indicators, but that's pure foolishness. For with-the-current techniques like the Hop, a strike indicator is absolutely essential. You, I, or anyone throw away half of our strikes when we don't use an indicator, simply because we will never feel all those light bites from fish that quickly reject our fly.

Regarding the issue of not hooking fish due to slack line: My guiding clients, many of just average skill, have hooked and landed thousands of big smallmouth. All the while, they were using their rod tips to animate the fly and often had a substantial belly in the line. However, I taught them to always keep the rod tip low (within 2 feet of the surface) and pointing towards the fly as much as possible.

From this position, when they get a strike they can come up forcefully with the rod, at the same time stripping in slack line with their non-casting hand. And if they think the first hook-set was a little light, they immediately hit 'em again with a second hard yank of the rod. Despite smallmouths having extremely hard mouths and legendary head-shaking abilities, this hooking method misses darn few fish. Learn it and you'll love it, too.

DOING THE CRAYFISH HOP

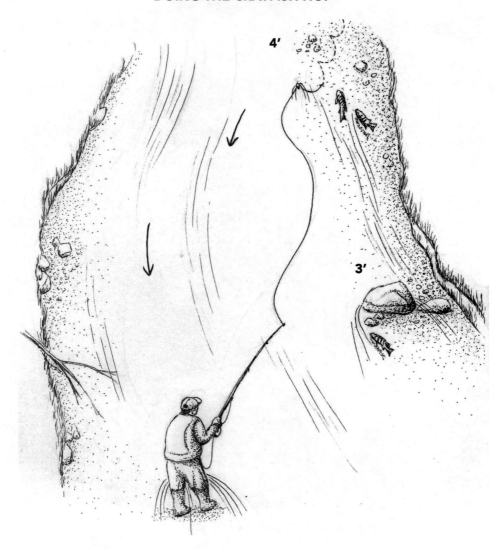

Using a floating line, long leader, a weight-forward fly and strike indicator, the angler hops a fly along the bottom slightly faster than the current. With this method you can work 30 to 40 feet of water per cast.

Doing the Crayfish Hop with a Holschlag Hackle Fly from a boat yielded this fine fish.

Hellgrammite Too?

Don't be confused by the strike indicator; the Crayfish Hop is substantially different than dead drift nymphing. Dead drifting is only infrequently a superior technique for bigger smallmouth. Even on rivers where hellgrammites are abundant, a productive way to fish hellgrammite patterns is to give them an action beyond pure dead drifting. In this situation, as the fly is being pulled downstream by moderate current, slight tugs or twitches of the line translate into mini-hops by the fly. By using a large hellgrammite pattern with a sizable tail and/or legs, you end up with fly action that probably looks to the fish a lot like my Crayfish Hop technique.

> **PLACES TO DO THE CRAYFISH HOP**
>
> Slow and Moderate-flowing Pools,
>   (5 feet deep or less)
>
> Moderate-flowing Runs
>
> Current Breaks
>
> Large Eddies
>   (at least 30 inches deep)

The Minnow Swing

This may be the most popular smallmouth technique. Strike detection is simple, it's easy to learn and it's a fine way to fish runs, small eddies and tails and heads of pools. Somewhat similar to streamer fishing for trout, the Minnow Swing is an against-the-current retrieve that allows you to maintain a semi-tight line. It also offers the options of using either floating or sinking line. It's especially effective on fast-flowing waterways because the swing allows you to maintain reasonably good fly control in heavy current.

The way I use the Minnow Swing to work bank eddies on shallow streams is by wading slowly downstream, staying 25 to 30 feet out from the eddies I intend to fish. When I'm still a little upstream of perpendicular from the target, I cast into the eddy and immediately throw a small upstream mend in the line so the fly has time to sink before the current pulls it downstream. As the slow-sinking fly moves down and across stream I give it extra animation. Depending on the fly type, I animate it with either short line strips or small twitches of the rod tip. If I'm using a lightweight Deceiver or a Flash Dancer (with its bright undulating wing) I use slow 12-inch strips. For more-darting patterns like the Shenk's Streamer and Whitetail Hare, shorter rod twitches are better. Whatever fly you use, imparting this extra action is key to maximizing strikes. When first trying a pattern for the Minnow

THE MINNOW SWING

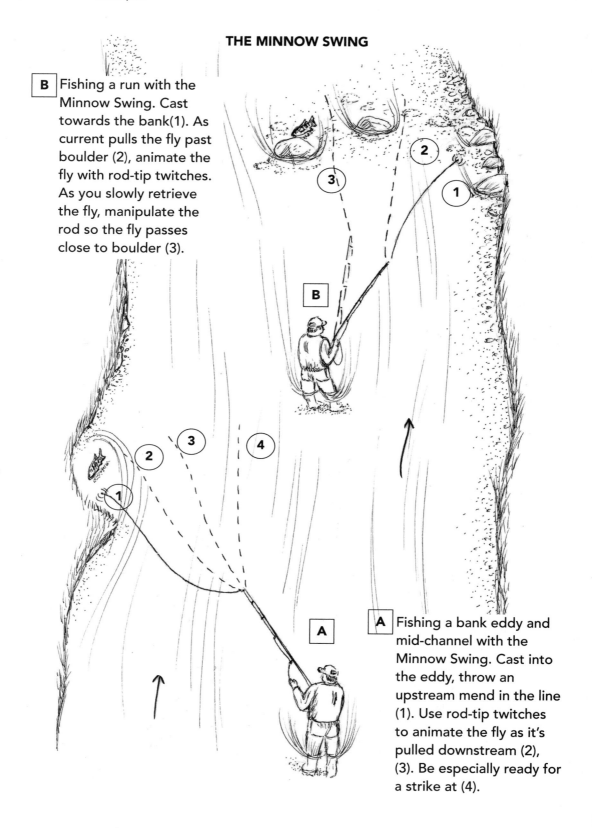

B Fishing a run with the Minnow Swing. Cast towards the bank(1). As current pulls the fly past boulder (2), animate the fly with rod-tip twitches. As you slowly retrieve the fly, manipulate the rod so the fly passes close to boulder (3).

A Fishing a bank eddy and mid-channel with the Minnow Swing. Cast into the eddy, throw an upstream mend in the line (1). Use rod-tip twitches to animate the fly as it's pulled downstream (2), (3). Be especially ready for a strike at (4).

Swing, carefully observe it to make sure it's properly balanced and doesn't spin in the current and twist the leader.

If no strikes occur in the eddy, I continue the retrieve until the fly has swung almost directly downstream of me. Sometimes fish will follow the fly out of the eddy and, like trout, wait until the fly gets to the end of its downstream swing before making their move. In fact, on many days you can tease more fish into striking by twitching the fly several times while it is trailing directly downstream before you pick up the fly to cast again. This against-the-current motion is how many minnow and shiner species dart forward and back while they feed in fast flows. So it has powerful appeal to riverine predators like smallies.

The Minnow Swing also works well in runs. If the run is long with scattered boulders, start at the upper end of it and move downstream 8 to 10 feet between retrieves. Cast to the fishiest side of the run and, as the fly is pulled downstream and away from the bank, try to maneuver the fly past the most likely fish locations—subsurface boulders, logs or patches of weeds. Manipulating your rod and line to get your offering to swing right past the most likely targets will significantly increase strikes.

Lines and Sink Rates

You can do the Minnow Swing with almost any fly that can produce darting minnow-like action, but the sink rate of your fly is critical. With a floating line, too heavy a fly will swing very little; instead it plummets and quickly hangs bottom. Too light, and the fly rides high in the water column, while it's dragged quickly downstream. Just right, and the fly will sink to at least mid-depth and swing slowly in the current.

Because a floating line is more versatile than a sink-tip line and because I enjoy casting them more than I do sink-tips, I often use a floater for the Minnow Swing. This means I carefully calibrate my fly weight depending on the current speed and water depth. So for a series of shallow slow-flowing eddies I might use a lightly weighted Shenk's Streamer. Then for a deeper, faster-flowing run I'll switch to a heavier fly, perhaps a Deceiver-style streamer. In fact, over the course of a single day I often use flies of 3 or 4 different weights (sink rates) depending on the conditions I encounter.

Of course, the other way to influence fly depth with a floating line is to add split shot to the leader. But it often comes off the leader and interferes with the fly's action, and very much split shot casts poorly. Still, I use it now and then when I want to add just a little more weight to a specific fly.

Sinking Lines

A better alternative to lots of split shot is to use a sink-tip or even full-sink line. In fact, plenty of less-experienced fly casters like sink-tips because they have trouble throwing heavy flies. They avoid the heavy fly issue by using a slow or intermediate sink-rate line and a lightweight fly. With this set-up you can still do the Minnow Swing—very well. By varying the leader length you can also vary how deep the fly goes! A very light fly on a sink-tip line will be pulled deeper on a short (3-foot) leader. This same fly on a longer (7-foot) leader will ride higher in the current.

And where currents are really strong, a few highly experienced anglers use a full-sink line to productively fish against the flow. They feel they don't get as much line belly with the full-sink, giving them better fly control and strike detection. The danger is allowing the line to pause too long in snaggy areas where it can sink completely to the bottom and snag around multiple rocks.

No matter what type line or fly you use, you always need to know how deep you want the fly to go and make sure it stays there. I've said this a couple times already, but it bears repeating: controlling fly depth is key to successful smallmouth fishing; it's one of the most important pieces of the subsurface puzzle.

The In-Their-Face Technique

With the Minnow Swing, I talked about twitching the fly while it trails directly downstream from you. The In-Their-Face technique carries that concept to the extreme. The idea is keep a fly in the same small zone for as long as 45 seconds. Using rod twitches and the pull of the current to keep a sleek-profiled, lightweight fly from snagging bottom, you can make a fly hover and dart forward and back, while it remains nearly stationary. For reasons known only to the smallies, sometimes they love this non-retrieve. Plenty of times, I've worked a fly this way for what seemed like an eternity, and just when I was ready to cast to another spot— bingo, a fish whacked it.

The tail-end of pools and log jams are two good places for the In-Their-Face technique. Log jams can be hard to fish and easy to snag on. Letting a fly drift so it is right in front of the jam and then twitching it there for long periods sometimes draws out fish that may have been far back in the cover.

The Drag-and-Pause Retrieve

Type A personalities, you might have trouble with this one, because "slower is better" is the key to success for this retrieve. Sometimes when smallies are inactive, dragging a fly ever-so-slowly along the bottom is one of the best ways to entice 'em.

IN-THEIR-FACE TECHNIQUE

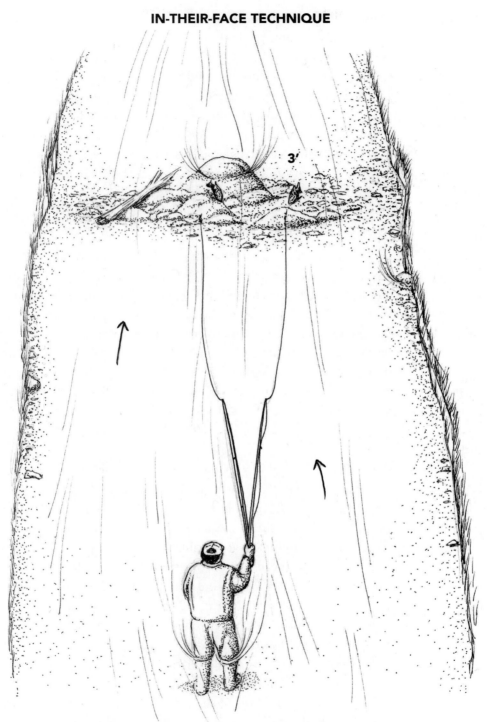

Fishing against the current, thoroughly work a small spot with up-and-down and side-to-side rod tip manipulation.

The Drag-and-Pause retrieve doesn't work well for snaggy areas or where there is substantial current, but in slow-flow pools with clean bottoms, it's irresistible.

Instead of a steady drag, pull the fly slowly along the bottom about 6 to 8 inches, then pause for about 3 seconds. If that doesn't produce, drag the fly even slower and pause even longer. Drag-and-Pause retrieves can be either with, against or across the current. Patterns tied with considerable weight and with upriding hooks (to reduce hang-ups) are best. One of my favorites is the Holschlag Hitail Craw because when the fly is at rest its tail is still waving enticingly. Strikes will be very light, often just an increasing pressure when you try to drag the fly. A sink-tip line will work, but to increase my hook-ups I like to use a floating line and a strike indicator.

The Float-and-Fly

Though this superb technique is presently known to only a handful of fly rodders, I predict it will gain great popularity in the coming years. Its essence is simply suspending a fly below a strike indicator buoyant enough to support the fly, and moving the fly extremely slowly. It is similar to the southern spin fisher's method of suspending a jig below a bobber for smallmouth in winter reservoirs.

Besides being excellent for winter fishing in mid-south lakes, I've found the Float-and-Fly to be unrivaled for river smallies during winter. It also works for spring and summer smallmouth in both lakes and rivers. The "Smallmouth Through the Seasons" and "Difficult Water Conditions" chapters explain how to use this technique for very specific situations. Here I'll describe the general principles behind it.

Precise depth control and the ability to work the fly extremely slowly are the key components of the Float-and-Fly concept. When the fish are suspended at specific depths, when they are sluggish and holding tight to the bottom or even when you want to fish subsurface in very shallow water, being able to keep your fly at an exact depth comes in mighty handy. This is possible with a fly suspended directly below a large indicator. And I do mean large—sometimes I use a 1/32nd-ounce fly that requires an indicator almost as big around as my thumb. However, experienced casters should have no trouble casting this rig on a 7-wt.

The slow retrieve aspect is married to the precise depth component; retrieve at more than a snail's pace and the fly gets immediately pulled out of the intended depth. The slow retrieve is also critical in its own right. Especially in the cold water of early spring, late fall and winter, the fish are sluggish and what you most need is a painfully slow retrieve—exactly what the Float-and-Fly can deliver.

FLOAT-AND-FLY TECHNIQUE

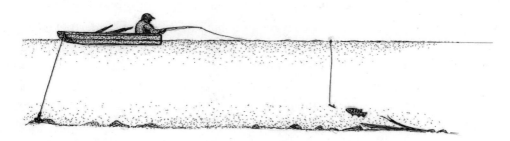

This technique can be used any time fish are extremely inactive, but the Float-and-Fly is best in cold, slack water. A horizontal-riding fly can be suspended at fish-eye level and worked ultra-slowly.

Pepper Casts

No this isn't about some special flavoring, but about "peppering" the entire area with casts. Where the banks are low and the bottom is hard, riffles and runs on large rivers sometimes spread out wide and shallow, creating boulder fields. By mid-summer, dozens of emerging boulders create a huge array of fish-holding locations in the form of small eddies, pockets and slack-water zones. In this target-rich environment, an angler who can quickly pepper the area with accurate casts is the one who will connect with the most fish. Just remember to choose your route carefully and to wade quietly.

Because each spot is generally small, just a cast or two to each should suffice. And because target zones are all around you, retrieves can be from any direction—with-the-current, against or cross-current. Since depths are probably just a foot or two, start the retrieve almost as soon as the fly hits the water. Sometimes a small, accurately placed topwater is the ticket; more often it's a slow-sinking hare leech or similar subsurface pattern. For smaller fish, these shallow boulder areas are some of the most action-packed places you'll encounter, and on rivers where they're common, they offer a pepper caster hours of enjoyment.

7

Topwater Techniques

It makes even tough guys tremble. Eighteen inches of bronze power engulfing a popper is one of the most thrilling phenomena in angling. I've long thought so, and an increasing number of other fly fishers agree. And plenty of clients say one smallie on top is worth ten subsurface. That may be a little extreme, but nearly everyone who has ever taken a smallmouth off the surface is hooked on the experience. We dream about the explosive take, we dream about the quiet sip, we dream about the strike when we're expecting it and dream about those that take us completely by surprise.

Thankfully, consistently taking smallmouth off the surface doesn't have to be just the stuff of daydreams. I'm called "Mr. Popper" by many who know of my long-standing passion for coaxing big bronzebacks to the top. Here's the nitty-gritty on topwater smallmouthing.

Topwater Tales

BIG smallies love topwaters! If you're skeptical, consider this. For each of the past dozen years, at least 7 of the 10 biggest fish my clients caught came off the top. This same ratio holds true for individual guiding days. Nearly 75% of the biggest smallmouth caught and released each day were taken on surface flies. These are 19- to 21-inch (4- to 5-plus-pound) fish! And these weren't from remote wilderness waters; many were caught from easily accessible rivers and streams across a wide geographical region.

'Course this doesn't include all the topside big boys that I and friends have caught while fishing for fun. These total hundreds over 18 inches, including two 5 1/2-pound beauties that were a couple of my personal best. Again, only a minority of these lunksters came from wilderness waters; most were caught from close-to-home rivers and streams. Plus, thousands of "smaller" 12- to 17-inchers also took my or my clients' topwaters. And these records aren't from some bygone era. Just last season, I had many days of great topwatering, including 73 fish in just five hours, and an even more impressive two-client, 103-fish day.

Why on Top?

So why do smallies take surface offerings with such gusto? Forget the "match the bug/frog/mouse" idea. Some the most consistent waters for topwater action are rivers where smallies seldom eat anything off the surface. There are few insect hatches or juicy terrestrials like grasshoppers or crickets, and frogs are virtually nonexistent. In fact, I've guided thousands of hours on rivers where smallies eat mostly crayfish and it is unusual to see fish ever break the surface—except when they're striking a popper, which they do with amazing regularity hour after hour, day after day, year after year.

Why? Only the fish know for sure, but I think I partly answered it in the "Understanding Smallmouth" chapter. *Micropterus dolomieui* is a curious and opportunistic predator. Your topwater, so unusual, is an offer the smallie can't refuse. It's making an odd, yet appealing noise, it's slow-moving, it's obviously struggling and very vulnerable. And just maybe, it reminds him of something he does occasionally see: minnows that are injured or dying and are struggling on the surface. This type of injured prey isn't an everyday occurrence, but predators are always on the lookout for cripples.

I'll leave it like this: If you're the sort who gets peace of mind believing that the yellow piece of foam or cork on the end of your leader really does imitate a mutated frog, giant grasshopper or baby beaver, by all means continue to believe that. Or you could adopt my more tongue-in-cheek observation: "Crayfish and minnows are the smallie's meat and potatoes, poppers and sliders are its ice cream. It eats craws and minnies every meal, but it always leaves room for dessert."

A big smallie caught off the surface. Does fishing get any better?

Tim's Ten Topwater Truths

1. BIG ONES BITE ON TOP

Topwaters aren't just for small fry. In many places the biggest bronze are the ones most susceptible to surface flies.

2. WARMER IS BETTER

Surface fishing for river smallies often gets better as the water gets warmer. Seventy degrees is great, 80 is better. Normally, once water temps fall below 58 that's the end of consistent surface activity. But if the fish are in very shallow water (and you work the fly very slowly) some fish may be coaxed up even at 50 degrees.

3. CLARITY IS KEY

Extremely low water visibility (less than a foot) is generally poor for topwatering. Extreme clarity (especially combined with low flows) is also poor, except during early mornings and evenings. Many waterways with the most consistent surface bites have visibilities in the 2- to 4-foot range.

4. IT'S NOT JUST AN EVENING AFFAIR

Midday surface fishing can be as good as the evening, both where the midday sun noticeably warms the water and where water visibility is less than 3 feet.

5. CONQUERING CURRENT

It isn't dry fly fishing. Don't let your topwater drift quickly downstream with the current. A fly kept over a targeted spot for several seconds is much more effective than one swept quickly away. The best on-foot method is to cast from an upstream position and work the fly against the current.

6. SHALLOW AND CLEAR = QUIET AND SMALL

Be it lake or stream, if the water is clear and shallow, quiet topwaters like small sliders or tiny poppers are often best. Big, noisy offerings may spook 'em.

7. DEEP AND DIRTY = BIG AND NOISY

If the water is deep, visibility is low or there is a surface chop, big bugs and poppers are the way to go. In these conditions, it takes a fly that makes plenty of noise to be noticed by the fish.

8. SOUND AND MOTION MATTER MORE THAN COLOR.

Occasionally fish will exhibit a strong color preference, but in most circumstances what a surface fly does is far more important than its hue.

9. TWO GOOD CASTS

A few accurate casts to each specific target are much better than a barrage. On many days, the first 2 casts to a spot produce about 90% of all strikes, no matter how many more are delivered. So make those first casts count, getting within a foot of the target.

10. YOU WON'T CATCH 'EM IF YOU DON'T USE 'EM

You can't catch fish on topwaters if you don't use topwaters. It's an obvious truth, but too often ignored. Because they don't have confidence in topwaters, many anglers only fish the surface briefly or haphazardly. Hence, they seldom catch fish on top, thereby ensuring they never gain the confidence and expertise required. The way to break this cycle is to use topwaters regularly. Try them for an hour, if no interest go subsurface for a couple hours. Repeat that sequence over the course of the day. Because there wasn't a top bite at 10:00 doesn't mean they won't hit like gangbusters at 2:00.

ON-FOOT TOPWATERING

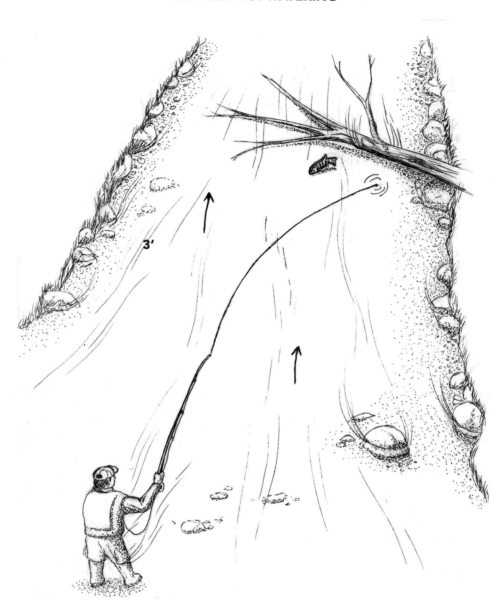

When fishing wood cover with a topwater, put the first cast near the bank-and-wood junction. As you animate the fly, the current will pull it towards mid-channel.

Topwater Tactics

Casting Positions

A surface fly drifting quickly away in the current is what neither we, nor the smallies want. So controlling the downstream drift is key. On smaller streams with slow to moderate flow, the on-foot and boat fisher can obtain pretty good fly control by casting *across and downstream* to targets along the opposite bank. The fly will gradually be pulled away from the bank, but often slowly enough that you'll have time to work the fly appealingly.

Casting directly downstream is another good option, especially if the current is quick (or the water too deep to wade, forcing you to fish the same bank you're standing on). Fishing directly across stream (perpendicular to the current) is practical on very slow-flowing pools or other areas with low current.

Topwater Hotspots

Many fishers use topwaters in only "classic" locations—water near the bank 2 to 3 feet deep, with slow current and lots of rock or wood cover. But you can take smallies on top in many other places, too. If water visibility is low, banks barely a foot

An angler casting across and downstream to a log. This is often the best angle to work targets from when you're on-foot topwatering.

deep can be worth fishing if they have cover. Shoreline cover can be in the form of cobble or boulders, overhanging grass, undercut banks, aquatic vegetation or wood (especially the largest limbs, logs and jams available). In fact, downed trees and log jams are often the hangouts for the biggest bronze in the river.

Smallmouth will also eat topwaters in mid-river and mid-lake locations. The fish only care how far the fly is from them, not how far away dry ground is. Boulders and weed beds, as well as head-of-pool eddies can all be far from a bank, but still produce. Two other mid-channel locations worth targeting are tails of pools and big river "flats." (Flats are essentially shallow, slow-flowing pool areas, often with weed growth.) Many guys seem to believe it's a grievous sin to ever drop a topwater more than a foot from a lake shore or stream bank. But I quit that religion long ago. Over the past quarter century, I've coaxed thousands of surface strikes from spots nowhere near shore.

Tim's Top Presentations

The topwater question I'm asked the most is "What's the best way to fish a popper." My answer is always: "However the fish want it that day." A smart-mouth response? Sort of, but it's also true. The most productive topwater presentation varies significantly from day to day, sometimes even from hour to hour. Why? Only the fish know for sure, but it is likely the interplay of water conditions, weather factors and fish activity levels.

Here are more specific recommendations. When using a popper or any noisy surface fly try my money-in-the-bank presentations:

The Old Reliable

Start with the Old Reliable. Drop the fly on the target. If it isn't drifting, wait 4 seconds, then give it a moderate "pop" (using a short sideways snap of the rod tip). If the current quickly pulls the fly off target, pop it after just 1 second. After the first pop, let the fly sit or drift for 3 seconds, then pop again. Continue this cadence for 5 or 6 more pops. If no takers, pick up and cast again to the same general area and repeat.

Be ready to set the hook as soon as the fly hits the surface (some days there are lots of these instant strikes). More often, takes occur after the first few pops, but sometimes fish will wait until you're thinking about the next cast and ready to pick up the fly. Sneaky fellas, huh?

The Slow Poke

If the Old Reliable isn't so reliable, try the Slow Poke, a significantly slower retrieve. Instead of 3 or 4 seconds between pops, double and triple the pauses to at least 10 seconds. A nice leisurely way to fish, so it should be easy, right? Actually, the Slow Poke is the absolute hardest presentation for Type A personality folks. On plenty of occasions, I've had two clients in the boat: one was following my advice, using an ultra-slow presentation and catching oodles of smallies. The other, a hard-charging type, was catching little and knew why, but just couldn't let his fly sit still long enough to interest the fish.

TOPWATERING BY WATERCRAFT

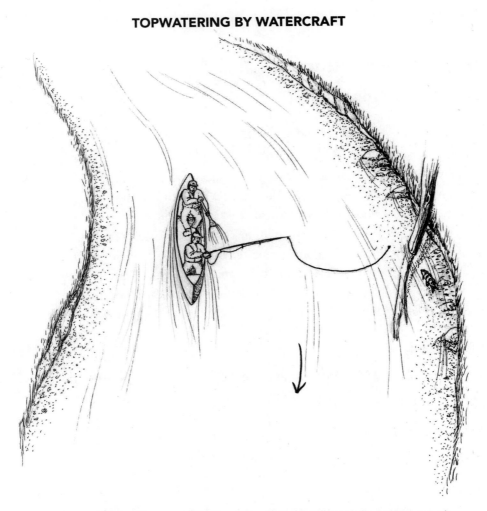

While the bow angler makes accurate across and downstream casts, the stern person should slow and carefully position the craft.

The Machine Gun

Okay, you've tried the two primary presentations and your quarry shows little inclination. Time to pull out the gun, the Machine Gun. This is a rapid fire "pop, pop, pop" retrieve with no more than a 1-second pause between each sound. It only works about 10 to 15% of the time, but on those days, it's a life saver.

On most days and on most waters, one of these three topwater presentations will pay off. But most isn't all. Sometimes those finicky smallies want a combo meal: maybe 4 Machine Gun pops, then a painfully long pause, or maybe vice-versa. You need to be willing offer whatever the fish want that day. And I think that's a big part of the enjoyment and challenge of topwatering—Mr. Bronzeback is a tricky and fickle fella, not tied to obvious insect hatches.

Special Techniques

Skating for Bronze

No, this isn't an Olympic sport. Trout fans sometimes allow their flies to be dragged across the surface, and "skating" a dry fly can be productive for smallies, too. It may not pull up a lot of lunksters, but seeing even a 10-incher slashing away at a fast-moving fly is always exciting. The idea is to use a fly so lightweight and buoyant that it rides very high on the surface. You can use any large, bushy dry fly (one tied on a #8 hook or larger) for this.

After the fly is cast across current, and the current starts pulling the line and leader, the dry fly should skate or skitter quickly over the surface. This causes enough of a surface disturbance that fish often key in on it. Skating is often the best in the evening on clear streams, especially in shallow areas where many small to mid-sized fish gather. Cobble-strewn banks and tails of pools are good places to try.

Popping in Place

Here's another one of those techniques that doesn't work all the time, but saves the day when it does. Actually, Popping in Place is sort of like the In-Their-Face sub-surface technique. It attempts to dazzle 'em with repetition. When the fish seem especially uninterested in standard topwater presentations, keeping a fly over them for as long as 30 to 45 seconds can bring up the most persnickety of them.

Popping in Place works best in slow current and when your popper or bug is directly downstream. The upstream edge of a log jam is a prime location. Without retrieving any line, make the fly pop, gurgle or chug every 3 to 6 seconds using short twitches or snaps of the rod tip. And keep doing it for what seems like forever. I'm not kidding, a number of times I've Popped-in-Place so long I nearly dozed off. Then—BAM! A rip-snorting strike yanked me out of my slumber.

8

Smallmouth
Through the Seasons

Year-round smallmouthing? It's true, fly fishers can catch smallies during every season—not just in the warmer weather from late spring through early fall, but also the chilly days of late fall and even mid-winter.

Of course, to be successful under these widely varying conditions you need to tailor your techniques to each season. I can't emphasize this too strongly. While river smallies can indeed be caught every month of the year, understanding where the fish are and what they are doing in each period is essential for success.

Spring

Ah, glorious spring! For a lot of anglers suffering through the winter doldrums, this is their favorite time for smallmouth. However, most of these folks actually only get out during the end of spring—the spawn period. They miss the first half of the season. If you want to maximize your angling enjoyment, don't neglect early spring.

Early Pre-Spawn Period

Spring on the angling calendar is only about 10 weeks long, yet it's a highly variable time and encompasses at least three distinct periods. It starts with the early pre-spawn. This is when water temperatures reach the upper 40s, which can be the beginning of March in warmer latitudes or early April in northern climes. Historically, few river anglers targeted smallmouth this early. With cold water and often strong flows, it seemed logical to stay away until the rivers became warmer and easier to fish.

However, with increasing interest in river smallmouth and greater angling expertise, more and more folks are now successfully trying for early pre-spawn fish. Certainly the cold, heavy flows present challenges, but those with early-season savvy can still experience great fishing. Here's what you need to know to get in on the action:

During early spring, smallmouth are becoming hormonally primed for upcoming reproduction, but are still several weeks away from actually building nests and laying eggs. In rivers where spawning sites are distant from wintering pools, this early period is when fish start moving upstream to areas where they will later reproduce. In waterways where spawning and wintering habitat are close together, early season movements will be slight.

Warmer Is Better

Virtually everywhere early spring smallies are looking for two things: slower current and warmer water. In these areas, they will acquire energy reserves by feeding on minnows until water temperatures reach the upper 50s and the males start staking out spawning sites. So forget the riffles, runs and mid-river pool locations. Instead, target early bronze in eddies below islands, slack water around shoreline

Spring can be a time of high water and strong flows, but dams can concentrate fish.

wood, side channels and the mouths of tributary creeks. Pools below dams and waterfalls are also hotspots.

Warm water zones, especially, can be easy-money spring locations. Solar heating can make slow-flowing creeks several degrees warmer than the rivers they empty into. Even culvert flow and intermittent creeks, if they are putting warm water into the river, can concentrate fish. So can the plunge pools below dams. The afternoon sun will warm the upper layer of still water above the dam, and as this surface layer peels over the top of the dam it can make the plunge pool 6 to 8 degrees warmer than it was in the early morning.

In fact, all parts of a river will warm significantly during sunny afternoons. Water can be a frigid 47 at 8:00 AM and a toasty 53 by 3:00 PM. This has such a dramatic impact on fishing that I seldom hit the water before 10:00 AM at this time of year. So fish during the afternoons if possible. And try to get out there after several consecutive days of unusually warm spring weather. Water temperatures can easily soar 10 degrees after one of these episodes. Wherever I fish in the spring, I regularly check the temperature in the main channel, creek mouths and side channels, always looking for warmer water. The old credit card slogan definitely applies to your thermometer in early spring—"don't leave home without it."

Slower Is Better

Certainly, early-season smallies are feeding, but not like they do in summer. As cold-blooded critters, both the bass and their prey will be in slow motion. Especially when water temps are below 52 degrees, retrieve your flies ultra-slowly and very near bottom. Dragging a weighted fly along the bottom with short pauses every 12 inches sometimes works, but suspending your fly just off the bottom using the Float-and-Fly technique is often better. (This technique is fully described in the "Subsurface Smallmouthing" chapter.) For fly color, bright hues (white, yellow and chartreuse) have long been my early-season favorites, but basic black is also a winner.

Late Pre-Spawn Period

This period sometimes lasts only a week or two, but it can produce phenomenal big-fish angling. When water temperatures reach the mid-50s, fish activity increases and both sexes start moving near their spawning sites. More than once while lake fishing during this time, I've landed several smallies over 19 inches from a single tiny bay. It's the same in rivers; a single large bank eddy or side channel can now hold numerous big fish. Catching a dozen fish over 15 inches from a single spot is possible. Where spawning sites are shallow, many fish will hold nearby in slightly deeper water. The males haven't yet fanned out nests, but reproduction is on their minds and both males and females will readily strike a variety of subsurface offerings.

Your retrieves should still be slow, but not as painfully slow as required when the water is colder. A Clouser Minnow, an Ice Bugger, the Holschlag Hackle Fly and other weight-forward patterns all do well during this period just before the spawn. The key factor is accurately targeting the fish-holding zones.

Spawn Period

This is the time most anglers dream of when they think of spring smallmouthing. As water temperatures approach 60 degrees, reproduction becomes primary and male fish start fanning out nesting sites along stream banks or lake shores. Then over the next several weeks they engage in an rigorous ritual. First they spend days defending their site from other males and coaxing a female (or females) to lay eggs in the nest. After egg-laying, the female plays little role in parenting and quickly drifts away from the nest to recuperate.

But the male's duties are far from over. Each male diligently guards his eggs for several days until they hatch, then works around the clock for an even longer period of time to protect his swarm of newly hatched offspring. This entire process from nest building until fry dispersal can take nearly a month if water temperatures remain in the low 60s.

Perhaps the most amazing part is that these devoted dads hardly eat during this whole period. Likely as a biological adaptation to avoid accidentally ingesting their young, spawning bass attack, but don't eat, intruders. And they will attack things far larger than your fly.

For instance, during a recent spring, a 19-inch spawning lake smallmouth grabbed the tail of a 34-inch pike my client had inadvertently pulled over the smallie's nest. Think of it—this four-pound smallie bit a ten-pound pike so vigorously it tore the pike's caudal fin. And it only let go when I lifted the pike from the water! Now that's protective behavior. But of course, this is also a source of great danger for smallmouth, since their aggressiveness makes them extremely vulnerable to overharvest during the spawn period.

To Fish or Not?

In some states, waters are closed to bass fishing during much of the spring period. These regulations are based on the notion of protecting fish from harvest when they are unusually vulnerable. And historically, tremendous harm has been done to smallmouth populations by kill anglers targeting spawning fish when they are shal-

SPAWNING LOCATIONS

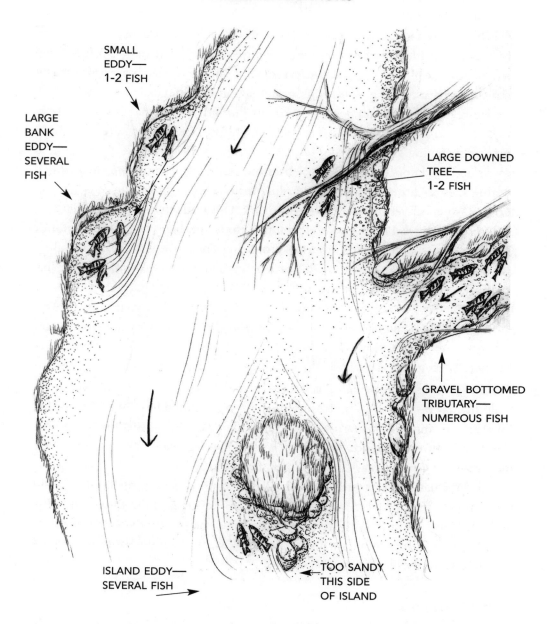

SMALL
EDDY—
1-2 FISH

LARGE
BANK
EDDY—
SEVERAL
FISH

LARGE DOWNED
TREE—
1-2 FISH

GRAVEL BOTTOMED
TRIBUTARY—
NUMEROUS FISH

ISLAND EDDY—
SEVERAL FISH

TOO SANDY
THIS SIDE
OF ISLAND

Spawning smallmouth require gravel substrates and slow current. The most
preferred nesting sites are near wood cover or large rocks.

low and easy to catch. But killing larger smallies anytime hurts the average size of the fishery and shouldn't be done.

On most waters, low to moderate amounts of catch-and-release angling during the spawn has little effect on overall reproductive success. I believe this includes well over 85% of the places where people fish smallies. So if these waters are protected by immediate-release spring regulations, reproduction should remain adequate.

However, on the small percentage of smallmouth waters that are particularly fragile, research indicates that moderate to heavy fishing pressure negatively impacts spawning success *even if all fish are released*. It works like this: on these waters nest predators (like perch, rock bass and sunfish) are abundant, smallmouth nesting sites are limited, and nest-guarding males are caught so often that they're too tired to effectively defend their eggs or fry. This leads to heavy nest predation and few fry survive. I offer a possible solution to this problem in the "Smallmouth Conservation" chapter, which discusses protecting smallmouth in greater detail.

If you're concerned about the impacts of angling during the spawn on certain waters, you should forego fishing during the 2 or 3 weeks when the majority of males are actively guarding their nests. If you do choose to fish, target areas where spring angling pressure is low, and of course immediately release every fish.

Spawn Fishing

This bears repeating: spawning is highly temperature dependent. One year nest building may be as early as mid-April, the next year it could be as late as mid-May (or even mid-June in northern waters). And waters near each other can also warm up at different rates. Hence, smallies in a slow-flowing, wide-open pasture creek may spawn two weeks earlier than those in a nearby heavily shaded spring-fed stream. Fluctuating water temperatures can even cause different smallmouth in the same river or lake to spawn at different times. All this means the spawn period is highly variable and can last several weeks in the same region. Don't try to determine spawning times by a date on the calendar; use up-to-the-minute water temperatures from the places you intend to fish.

Target Casting

When the water is clear and the light is good, spawn fishing can be an exciting visual affair. Nests on open bottom are often light colored and easy to spot and cast to. However, smallies often build nests next to boulders or under logs, and these require careful observation to identify. If the water is shallow and the surface flat, topwater fishing is often effective around nests, and is great fun. The "Topwater Techniques" chapter discusses surface fishing in detail.

If nesting fish aren't willing to come up, one excellent subsurface alternative is the Slow-Sink technique. It requires a bulky, slow-sinking pattern, such as a lightly weighted rabbit bugger. Cast the fly to the far edge of the nest and watch as it slowly settles towards the bottom. Some strikes will occur on the initial drop. If not, when your fly gets about a foot from bottom start retrieving it ever so slowly. Work it with very short (6-inch) twitches and pauses, right over the nest. Try to keep a close eye on the fly as you retrieve it, since some strikes will be fish lightly biting down on the fly. The Slow-Sink technique is especially good when there's wood around the nest, because with such a slow-sinking pattern you can fish around and over the wood but seldom snag.

Another tremendous subsurface technique for this situation is the Drag-and-Pause retrieve discussed in the "Subsurface Smallmouthing" chapter. Just as it sounds, this technique calls for dragging a heavier fly (like a tube fly or the Holschlag Hackle Fly) across the bottom. Cast a few feet past the target, let the fly sink completely, then slowly pull it 6 to 8 inches at a time with a 2- or 3-second pause between each pull. This retrieve often persuades the more hesitant fish to strike.

Top, bottom or mid-depth retrieve, approach every nest cautiously and keep at least 35 feet away from them. If you get very close, some bold fish will remain on the nest, but your presence often stops them from striking. And some males are much less aggressive than others. I've seen plenty of nest-guarders charge 15 feet to strike, and I've seen others refuse to strike an offering only inches from their nose. With these shy guys, the wisest strategy may be to move on to more cooperative fish.

Summer

No question, over much of the smallies' range summer is the prime time. Summer is often the most consistent and the easiest time to fish. Many of the basic techniques described in the other chapters apply to the summer, but to get the most out of this wonderful season, here's a few more things you should know.

Post-Spawn Period

Summer, like spring, is really 3 different periods. It starts with a short, but tough fishing time—the post-spawn. (Or as I mournfully call it, the "post-spawn funk.") It's when the majority of male fish in a given area have just finished nest-guarding so they (and most of the females) are recuperating from the rigors of spawning. On some waters it only seems to last a week or so, and other places it can linger three weeks. Honestly, post-spawn smallmouthing can be mighty slow. I've seen plenty of hot-shot anglers do poorly during this period.

By mid-summer, rivers are often low and warm and the smallies eager. Wet wading is a good option.

But here's a way to counter the post-spawn blues—fish fast! Sure, you can catch some funky fish by pounding a likely location with multiple casts using a very slow retrieve. But quickly covering water using a fast and erratically retrieved fly often produces more post-spawn bronze. I know this seems counter-intuitive (since many fish are lethargic) but it often works.

Don't continue to flail previously productive, but now abandoned, shallow nesting zones. Instead, direct your efforts towards slightly deeper water. Slow-flowing pools and large, deep eddies, as well as rocky flats in lakes, are good for post-spawn fish. Try a moderately weighted Shenk's Streamer fished rapidly with sharp twitches. This calls for a rod-tip retrieve that really makes the fly dart. And if the fish seem extra-finicky, try a more lightly weighted fly that almost suspends while at rest. A retrieve with long pauses (so the fly stays right in the fish's face between twitches) will sometimes elicit strikes when nothing else will.

Early/Mid Summer Period

Early and mid-summer may be the most consistent fishing period of all on many streams. Fish have recovered from spawning, they've moved into their summer feeding zones, but forage abundance is still low. (The young-of-year minnows and crayfish are still very small, so don't offer a lot of easy protein.) And most rivers haven't yet become extremely low and clear, so fish aren't overly spooky. Thus, barring heavy thunderstorms, the early/mid summer period offers the easiest angling of the year, at least for high numbers of fish. Water is likely near 70 degrees, so top-watering can be excellent, and a variety of subsurface patterns and presentations will pay off, too.

Late Summer Period

Late summer is truly a tale of two types of rivers. Some eastern and mid-south waterways present difficult midday fishing by late July. In contrast, hundreds of northern and midwestern rivers offer spectacular fishing from late July through early September.

Why such a difference? It's mostly an issue of clarity. On streams that become low and crystalline during late summer, bigger smallies often become light-shy and do much of their feeding in the mornings, evenings and at night. These big ones are still feeding heavily, but not necessarily during the 8:00 AM to 6:00 PM shift when most anglers are fishing. To improve your clear-water odds, make sure you're on-stream during the first and last two hours of daylight.

Low-Light Magic

A clear pool that seemed totally devoid of any fish over 10 inches during midday often comes alive with bigger smallmouth during the last hour or so of daylight. The smallmouth has the ability to see and hunt effectively when crepuscular prey such as crayfish leave their daytime hideouts. During this twilight evening period (and early morning, too, on many streams) smallmouth often start to hunt actively. Radio tracking and visual observation have found that some fish cover an entire pool during their low-light patrols, rather than staying in a single ambush site. In larger rivers, they may confine their hunting to a flat or the head or tail of the pool. To fully exploit this opportune time, the smallmouth are aggressively seeking prey and have lost much of their caution. An angler covering a lot of water with a very noticeable fly (such as a topwater or a shallow-running streamer) can experience spectacular fishing in these magic hours.

Midnight Madness?

While I'm personally no big fan of night fishing, after-dark summer smallmouthing is an option in some areas. On rivers with reduced water clarity, smallmouth quit feeding at full darkness and go into a sleep cycle. Biologists diving at night have observed the fish hugging the bottom or tucked against a rock or the bank, remaining stationary the entire night. On these rivers, night fishing is very poor.

SUMMER SMALLMOUTH LOCATIONS

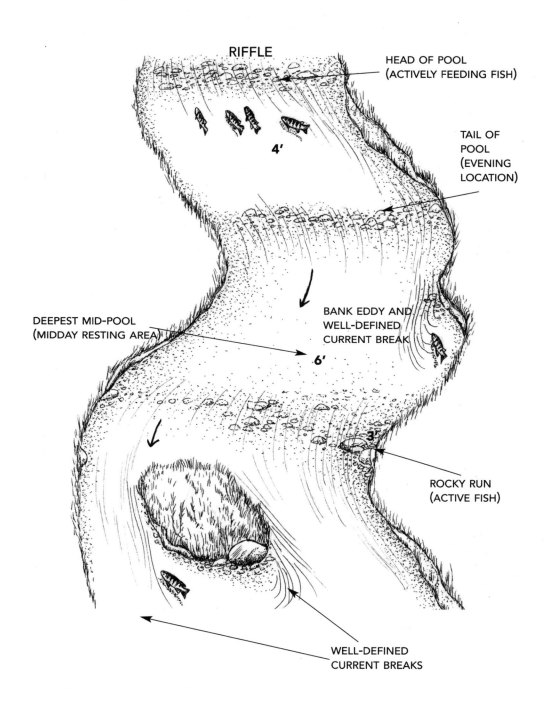

RIFFLE

HEAD OF POOL
(ACTIVELY FEEDING FISH)

TAIL OF
POOL
(EVENING
LOCATION)

4′

DEEPEST MID-POOL
(MIDDAY RESTING AREA)

BANK EDDY AND
WELL-DEFINED
CURRENT BREAK

6′

3′

ROCKY RUN
(ACTIVE FISH)

WELL-DEFINED
CURRENT BREAKS

On high-clarity waters, however, there seems to be enough light for the fish to continue to feed after nightfall, especially during moonlit periods. A few areas have a long tradition of spin anglers fishing at night. Before dark, fishers float or walk to a large pool where they know big fish reside and familiarize themselves with the pool while it's still light. Then they wait until the night bite kicks in, generally about an hour after full darkness. Traditionally these hardware guys worked the pool with black-colored topwaters like Jitterbugs, setting the hook whenever they heard or felt the strike. Often the fish will strike and miss the lure multiple times. Naturally, this same method of fishing can pay off for a fly rodder slowly working a black popper. While night fishing can produce plenty of exciting strikes, it has drawbacks: you can't clearly see where you're casting, you won't see the strike, wading can be challenging and unraveling leader tangles is frustrating in the dark.

Far-and-Fine Tactics

But what about the many hours between first and last light, when most of us do all of our fishing? One way to counter the clear-water blues is to use Far-and-Fine tactics. Sort of like angling for spooky trout, the idea is to finesse some fish into hitting. The "far" aspect means you should keep as far from your target areas as possible, make as little noise as possible and keep a low profile. The "fine" presentation means using a longer and lighter leader than usual (3X or even 4X). Flies should also be smaller and quieter than standard fare. A small woolly bugger or Geibe's Damsel Nymph are two good ones. Because light-shy smallies are almost always hugging bottom, slow-moving subsurface offerings are generally best.

Time to Travel

Of course, there's another great way to beat the late summer slump—go where the dogdays are doggone good. Streams in agricultural areas and bog- and algae-stained rivers often become outstanding in the late summer. Earlier in the summer, these waters can have such low visibility that catch rates are depressed. But when clarity finally improves to 3 feet or so, the fishing becomes red hot! For many years, I've guided on stained and moderately turbid rivers. Here, August is the best month of the year, both for numbers and sizes. The fish aren't shy any time of day, and my clients catch thousands of high-noon lunkers, often off the surface and often when water temps are over 80 degrees.

If your local streams become gin-clear in August and fish become tough customers, why not take that time to try new waters? In many northern and midwestern states, there are scores of rivers where smallmouthing is stellar during late summer. For information about such places check out Part 3 of this book. There you'll find hot-fishing late-summer destinations in the Upper Midwest, Lower Midwest and parts of the Northeast region.

Fall

FALL's FEEDING FRENZY!! For decades I've seen articles with such titles extolling fall smallmouthing. But alas, this magazine hyperbole is only partially true. Yes, on some waters and on some days, early fall fishing can indeed seem like a frenzy. Other times, cold weather and plummeting temps can make for slim pickins. And on other waters, fall is when the smallies pack up and abandon their summer residences for more distant haunts.

This means two things: First, you gotta figure out what fall smallies do in the rivers or lakes you intend to fish. Second, use a thermometer—a lot! As I explain in the "Understanding Smallmouth" chapter, smallmouth in many northern rivers migrate in the fall. In fact, in some of the smallest, shallowest waterways fish completely evacuate the stream when water temps dip into the 50s; they move many miles downstream into the still, deep water of a larger river. It's literally a case of here today, gone next week.

On small, clear streams farther south, the fish don't migrate, but many concentrate in the deeper pools in the fall. This is primarily because the fish feel vulnerable in the stream's low flows and high clarity. However, on streams where smallies stage significant fall migrations, biologists believe it's primarily temperature-triggered. This makes your trusty thermometer an essential fall accessory.

Early Fall Period

When writers hype fall fishing, this is the time we're talking about. The early fall period is when water temperatures are still in the low 60s or upper 50s, so the smallie's metabolism is relatively high. Plus the fish require plenty of nutrients to aid in gonad development. Thirdly, no new minnows or craws are being produced, so food sources are declining. On larger waterways, in early fall, fish often move into runs and flats and feed heavily, especially on minnows. (The cooler temps means crayfish are no longer as active/available, plus they quit molting, which means they are hard-shelled and less appealing.) This prime period can occur as early as the beginning of September in cold climes or as late as October in southerly zones. If current isn't too strong, early fall topwater fishing can still be tremendous, but more often mid-depth minnow imitators are the flies of choice. The Minnow Swing described in the "Subsurface Smallmouthing" chapter is an excellent technique.

Mid/Late Fall Period

I define the mid- and late-fall period as when the water is between 54 and 47 degrees. Smallies that migrate have likely settled into their hibernacula (wintering

FALL/WINTER SMALLMOUTH LOCATIONS

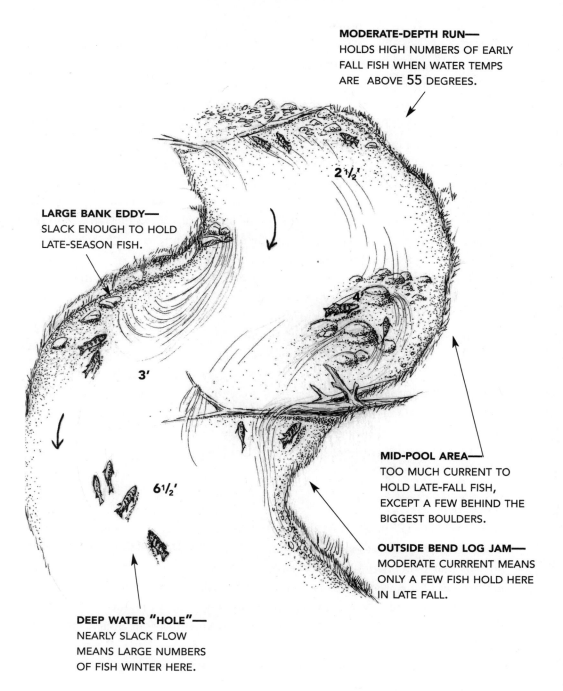

MODERATE-DEPTH RUN—
HOLDS HIGH NUMBERS OF EARLY
FALL FISH WHEN WATER TEMPS
ARE ABOVE 55 DEGREES.

LARGE BANK EDDY—
SLACK ENOUGH TO HOLD
LATE-SEASON FISH.

2 1/2'

4'

3'

6 1/2'

MID-POOL AREA—
TOO MUCH CURRENT TO
HOLD LATE-FALL FISH,
EXCEPT A FEW BEHIND THE
BIGGEST BOULDERS.

OUTSIDE BEND LOG JAM—
MODERATE CURRRENT MEANS
ONLY A FEW FISH HOLD HERE
IN LATE FALL.

DEEP WATER "HOLE"—
NEARLY SLACK FLOW
MEANS LARGE NUMBERS
OF FISH WINTER HERE.

pools). And even on rivers where smallmouth don't make dramatic movements, the fish have moved into slower water. Depending on the latitude and the weather, this period can start any time from the first of October to early November.

This is a time that really stymies some smallie fans. On most waterways, the fish are no longer in riffles or runs, they won't strike on the surface, and in some streams they may not even be present anymore. To top if off, fish activity can vary widely from day to day. Despite these challenges, I love this period.

No matter what I catch, just being out during the golden days of fall is a joy. And the bronze on the line can be more impressive than the gold on the trees. Fish are at their heaviest of the year, they're concentrated, and on the warmer days they're still eager to bite a fly. I really mean it about warmer days. Late-season weather is notoriously fickle, and days with frigid winds or icy rain can put the smallies in a funk. So do whatever you can to get out on those grand sunny days when the sun warms the water and energizes fish, and make sure you're fishing from 2:00 to 5:00 PM. Water will be warmest then and fish more active than in the morning.

In mid- and late fall, the Crayfish Hop using bottom-scraping patterns is an indispensable technique. Many times, I've landed a dozen nice fish from a single small pool this way. And plenty of times, one of these concentrated fall fish has been my biggest bronze of the year. Other times I've caught a bunch of 16-inchers. All of these fall outings have been truly memorable occasions.

However, there's one short period to avoid during fall: the peak of the leaf drop. On windy days after the first hard frost, there's often a blizzard of falling leaves. On heavily wooded waterways, fishing is impossible at this time because leaves fill all parts of the water column. Fortunately, on most streams drifting leaves quickly dissipate and fishing becomes good again within 3 or 4 days.

Winter

Fifteen years ago, in my first book, *Stream Smallmouth Fishing,* I talked about a 9-month smallmouth season. One of many things I've learned since writing that book is that river smallmouthing can be a year-round affair. Winter fishing may not be possible or productive in every river in North America, but even in states as far north as Pennsylvania and Illinois the hardy angler can score during the dead of winter. In more southerly states like Virginia and Missouri, spin anglers are catching hordes of winter bronze nowadays.

Here's how fly fishers can get in on this cold-water action: *first identify the wintering locations* (generally the same slack-water areas where fish were in mid- and late fall). This winter habitat can be pools 10 feet deep, or bank eddies just 3 feet deep, if these areas have almost no current. On rivers with incoming springs or spring seepage from the bottom (common in some hilly limestone regions) winter smallmouth will concentrate near the spring flow because it's warmer than the river.

Next, properly prepare for cold weather angling. That means *using the best flies* (such as Tim's Winter Minnow or an Albino Clouser Minnow). Proper preparation also means *dressing adequately*. If you're fishing on foot, good waders with multiple insulating layers underneath are essential, plus a warm hat and good fishing gloves. Clothing for fishing from a boat should be equally warm and layered.

Another way to stay warm and catch more fish is to go out on the warmest winter days, when the smallies are more active. In some locales, that may only mean a high of 40 degrees in January. A little farther south it might mean a "balmy" 55. But no matter where you fish, avoid air temps below 32 degrees. Your fly line constantly freezing in the guides won't lead to productive or enjoyable angling.

Winter smallmouthing requires warm clothing, but can produce great fishing.

The Float-and-Fly for Winter Bronze

One big reason we caught so few smallies during the winter a decade ago was because we didn't present our flies properly. In recent years a few of us have adopted the Float-and-Fly technique (described in the "Subsurface Smallmouthing" chapter) to entice icy-water bronze. When the water is in the low 40s, the smallmouth is one sluggish fish. It doesn't feed often and won't chase anything far or fast. But by using a large strike indicator buoyant enough to suspend a fly, setting the indicator so the fly rides just a few inches off bottom, you can present your offering at eye-level and tantalizingly slow. Really, really s-l-o-w.

In a completely slack eddy a little over 3 feet deep you'll be able to use a 1/50th-ounce fly. In a pool 6 feet deep, you will need a 1/30th or 1/36th-ounce fly. To help it stay down, use an untapered fluorocarbon leader of just 6-lb test. Let the fly settle and hang directly below the indicator. Slowly pull the indicator a foot or less, then pause 4 seconds. Keep the entire retrieve at least this slow. Strikes will likely come when the fly is at rest, and will be very light.

Like during the fall period, a warm spell in December, January or February can boost the water temperature several degrees and lead to a veritable feeding frenzy. During a recent winter, a pal and I hit one of these January thaws. Though the water was just 42, it was warmer than it had been previously and the fish appreciated it. In 5 hours we released 65 fish, many over 16 inches. A great day anywhere or anytime, phenomenal in mid-winter Minnesota.

Weather, Barometric Pressure and Lunar Cycles

A lot of folks wanna know. When is the best time to go fishing? Some think I'm being flip when I answer "whenever you get the chance." But I sincerely mean this, since most people don't get that many fishing opportunities. When you do, make the most of it—get out there and enjoy it.

Of course, that response isn't what most anglers are looking for. They want to know what type(s) of weather make the fish bite the best. Yikes! That's a mighty complex question with no simple answer. One problem is that there may be three different meteorological factors influencing fish activity: *weather conditions, barometric pressure* and *lunar cycles.*

Regarding weather, I give general guidelines throughout this book. For instance, a period of sunny, warm weather during early spring or late fall often increases fish activity. Conversely, in the summer, dark cloudy weather often improves fishing if the water is extremely clear. The complication is that water conditions (on rivers especially) can also enhance or even completely negate the favorable weather factors. The rule of thumb is: *fishing is better when water temps are stable or rising, levels are normal and clarity is moderate.*

Too Much Pressure?

Here's my view on barometric pressure: It seems likely that many lake species, including smallmouth, are significantly impacted by air (barometric) pressure. And that's why so many lake fishers live in terror of the "cold front." Besides cooler weather, a cold front means high air pressure, clear skies, and often reduced fish activity. There's little agreement among scientists regarding the cold front/high pressure phenomenon, though there are 3 or 4 layman's theories why fish activity seems to decline at this time.

However, river fish do not seem as strongly affected by barometric pressure, especially the negative affects of high pressure, as lake fish are. I've had many fair-to-good cold-front days while fishing rivers. These days aren't spectacular, but the fishing is seldom as poor as what you would likely experience on a lake during high pressure times. So if a river's water conditions are good, don't hesitate to fish during a cold front.

Hot, Muggy Frenzy

In contrast, fish sometimes become extremely active *just before a cold front*, when the barometer (air pressure) is falling sharply. Again, scientists don't agree on why (or even if) this is the case. But countless anglers over the decades have experienced fast fishing just before an approaching cold front, so I believe there's some validity to the pre-front frenzy idea.

If you can be fishing the day before a strong cold front arrives, be sure to get out there. Often these low pressure conditions bring hot, muggy weather, including thunderstorms. Fish activity isn't always high on these days, but perhaps half the time smallmouth will be unusually aggressive during low-pressure periods. A hot, sweaty day of battling big bronzebacks between cloudbursts is one my clients reminisce fondly about years afterwards.

Moon Watching

Okay, what about *lunar cycles?* For decades, magazines and outdoor calendars have published daily schedules for "peak fish and game activity" based on the moon's location relative to the earth. A small segment of anglers are devoted disciples of this lunar theory and try to arrange their fishing to coincide with the peak days and hours.

Is there any solid evidence the moon significantly influences fish behavior? Fisheries scientists haven't given much attention to the moon theory, but I've known a few methodical anglers who kept accurate records of their fishing based on those peak periods. Some days the best catch rates coincided with the prime lunar times, but during other periods of the month there was not much correlation between them. The lunar calendars almost always include a disclaimer along the lines of "local weather extremes can affect fish/wildlife activity." I take this to mean other factors often trump the lunar cycle. And that's why I pay much more attention to water and weather conditions than to the moon. Fish when you have the opportunity!

SMALLMOUTH SEASONS IN BRIEF

SPRING
EARLY PRE-SPAWN (WATER UNDER 55 DEGREES)
Smallmouth: Seeking warmer water, slower current
Fishing: Near bottom, ultra-slow retrieves

LATE PRE-SPAWN (WATER 55 TO 60)
Smallmouth: Concentrate near spawning sites
Fishing: Target near-spawn zones, slow retrieves

SPAWN (WATER LOW TO MID-60s)
Smallmouth: Males guard nests, aggressively attack intruders
Fishing: Visual target casting, immediate release

SUMMER
POST-SPAWN (WATER UNDER 70)
Smallmouth: Sluggish recuperative mode
Fishing: Deeper, erratic retrieves, cover water

EARLY/MID-SUMMER (WATER UPPER-60s INTO 70s)
Smallmouth: In summer locations, actively feeding
Fishing: Consistently good, many presentations work

LATE SUMMER (HIGHEST TEMPS OF SEASON— TO UPPER 80s)
Smallmouth: Big fish, actively feeding, can be spooky in clear water
Fishing: Fish mornings and evenings, Far-and-Fine tactics for
    daytime, or target stained/murky/less-clear waters

FALL
EARLY FALL (WATER 60s TO UPPER-50s)
Smallmouth: Actively feeding
Fishing: Mid-depth Minnow Swing, sometimes topwaters

MID/LATE FALL (WATER 50s TO UPPER-40s)
Smallmouth: Concentrate, move to wintering pools, may migrate
    long distances
Fishing: Check water temps, fish afternoons on warmer days, Crayfish Hop
    near bottom

WINTER (LOW-40s OR COLDEST WATER OF YEAR)
Smallmouth: Sluggish, concentrated in wintering pools and slack water
Fishing: Dress adequately, choose warmest days, Float-and-Fly
    technique

9

Float Fishing for Smallmouth

It's been a long journey for me. So many years of floating rivers have added up to nearly a trip 'round the planet. But I'll tell you. Every time I push off on yet another float I'm as excited as I was four decades ago when that first trip down a serpentine stream opened up a wonderful new world. And what's not to love about river float trips?

Gliding down a winding waterway, deeper and deeper into the river's secret reaches, you experience new sights and sounds around every bend. Slinky mink bounding along the bank, gaudy wood ducks taking flight, power-diving kingfishers, majestic maples anchoring the shore, scarlet sumac in the late-summer sun, the murmur of fast water around smooth boulders. Floating down a wild waterway is a true outdoor adventure and a feast for the senses. Even on "civilized" streams flowing through urban or farm lands, a float trip can make you feel you've discovered a private piece of paradise. Though the harsh hands-of-man may be only yards away, while drifting down that quiet stream with its verdant shores, you can thoroughly relax and enjoy the soothing sights of nature.

Angling Advantages

Floating a stream in a quiet craft is a grand way to commune with nature; moreover the advantages to the angler are enormous. Floating allows you to cover more good water in a few hours than you could in several days of wade fishing. And of course, many stretches of deeper rivers are impossible to effectively fish on foot, making a watercraft mandatory.

Floating quietly down a beautiful river and hooking large, hard-fighting fish. It will put a smile on everyone's face.

Even on some small streams a craft is superior. Thick, brushy banks and shallow stretches hundreds of yards long separate the fish-holding pools, making wading a Herculean effort. A float angler may occasionally have to pull their boat over logs, riffles or sand flats, but it's still much easier than wading/walking that stream. And while a hard-core wader might be able to cover a couple miles of water, a floater can easily travel four times that distance.

Other obstacles such as soft, silty bottoms, slippery rocks and stiff currents also stymie on-foot folks. Float fishing surmounts them all. And of course, a watercraft is perfect for escaping the crowds and reaching those remote honey holes far from an access. Even casting can be easier while floating. Deep water can prevent wading away from the bank, where tall trees make backcasts impossible. Being in the middle of the channel in a boat allows ample room for a cast.

Perhaps the least-acknowledged attribute of float fishing is the togetherness it affords. I know plenty of anglers, including many of my guiding clients, who immensely enjoy the 8 or 9 hours they get to spend in a boat with a friend or a family member. Sure, they may say it's all about the fish, but often it's the time spent together that they seem to value most.

Of course with all these attributes, if float fishing was always easy, every stream would have wall-to-wall watercraft. Actually, fishing a river by boat presents plenty of challenges. Constant current, fluctuating water levels, shallow riffles, tricky rapids, blocking trees and rugged launch sites are just some of the things that make boat handling and float fishing so challenging. This is why river guides make the "big bucks." (I'm kidding about the big bucks, but we are in demand because many anglers realize that a good guide has the skills and equipment to make their trip down the stream easy and enjoyable.)

Bank Shooting

Bank shooting can be oh-so pretty and productive. The perfectly positioned boat: moving quietly downstream at just the right speed, and just the right distance from the bank. The well-executed cast: smoothly delivering a fly to exactly the right spot. And (when the fish follow the script) a heart-pounding strike followed by a heart-stopping jump.

Or it can be downright ugly: two frustrated guys bumping and banging down the river, their craft out of control, both fruitlessly flinging casts to targets that go by too fast, and are too close or far away.

One person making accurate casts while the other keeps the craft 45 feet from the bank leads to hook-ups like this.

BANK SHOOTING

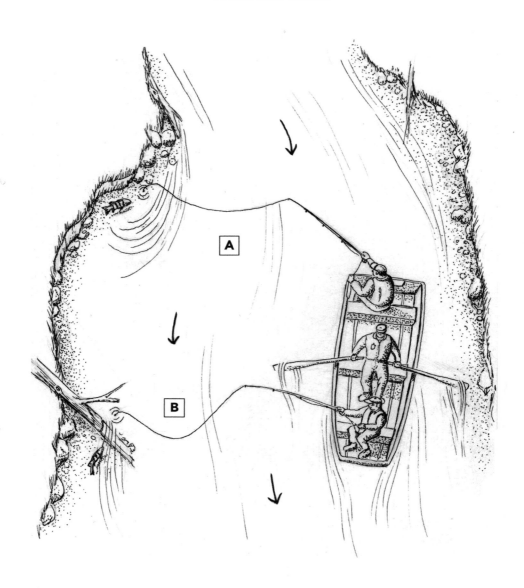

A The stern angler casts a **subsurface** fly slightly **upstream** to targets as the boat passes them.

B The bow angler casts a **topwater** slightly **downstream** to bank targets.

When guiding, I get paid to create that postcard-perfect scene. But too many of the other float fishers I see fall into the other scenario. So where do they go wrong? And what the heck is bank shooting, anyway?

Bank shooting is simply making a controlled downstream drift in a boat, while one or more anglers "shoot" the bank (cast to shoreline targets). It's often the most effective way to fish mid-sized and large rivers because it allows anglers to cover huge amounts of water, hitting the hotspots and easily bypassing marginal areas. And though I've done it thousands of times, I still marvel at how enjoyable and productive the technique can be. Not only is it a first-rate way to fish a river you're familiar with, but it's also by far the most effective way to quickly investigate new waters.

Bank Shooting Dos (and Don'ts)

Successful bank shooting starts with good craft control. The reason so many float fishers do a third-rate job of boat handling is because neither person puts enough effort into the task. When using oars or paddle, one person needs to spend 100% of their time keeping the craft in the best position for the caster to work the target areas. And I can't equivocate on this point. Try to control the boat and fish at the same time, and you'll be out of position more often than not. This will frustrate both you and your fishing partner. Instead, take turns fishing and you'll both catch more.

As the "Bank Shooting" illustration depicts, proper boat positioning generally means keeping the boat 40 to 45 feet away from the target zone. It also calls for constantly adjusting your speed. At large targets, where several casts are required, you'll bring the boat to dead stop for several minutes. At smaller one-cast spots, you may slow the boat to just half the current speed. Through long stretches of good water, you should move slow enough so the angler has time to place a cast every 6 feet along the bank. In shallow stretches, the boat handler should speed up to quickly move through these fishless zones. On smaller rivers, you'll also ferry the boat back and forth from one bank to the other, so you continuously fish the deeper (outside bend) side of the river. All the while, fluctuating currents will constantly try to stymie you, by pushing the boat too far from the bank, too close, or making it go too fast or too slow.

Secrets of the Pros

Here are the secrets of handling a boat like a pro: first, take the time to learn the proper paddle or oar strokes. They aren't complicated or particularly difficult, but you must practice enough to be quick and comfortable with them, and clearly understand which strokes work best to turn, stop and ferry the craft. Most importantly, learn to be proactive rather than reactive. You should start slowing *before* you reach the target or *before* the boat is racing downstream, and start controlling a turn before you're pointing the wrong way. Small preventive strokes are much better than trying to make major corrections after the boat veers off course.

Motor Power

While many boat control situations call for human power, there are places (primarily on big rivers) where an electric trolling motor will also do the job. In slow-flowing stretches and in long pools, a bow or even a transom-mounted motor can often slow the craft and keep it on course well enough for both anglers to fish for limited periods. However, even with a foot-operated electric, you must pay careful attention to the changing current speeds and the minor course corrections that will be required. Therefore, the person operating the motor should give top priority to craft control, and their fishing should be secondary.

Once in a while, I also use a motor to bank shoot while solo fishing. It's seldom as effective as tandem angling, but if a deep stretch is at least 100 yards long and the current is slow and uniform, it can be productive. I try to adjust the motor speed so I'm moving just slightly slower than the current. When I use a side-mounted motor on my Smallmouth Angler canoe, I run the motor in reverse and make the course adjustments on the tiller between casts. If a bank is particularly good, sometimes I'll also motor back up to the top and float down again, hoping to contact fish I missed on the first pass. A 30-pound-thrust motor will move a solo canoe well; you'll need at least 50 pounds of power for a jonboat.

Playing the Angles

Now that the boat's under control, it's time to consider your casting. Most floaters quickly realize that accurate casts are crucial while bank shooting, but far fewer understand that their angle from the target is also key.

For surface fishing in substantial current, presenting your offering from the wrong angle means severe line drag, a skittering fly and lots of missed strikes. As the "Bank Shooting" illustration on page 102 shows, the way to correct this problem is to present the topwater about 30 degrees downstream of perpendicular. This slightly downstream cast significantly reduces the line belly and drag that develops when you cast at a 90-degree angle (perpendicular) to the shoreline and the current. Because the boat should be traveling slower than the current, the line will remain tighter when the fly is at a downstream angle from the boat. This presentation keeps the fly from being pulled away from the target so quickly, makes a popper "pop" better and makes hook-setting much easier. I'm not exaggerating, following the 30-degree-angle rule can easily double your catch rate, especially in fast current.

The 30-degree rule also applies to subsurface fishing, just in reverse. Instead of casting towards the bank and slightly downstream, angle the cast 30 degrees upstream of perpendicular. Then as the boat moves slowly downstream you will be able to fish a weight-forward pattern with a modified with-the-current retrieve. It's sorta the Crayfish Hop while moving. Your offering will ultimately get pulled away from the bank, but with the line belly pulling the fly downstream, it should remain in the target zone for at least 12 to 15 feet—plenty of time to interest a fish.

FLOAT TRIP MISTAKES TO AVOID

1. NOT AGREEING BEFOREHAND HOW MUCH EACH PERSON WILL CAST VERSUS PADDLE.

To avoid conflict between you and your fishing partner, agree before starting the day on when you will switch roles. You might switch every 2 hours, or perhaps after the caster has caught 2 or 3 fish.

2. TRYING TO COVER TOO MUCH WATER.

Floating a dozen miles of river might sound great while you're at home poring over the map, but on-stream 6 to 8 miles is plenty to thoroughly work the fishable water. Only consider more distance on fast-flowing, shallow or low-fertility streams where good water is very limited.

3. NOT PACING YOURSELF.

You only have 7 miles to float in 9 hours, but you fish the first miles so hard that you're still only halfway down the river by sunset. You miss fishing half the water and end up having to navigate in near-darkness. To avoid this unsavory scenario, set a schedule and stick to it (the old railroad bridge by noon, the big tributary by 3:00 PM, etc.).

Targets to Shoot For

Bank shooting targets are multitudinous, and not all of them are along the bank. Shoreline eddies are obvious bulls-eyes, as is wood cover, including the eroded root systems of large trees. Ditto for riprapped banks (artificial or natural). Outside bends are prime locations, too, since these are invariably the deepest, rockiest banks, where current scours away sand and silt. The outside edges of weed beds can also be quite productive, and even overhanging bank grass can hold fish.

However, as rivers clear and levels drop during late summer, many shallow banks become devoid of larger fish. Now it's time to shift your target zone to depths of at least 2 feet. This might be only 5 feet from shore or it might be 75 feet, but you must be willing to fish water with enough depth to hold adult smallmouth, no matter how far it is from dry ground. This can't be emphasized enough.

The failure to move out from shallow shoreline zones is the most common float fishing mistake I see made during the late summer period. Because so many fly anglers seem so fixated on laying their fly inches from land, they continue to flail the shallows long after any fish of size have retreated. There's no reason to make this error; fishing a little farther from shore isn't difficult. You can use exactly the same flies, techniques and presentations as when casting tight to a bank. Once river flows slow, numerous targets far from the banks are productive. Try mid-channel boulders, logs, current breaks and the eddies below small islands. Bypass the shallows and near-bank areas that are very sandy, silty or fast-flowing.

Anchors Away!

The anchor is probably the most underrated item in the float fisher's bag of tools. Many anglers seldom use one and others don't even have one onboard. But not me. I regard anchors as indispensable. I use them constantly and make sure all my boats' anchoring systems are quick, easy and reliable—for several reasons.

1. On many rivers there are deep or wide areas where anchoring is essential to success.

2. Anchoring is one of the few times when both people in a boat can fish simultaneously.

3. For the solo angler, anchoring is often the primary (sometimes sole) boat fishing technique.

4. Even when you're bank shooting, you need an anchor. Stopping as soon as you hook a bass keeps you from drifting past good water while you're fighting the fish.

ANCHORING

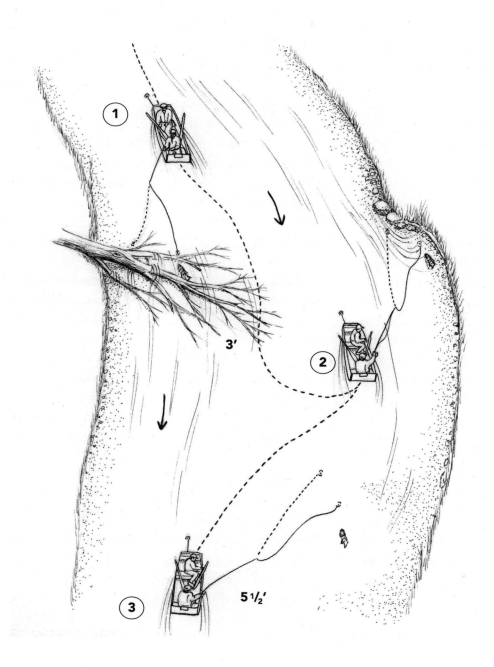

Careful anchoring in select locations from which to cast. (1) Anchor upstream to fish large log jam. (2) Anchor parallel to bank eddy. (3) Anchor next to and slightly downstream of deep part of pool.

So even on a slow day of fishing I'll anchor 25 times, on a busy day maybe 50 times.

Of course, to stop that much your anchor system has to be a good one. This means a system you can operate quickly and easily with one hand from where you're sitting. On my larger boats I use a bow mounted 10- or 12-pound mushroom-head anchor that's winch-operated. On my canoes it's a 6- or 8-pound front anchor that rides outside the hull, with its rope running under the gunwales and secured near the stern seat by a jam cleat. Both of these systems function nearly effortlessly, so I can anchor as many times a day as the fishing demands. In contrast, an anchor that must be picked up and thrown overboard then hand-lined in will dirty up the boat and is very tiring to use. And because it's such a hassle to use, it won't be, at least not nearly as much as it should be.

Anchoring—Where and When

Fishing big pools with subsurface presentations nearly always requires anchoring. But before dropping anchor, consider where the best places to cast from are. Then quietly move into position and set the anchor. On a long, deep pool you might anchor 3 or 4 times, starting at the head of the pool and working downstream until you've covered all the good water.

For a small pool or a log jam, one stop might do it. At a log jam that extends partway into the channel, anchor so the boat stops about 30 feet upstream of the wood and slightly out in the channel. From here you can use the Minnow Swing to carefully work a sinking fly or topwater along the upstream edge of the wood cover, tempting bog smallies. Often these log-jam bruisers want the fly just inches from their woody lair.

Sneaking by Boat

I mentioned the "sneak technique" for wading, and small-water floaters would also be wise to practice sneaking. If you intend to anchor at the bottom of a small pool, drifting down through the center of it may alarm the fish. Instead "sneak" tight along the bank on the side of the pool that's the shallowest or farthest away from the area you will fish. Once you get to the bottom of the pool you can move into mid-stream, anchor, then employ a with-the-current retrieve, such as the Crayfish Hop. If you approach a pool that may be deep enough to hold fish, be cautious and sneak. If it turns out to be shallow, fishless water, no harm is done. But if the pool looks good as you edge around it, you'll be in an excellent position to effectively fish it.

SNEAKING BY BOAT

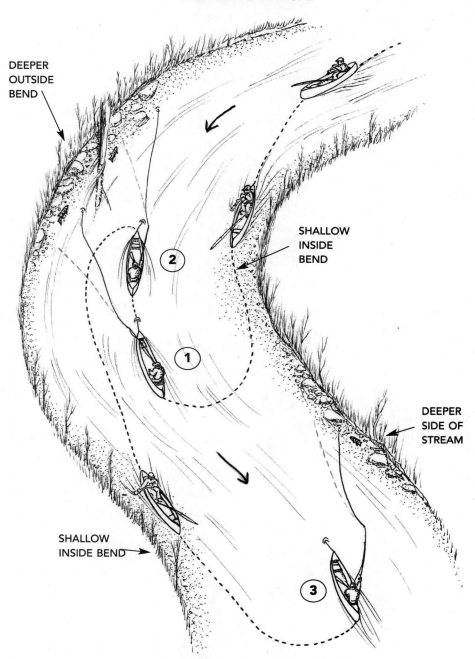

DEEPER
OUTSIDE
BEND

SHALLOW
INSIDE
BEND

DEEPER
SIDE OF
STREAM

SHALLOW
INSIDE BEND

②

①

③

On shallow, narrow or clear streams, "sneak" your craft along the shallow
bank to avoid spooking the fish. Float past the target, then approach
from downstream. Anchor at (1) to work the downstream end of the
target area, then move upstream to position (2). As the river winds, sneak
along the other (now shallower) bank to fish the deeper outside bend
from position (3).

The 70-Foot Hop

Anchoring in a pool or run allows the float fisher to do the enticing Crayfish Hop. Even better, from an anchored position you can actually double the standard hop distance, making impressive 70-foot presentations. Here's how:

Paying attention to water depth, current speed and fly weight is always important when doing the Crayfish Hop, but they're especially critical when performing a 70-footer. This long retrieve is best performed in a run or pool with uniform

THE 70-FOOT HOP

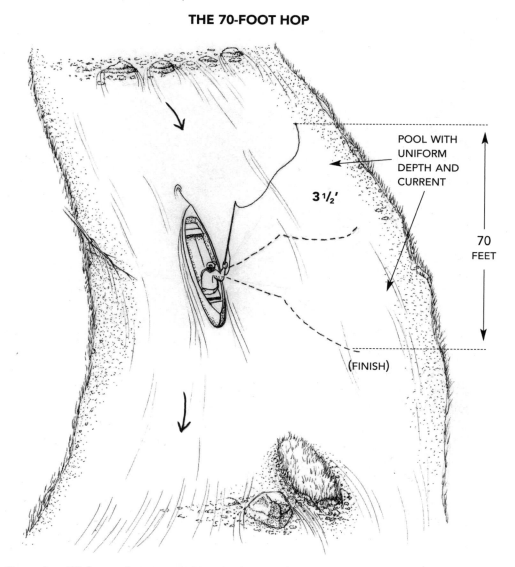

POOL WITH UNIFORM DEPTH AND CURRENT

3½'

70 FEET

(FINISH)

Covering 70 feet of water with a single Crayfish Hop retrieve is possible when wading or from an anchored craft.

depth and current speed (3 to 4 feet deep and moderate current). Use a fly barely heavy enough to tick bottom (no heavier than 1/50th oz.) with a floating line, long untapered leader and strike indicator. (Rigging for the Crayfish Hop is fully explained in the "Subsurface Smallmouthing" chapter.) Anchor the craft to one side of and mid-point to the area you want to fish, then cast 40 feet upstream and left or right towards the target area.

Once the fly sinks to the bottom, do the Crayfish Hop as you would while wading, then as the indicator gets perpendicular to the boat, make sure a small downstream belly remains in the line. And as the line and fly is pulled downstream of the craft maintain that belly by slowly feeding out line. If the fly isn't too heavy (and once you learn to maintain the correct amount of line belly) you can keep the retrieve going for at least 35 feet downstream of your position. This 70 foot retrieve allows you to cover a huge amount of water per cast and is very effective on long pools and runs. Just make sure to be alert during the entire retrieve. I've gotten strikes during all parts of the drift, including at the very end of the retrieve. In fact, when the fly halts its downstream movement and starts rising in the water column, that's often a cue for a fish to strike. Connecting with 19 inches of bronze power that far downstream is a real kick (er, pull).

Park and Wade

Many anglers love to escape the confines of a craft and stop to wade. Besides being a great way to stretch your legs, this is the best way to fish on some waterways. On wide, shallow rivers with hard bottoms, such as many in the East, parking the boat to thoroughly work areas below riffles and rapids is an excellent technique. And even deep rivers invariably have a few spots to get out and fish on foot, such as boulder fields.

The park-and-wade method really shines on our smallest streams— waterways barely big enough to float a boat and where an approaching craft sends the smallies into a panic. Here, the best bet is to stop the boat well before you drift into the pool. Quietly park the craft, then get out and sneak along the bank to the target area. This cautious approach skirts the water and allows you to get behind (downstream of) any spooky fish, so you can work them with the old reliable with-the-current retrieve.

This craft-as-transportation-only method is especially good on shallow waterways where good smallmouth locations may be hundreds of yards apart. Here a wade angler may only be able to reach 2 or 3 spots in a day. In contrast, by cruising quickly through the marginal water, then stopping to work the good stuff on foot, a park-and-wade angler can hit a dozen pools in a 5-mile stretch.

THE PARK AND WADE METHOD

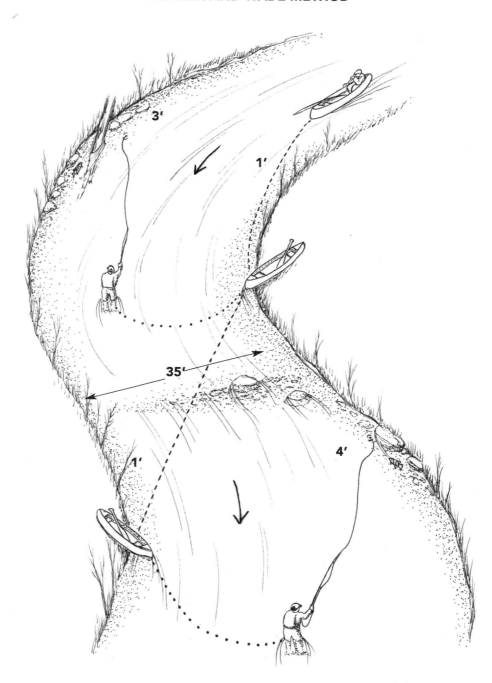

The Park-and-Wade method can be used anywhere water is shallow enough for wading. It's most valuable on small streams, where the method allows you to get out and cautiously approach a spot on foot.

Park-and-wade also frees float fishers from the task of craft control. Tandem anglers can both fish, and can escape the confines of a small boat, putting more casting distance between themselves. Park-and-wade may be most appreciated by the lone floater. Though organizing the shuttle takes a little extra work, I really enjoy the occasions I float small water alone. I can stop when and where I please, I don't have to share the hotspots, plus I can pile all the gear and goodies I want in the canoe. Sweet.

Special Tips and Techniques

The Come-Back Fly

One strike and you're out. Often big smallies will only strike a topwater once. If you don't hook 'em on that first attempt, the big one won't come up again no matter how many more times you cast to it. Unless . . . unless you "come back" with a sinking fly, and the sooner the better. When guiding I always keep a second rod rigged and ready with a "come-back" fly for missed surface strikes. It doesn't always work, but plenty of times it does, sometimes scoring the biggest bronze of the day. In slow current, a slow-sinking pattern is best; in a stiff flow, a get-to-the-bottom-quick fly is better. Four or 5 casts will tell you if the fish is interested.

Catching Doubles

Double your fish, double your fun. Sounds sorta like a chewing gum jingle, but I'm referring to hooking two smallies when two boat anglers are fishing at the same time. Everyone scores a double occasionally, but there's a way to dramatically increase the odds of these catches. When food sources are high and smallmouth are feeding heavily, they commonly regurgitate their recent meals when they're hooked. This causes other smallies to follow a hooked comrade in the hopes of getting a free meal. Sometimes several fish will follow, more often it's just one of similar size.

To catch these closely following shadow bass, quickly drop a sinking fly next to the hooked fish. The follower is most excited at the initial stages of the fight and is focused totally on its hooked brethren. So speed and accuracy is key. As fast as possible, put a fly that sort of matches the regurgitation next to the hooked fish (a plain brown woolly bugger or Holschlag Hackle Fly works good when the upchuck is crayfish). Over the years, my guiding clients have scored an impressive number of 18-inch doubles with this presentation.

When on Top, Go Barbless

To increase topwater hook-ups, pinch down the barbs. The line belly common with surface fishing by boat makes hook-setting tough, and the less experienced fail to land half their strikes. But it takes less force to drive in a barbless hook than a barbed one. And once the hook goes in to the bend smallmouth will seldom throw a surface fly—provided you maintain a tight line. Therefore, over the course of a season you'll land more surface smallies without the barbs than with them. And of course, barbless makes unhooking easier for you and the fish.

A double on smallies, caught when the second angler dropped his fly next to his boat partner's hooked fish.

One-Car Shuttles

Bikes and Boats. It may seem like an odd combo, but they can go together well. If you choose the land route carefully you can eliminate one of the two cars usually required for floating, by bringing along a bicycle (or a small motorized two-wheeler). First drive to the launch site and unload the craft, gear and one person. Then drive down to the take-out, leave the car, bike back to the put-in, secure the bike and shove off. Your vehicle will be waiting for you at the end of the day, and on the way home you can pick up the bike (I usually have it chained to a tree out of sight). For really short shuttles, you may not even need a bicycle; simply drop off the car and jog back to the put-in. This one-car method is especially good for solo floaters, so they can eliminate shuttle service. You'll have to leave the craft alone for a little while, but if you secure it discreetly you shouldn't have any trouble.

What to Bring?

Everything, maybe even the kitchen sink. That's what lots of folks try to pile into their craft for a float fishing trip. This is a mistake. Loose gear makes casting difficult and impairs boat handling. Things get kicked and stepped on, and the crowding makes it hard to find the items you actually need. In a small boat careful packing is critical, and even a big boat will quickly get cluttered if you don't pack your gear wisely.

Here are the 6 items I always bring on a float trip.

1. Rainwear and Extra Clothes:
Always bring a quality rain suit and extra shirt or jacket, but keep them together (and out of the way) in a waterproof bag or box. Never make the mistake of leaving the rain gear at home because it's sunny in the morning. Being 6 long miles from the landing in a downpour without rainwear will ruin the trip (and maybe give you hypothermia).

2. First Aid and Emergency Kit
My kit is the usual items like Band-Aids, headache medicine and cold remedies, plus a small tweezers, toilet paper and waterproof matches. During cooler weather a fire can save the day if you get wet.

3.Sunblock, Insect Repellent and a Small Flashlight.
Sunscreen and repellent should be no-brainers. But I've seen hundreds of guys come off the water with severe sunburn because they didn't bring sunblock. Badly burned knees and feet are common because many folks wear shorts and sandals while floating. And if you get caught on the water after dark you'll discover the value of a good flashlight.

4. Compact Coolers
If it's really hot and you're bringing lots of cold beverages, bring two coolers. In a johboat or other larger craft, I use two medium-sized rigid coolers, one full of ice and drinks and another with the food and chemical ice. In a canoe, to conserve

space it's often just a single flat-topped cooler, which also serves as a shore chair during lunch stops. On extra-long canoe floats in hot weather, I'll add a soft cooler with ice and extra drinks. (Soft coolers can be squeezed under a seat or fit into other odd spaces.)

5. Tackle Container

Vest, bag or box? These are your primary tackle storage options. If you intend to park and wade a lot, a vest or waist pack is the best choice, but if you stay in the boat to fish, most float anglers like their tackle near but not on them. Often I bring my float fishing tackle in a large plastic storage box with a lift-off lid. The box is uncrushable and waterproof both top and bottom (canoe floors are often wet), it doesn't have straps or handles to catch loose fly line, and I use its lipped lid as a handy table.

A conventional tackle bag also has its strengths. A bag is easier to carry, multiple pockets let you separate individual items and your buddy won't raise his eyebrows (which might happen if you use a box). With either a bag or box, I attach a nipper to my shirt and stow a small forceps in a pocket. Some anglers like to hang these and other doodads on a lanyard or strap around their neck.

6. Casting Aids

Loose fly line hanging up on assorted things in the bottom of the boat (especially your feet) is the biggest gripe floaters have. Any loose item, any little protrusion, and the line seems to magically find it. The nylon casting apron in my Smallmouth Angler canoe solves the line problem for that craft. If the boat allows you to stand, a large stripping basket is another line control option. What works reasonably well for most sitting anglers is to keep the floor and their laps clear of any loose items. And some go a step further; they remove their shoes and cast barefoot or in just socks, to keep the line from catching on shoe laces, straps or buckles.

10

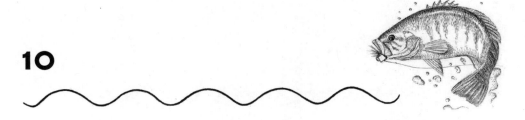

Float Fishing Watercraft

Many who take up smallmouth fishing ultimately find that they want or need a boat. A substantial percentage of good smallmouth rivers are best, or only, accessed by watercraft. And even on wadable streams, float fishing is often a more productive way to cover water because fish densities are generally much lower on smallmouth water than in trout streams. So having the right boat can be critical and can change your fishing life.

Yet as big a decision as boat buying is, very few fishing books or magazine articles offer detailed information on river watercraft. Because of this dearth of sound advice, I've seen scores of anglers get excited about river fishing, then run out and buy a boat, only to be quickly disappointed with it.

To avoid this common and costly mistake, you need to figure out what you really need and want in a boat before you purchase one. Then get accurate information about the pros and cons of the different watercraft on the market. There are several basic questions to consider before buying a boat (see the "8 Crafty Questions" box).

You may not be able to fully answer these questions immediately, but at least you'll know the key issues to consider when looking at boats. Of course, no single watercraft is ideal for every situation, and having a boat won't automatically enable you to catch more fish. Learning to handle the craft is just as important as what boat you have. But those who get an appropriate craft and learn to use it properly often find that float fishing offers them a lifetime of exciting outdoor adventures.

Getting the right boat for the waters you will fish helps ensure an enjoyable angling experience.

8 CRAFTY QUESTIONS
WHAT TO ASK YOURSELF BEFORE BUYING A RIVER BOAT

1. HOW MUCH USE?
If you're only going to use a boat a few times a season, you're not likely to want an expensive one (or maybe none at all). If you will use a boat often, it's worth investing time and money to get the one best for your needs.

2. SOLO OR TANDEM?
If you intend to fish with a partner at times, a one-person craft isn't the right choice. To fish solo, look for a boat you can handle on your own. If you want to do both, look for watercraft you can use solo or tandem.

3. TYPE OF WATER?
To float small, rocky streams you'll need a different type of craft than if you're going to only float big, deep rivers and launch at developed boat landings.

4. THE SHUTTLE?
With most craft and on most streams, you'll need a motor vehicle or bicycle shuttle between the upstream launch site and downstream take-out . How will you organize the shuttles?

5. STORAGE SPACE?
Canoes, kayaks and small pontoons take up far less storage space than trailered boats. How much space do you have?

6. HAULING THE BOAT?
Some craft can be easily cartopped or hauled in the back of your vehicle; others require a large trailer (and a substantial vehicle to pull it).

7. HOW MUCH TO SPEND?
Some of the least expensive models go for only a few hundred dollars; some trailered rigs cost over ten thousand.

8. ESSENTIAL FEATURES?
What features (such as cushy seats, lots of gear space, standing capability) do you absolutely need to have?

Types of River Watercraft

There are dozens of specific brands and models of boats that can be used for river fishing, and new ones continuously coming to market. But most of the practical and popular river craft fall into one of 7 categories: Sit-on-Top Kayaks, Pontoon Boats, Canoes, Jonboats, Drift Boats, Rafts, and Jet-Drive Boats. A huge distinction among these 7 types is whether they require a trailer, or can be cartopped or carried inside your vehicle. Smaller, lightweight, non-trailered watercraft are more practical and economical for many fly anglers. So let's start by considering these.

Sit-On-Top Kayaks

Originally designed for recreational paddling in warm oceans, sit-on-top kayaks are now being used for nearshore saltwater fishing and some freshwater fishing. Unlike other kayaks, you sit on top the boat rather than down inside a cockpit, and they can't fill with water. A plastic-hulled sit-on-top can work for the solo fly angler looking for a very basic and inexpensive boat that's easy to cartop. And because kayaks are skinny and lightweight and you use a double-bladed paddle, they're quite maneuverable and good for snaking down small streams. Most solo models are 10 to 15 feet long and weigh 35 to 60 pounds A few models try to cater to anglers by offering an anchor system, more storage space, and other features.

However, a kayak's downsides are several. Even in the roomiest ones, seating and storage is extremely limited. Big guys who like plenty of room to stretch or move around will feel cramped in a kayak, and ditto for those who like to bring lots of easy-to-reach gear. Safely stowing a 9-foot rod is another vexing issue. And you'll contend with constant wetness from splashes and dripping paddles. Most importantly, as soon as you stop paddling, the kayak quickly drifts out of proper casting position. One innovative model has foot-powered fins; but even this kayak requires hand steering, and the danger of fin damage from rocks is considerable. Therefore, the best way to fish from a solo kayak is to anchor (making a good anchor system essential). Or you can use a kayak very effectively for park-and-wade fishing.

Pontoons

Solo pontoon boats have received a lot of interest lately, mostly because these small craft appeal to the solitary instinct of many fly fishers and because the fly fishing industry is heavily promoting them. An objective assessment gives them a mixed rating. Small pontoon boats are essentially just an aluminum frame with a seat and oars that's supported by a pontoon on each side. Those with inflatable pontoons are quite lightweight (under 50 pounds) and very inexpensive (just a few hundred dollars). They can also be deflated and disassembled for very compact storage and

THREE SMALL CRAFT

Small craft options such as kayaks, pontoon boats and canoes each have their strengths and weaknesses. To choose the right boat, you must understand your particular needs.

Sit-on-Top Kayak

Pontoon Boat

Customized Canoe

hauling. On the water, they are stable and fairly comfortable, and with their oars they are maneuverable and perform reasonably well in current. An anchor system allows you to fish from them while they're stationary.

More deluxe solo models with rigid plastic pontoons cost significantly more and take more storage space, but these models last longer and you don't have to pump them up. Larger two-person pontoon boats are much heavier and more expensive yet, but you have the advantage of being able to bank shoot from them— one person rowing, while the other stands and casts.

Of course, pontoons have their shortcomings. Their substantial width (often nearly 5 feet) means they can't squeeze between boulders and through narrow chutes as well a kayak or canoe can. And when assembled and loaded, a pontoon boat is awkward to lift and jockey around blocking obstructions. Rod and gear storage space is very cramped, seating is tight, and the disassembly feature means you spend some of your fishing time putting the boat together and taking it apart.

Canoes

The canoe has been around so long that many trendy fly rodders no longer seriously consider this venerable craft. That's a serious mistake. Here's a lightweight, durable, go-anywhere boat that's excellent for fly fishing if it's properly customized.

Lightweight and durable small boats like this 60-pound canoe can be launched and landed nearly anywhere.

Customizing a canoe such as this one with oars, an anchor system, comfortable seats and an electric motor can make it a fishing machine.

Consider my "Smallmouth Angler" models. The larger model can seat 3, while the smaller, lighter version is designed for either 1 or 2 people. Both models can be rowed, paddled or propelled by an electric or small gas motor. They're equipped with an easy-to-use bow and stern anchor system, have comfortable swivel seats, excellent fly rod holders and even a nylon casting apron to keep the line from tangling. These custom-rigged canoes work well for bank shooting. And with the oars or motor they also make decent solo craft. These plastic canoes are durable enough for rocky streams and light enough to be dragged, carried and cartopped. And my custom-rigged canoes can be used on lakes and ponds, too.

While most canoes aren't nearly this fishing-friendly, many other models at least are relatively inexpensive water transportation. They will carry either one or two people, and are extremely durable, yet light enough to be cartopped, and can be stored on a garage wall or hung from the ceiling. And like a kayak or smaller pontoon boat, a canoe can be carried down and launched off road embankments and other rough landings. Most weigh from 55 to 85 pounds and are from 13 to 17 feet long. Those made of plastic are best for rivers; aluminum is inflexible and hangs up on rocks, and fiberglass is too brittle. Canoes also have good resale value because they're so popular and versatile. Even after a decade of use, many models can be resold for most of their original cost.

Many anglers think the canoe's chief flaw is tippiness. But this concern is easily addressed by getting a wider, more stable model and some canoeing experience. In reality, the biggest downside of most canoes is that they're not adequately rigged for fishing. Therefore, to use them well you should at least rig up a decent anchor system and better seating. Another weakness of average canoes is the difficulty most paddlers have controlling them in current. I guide out of canoes and have paddled them for decades. But I will be the first to admit they are challenging to control for fishing. That's why most of my river canoes are equipped with oars; a set of oars is vastly superior to paddling.

In the hands of a skilled oarsman, a mid-sized jonboat like this one can be a good craft for bank shooting.

Trailered Craft

If you are going to fish bigger, deeper rivers, and you're willing to commit more money and storage space to your boat, there are 4 larger craft to consider. Most of these require a garage space or parking spot to store them, a trailer to haul 'em and a developed boat landing for launching.

Jonboats

Developed on Missouri Ozark streams generations ago, the low-sided, flat-bottomed jonboat is a very functional river craft. I've guided from one for many years and it has served me well. Jonboats come in a wide range of sizes (under 10 feet long to over 20 feet). The smallest models (under 12 feet long and made of aluminum or plastic) weigh just over 100 pounds and can be carried by two guys and slid into the back of a pickup. A boat this size is too small for safe standing, but either oars or a small motor will propel it well.

A mid-sized jonboat (14 to 15 feet long, usually made of aluminum) affords significantly more room for two fly rodders. It is still light enough to be rowed, yet wide enough for anglers with good balance to stand and cast. It requires a trailer, but at less than 170 pounds, can still be carried short distances. No-frills models are also quite inexpensive and can be stored on their sides or upside-down. And with its shallow draft and low sides, a mid-sized jonboat will do fine on small and mid-sized rivers, as long as there aren't too many rapids or shallow riffles.

Most factory jonboats are so basic that serious jonboat owners customize their craft to fit their needs. Many add oars, better seats, anchor systems, carpeted floors, storage compartments, and outboard or electric motors. But remember, every addition will add weight or take up space in the boat; choose your add-ons wisely.

Big johnboats (16 feet or longer) are popular with some guides and others who ply large rivers and like lots of room. Generally too wide and heavy to easily row or carry, they require gas motors and large trailers. They are roomy enough for 3 people and stable enough for easy standing. In deeper, slow-flowing rivers you can use a large bow-mounted electric motor to maneuver the boat for bank shooting. But in shallow, fast water, an electric motor does a poor job of controlling a big, heavy boat. This often makes good craft control difficult. Seventeen- and 18-foot jonboats are also too large for about 80% of smallmouth rivers. And naturally, they cost more than smaller models and require greater storage space. Big jons aren't a good choice unless you intend to confine your fishing to big rivers with developed boat landings.

Drift Boats

"What a beautiful boat," people say when they first see a drift boat. Besides having graceful lines, drift boats make good fishing craft on select waters. The flat-bottomed, high-sided drift boat was designed to be very stable, dry-riding and maneuverable on fast-flowing western rivers. Drift boats are propelled by oars, most range from 10 to 16 feet long, and many larger models are rigged so that two anglers can stand and cast while a third person rows.

But the larger drift boats are big heavy-duty watercraft weighing hundreds of pounds. Fully rigged, these boats cost thousands of dollars. They require full-sized trailers, need developed boat landings and are too heavy to carry. And on wide, windy rivers without much current, the high-sided models catch the wind and are tough to row.

TWO LARGER CRAFT

Bigger boats like these are great on larger rivers, if you can handle them and are willing to invest the money and space they require.

Jonboat

Drift Boat

Some manufacturers also offer smaller, lighter two-person drift boats. And some current models have lower sides and more versatile designs for non-whitewater rivers. The smaller boats are about 12 feet long or less and easier to launch, load and row. But even smaller drift boats require considerable storage space, and most must be trailered. And while they are less expensive than the big rigs, they're still quite pricey compared to a jonboat, canoe, or kayak.

Rafts

Heavy-duty inflatable rafts are mostly used on rivers with lots of boulder-filled rapids, because they can bounce off boulders unscathed and stay upright in large waves. Thus, an oar-equipped raft is a good bet for brawling rivers with lots of class III and IV whitewater. You see increasing numbers of 3-person rafts used by fishing guides on big western rivers or mid-south mountain rivers. But out of all the smallmouth rivers in North America less than 10% have serious whitewater. And because it is so wide and bulky, transporting and storing a large raft is a major hassle for the average person. Therefore, larger rafts, like large drift boats, aren't practical for most smallmouth anglers.

Jet Drives

Flat-bottomed boats (especially big ones) propelled by huge jet-drive gas motors have become the rage on some rivers. They're popular with tournament-oriented anglers from lake backgrounds, where "gun-and-run"-style competitive fishing, high speeds and mega-horsepower have long been standard fare. These extremely noisy and wake-producing craft are dramatically changing the nature of river floating on some waterways. Because they have no propeller, jet drives can blast upstream in only a few inches of water.

However, on relatively narrow river channels, jet boats are nearly as dangerous and destructive as that other jet-drive scourge, the personal watercraft (PWC). Traveling at high speed upstream around tight bends in narrow corridors, jet-drive boats have collided with canoes and other slow-moving craft coming downriver. Even when actual collisions don't occur, the large waves created by the jets swamp or at least terrorize the smaller craft. Even worse, from an ecological perspective, is the erosion caused by the large waves. On narrow channels where jet-drive traffic is pervasive, the banks get a constant pounding from wave action. Besides increasing bank erosion, this re-suspends silt in the shoreline water column, negatively impacting fish spawning and feeding, and it ruins near-shore fishing.

Heavy jet-drive use on smaller waterways can turn what was once a quiet experience into a front-row seat at a stock car race. While hard-core motorheads may love the drama and danger of high-speed power boating, it's an anathema for river users seeking a peaceful, ecologically friendly outdoor interlude.

I'm not totally against jet-drive boats; I recognize their merit on large, wide rivers. But unregulated, they have potential to create serious problems. Many states are increasingly enacting laws to control dangerous and disruptive PWC (jet ski) use. Such laws make it illegal for jet skis to create wakes within 150 or 200 feet of land or near anchored or slow-moving watercraft. Although anglers are notoriously slow to react to growing problems, in the future I believe more and more small river users, too, will see the necessity of more laws protecting their fragile waters.

WATERCRAFT RIGGING

For any river watercraft, proper rigging is essential. Here are the 5 basic components needed to fly-fish effectively from a boat:

1. PROPULSION AND CONTROL
Oars, paddles, gas or electric motor—whatever propulsion you choose should get your boat easily through or around riffles, rapids, rocks and downed trees. And if you intend to cast from the boat, you must also maneuver, position and control the watercraft for effective and accurate casting.

2. ANCHOR SYSTEM
Easy anchoring is essential for effective river fishing. The best systems have both a bow and a stern anchor, each operable from your fishing position and convenient enough to use dozens of times in a day.

3. CASTING EASE
For bank shooting or anchored fishing, you need a stable sitting or standing position from which you can easily cast out the front and both sides of the craft. The casting area must also be clear enough so loose line doesn't constantly tangle.

4. ROD STORAGE
Your watercraft should have an out-of-the-way, yet convenient, place to store a rod (or rods) when not in use and protect rods from breakage.

5. GEAR STORAGE
You need dry, yet accessible, places to put your extra flies and tackle, plus rainwear, clothing, lunch, and everything you need for a day on the water.

11

Hunting Big Bronzebacks

BIG FISH! They fire our imaginations and quicken the pulse like few other matters in the piscine world. While three pounders are thrilling and fours are fantastic, five pounds of bronze is unadulterated power. There's no slowing down for the small-mouth as it gets older. The bigger it gets the stronger its runs, higher its jumps and greater its stamina. All smallies are special, but five pound, 21-inch specimens are truly amazing.

One beauty of the quest for mammoth smallies is that, unlike some species, big bronze can be found across the fish's range. For example, brown trout can exceed 20 pounds, but in the places most of us fish they rarely reach one-third that size. Same for the ubiquitous largemouth; while it may be nearly everywhere, most anglers must be content with northern strain largemouth, which are less than half the size of the Florida strain. In contrast, there's barely two pounds of difference in the biggest smallmouth across the continent. *Micropterus dolomieui* tops out at 7 to 8 pounds in a handful of locations, but thousands of waters offer the possibility of 5- to 6-pounders. So no need to fly across the continent or halfway around the world in your quest, heavyweight smallmouth are probably finning nearby.

I'm not implying that 5-pound (or even 4-pound) fish are common, or that by simply modifying your fishing strategies you'll automatically hook hordes of hefties. But there are definitely things you can do to significantly increase the numbers of big fish you catch. Best of all, these aren't difficult or complex techniques off-limits to the average angler. Here are 6 simple strategies to put bigger bronze on the line.

1. Follow the Big Fish

Going to where the big ones roam is one straightforward way to score. While many places hold fine fish, at any given time only select rivers and lakes offer the very best chances for lunkers. Perfect water conditions, catch-and-release regulations, a previous reproductive boom, low angling pressure—these and other factors can all produce a "big fish bite." Being on the best water doesn't guarantee success, but targeting prime destinations will greatly up your odds of connecting with chunksters.

To make good destination choices you gotta both figure out which waters are truly good (rather than simply hyped) and which ones are fly-fishing-friendly.

You can increase your odds of catching big smallmouth like this by following the 6 big fish strategies.

Some deep, clear reservoirs might have hefty fish, but they're tough to fly fish effectively. And plenty of destinations are still heavily promoted by local businesses even though their big fish heydays have long since passed.

One good place to start prospecting for more reliable information is in Part 3 of this book, "100 Top Smallmouth Destinations." I've always disliked the blatant hucksterism the non-fly fishing industry often falls into, so I strove to keep the wild exaggerations and unsubstantiated claims out of the destination section. There are a number of waters listed that are consistent, current producers of out-sized smallmouth. Start with this general information, then contact local sources for more details and up-to-the-minute reports.

2. Prime Time

Choosing the best time is another easy way to increase your big fish percentages, yet it's often overlooked by fly rodders. Average-size smallies can be caught year-round in many waters, and in some places the big ones also bite pretty well throughout the season. But on most waters the prime period is abbreviated, sometimes just a few weeks a year. At other times, the lunkers may be too deep, too dispersed, too wary or well-fed to be easy targets. The best fishing periods will depend on the specific locale, but on lakes and clear rivers, it's often the late pre-spawn period. On many other rivers, the mid- to late-fall period is the most consistent for the serious lunker hunter.

For example, a few years ago I had a particularly busy guiding season and didn't get any personal fishing time on one of my local rivers until early November. Though my clients had caught plenty of fine smallies during the summer and early fall, my 4-hour late-season foray yielded the biggest of the year, a rotund bruiser over 5 1/4 pounds.

3. Prime Lies

Of course, even in the most fish-laden water, only a tiny percentage of it will hold biguns. Don't try to cast any and everywhere, concentrate on just the very best spots. On smaller and mid-sized rivers, identifying some of the best big bass hangouts is surprisingly easy. Simply look for the best pools, best rock and best wood.

For instance, in 6 miles of river, perhaps a dozen pools have water over 5 feet deep. Out of the several dozen pools in that section of river, these few deepest ones will attract the highest percentage of big fish. And you can narrow your search even more. Large logs or trees resting in at least 3 feet of water are lunker magnets; if some of the larger, deeper pools have this big wood, you can be almost certain they're prime lies.

Less obvious (but nearly as productive) big-fish lairs are large subsurface boulders. Everybody likes to flail away at rocks that jut out of the water, but those at least a couple feet below the surface are much better. A 4-foot-diameter boulder in a 6-foot-deep pool is often overlooked by anglers, but never by the smallies. I know deep water boulders where my clients or I have regularly caught big ones for 20 years. How's that for consistency?

4. Big Fly, Big Fish

It's a cliché you've heard before, but it's true—big flies equal big fish. Not always, of course, but often enough to make the big fly concept a viable strategy. In the realm of subsurface offerings, going up to 3½, 4, sometimes even 4½-inch long flies will increase strikes from the 18-inchers. These larger-than-average flies are particularly effective in low or moderate visibility water. Naturally, they are also harder to cast and will reduce the number of fish under a foot you'll catch. Some don't like these trade-offs; others consider them a small price to pay for greater chances of a trophy.

Another fly tactic is using unusual patterns or uncommon colors. This tactic is especially productive in clear streams that receive substantial angling pressure. Old fish in these environments have seen a lot of lures. So if spin boys mostly throw white jigs, offering the fish a black or olive woolly bugger can pay off. In fact, in these heavily pressured waters, an extra-fuzzy pattern (like an extra-bushy woolly bugger) in subtle colors often triggers a response.

Fighting a big fish from a small craft is exciting. The canoe handler can help by moving the boat away from shoreline snags.

5. Top or Bottom

Keeping your fly in the top or bottom of the water column is another proven big-fish strategy. I've mentioned before how anglers like to work the middle of the water column and fish become acclimated to these presentations. This is particularly true of the biggest fish. So to fool the big ones, fish either the top or bottom, depending on the place and conditions. If depths are under 5 feet and few others are using top-waters, trophy smallies can be suckers for a large-profiled slow-moving topwater. Conversely, where surface fishing is common, scraping bottom is a better way to go. In fact, slow with-the-current hop or drag retrieves are the most consistent big-bronze presentations there are. Even the most sophisticated lunkers will (at least occasionally) fall for a slow-along-the-bottom technique.

6. Stay Late

This is an easy way to dramatically increase hefty hook-ups no matter where you fish. Staying on the water through the last hour of light can turn a mediocre day into a spectacular one. So often rivers and lakes come to life at sunset. Even on crystalline summer streams, big fish almost magically appear where only dinksters roamed earlier in the day. No longer hugging the bottom, the biggest smallmouth leave their lairs and hunt aggressively. Now is the time for a large topwater, a stout leader and keen anticipation.

> **THE "BIG BRONZE EQUATION"**
>
>   Best Place
>
> + Best Time
>
> + Best Spots in the Stream
>
> + Best Cover
>
> + Best Fly
>
> + Best Technique
>
> = Big Bronze

Small Water/Big Bronze

There's something special about small waters and big bronzebacks. Sure, hefty smallies raise our heart rates no matter where we catch 'em, but hooking those same fish in a little creek produces even more adrenaline. Maybe it's the challenge of outwitting the biggest, baddest predator in the stream. Perhaps it's a combination of factors: Small streams are such intimate and enjoyable places to fish. You're so close to the water, it's so quiet, so uncrowded, so shallow—so perfect to fly fish. Add three pounds of bronze to this scenario and you've truly found nirvana.

Whatever the reasons, I've been passionate about hunting big smallies in small waters since a youthful experience with a high-jumping 19-incher in Bohemian

Creek. The little creek's extremely clear water allowed me to spot the fish before-hand, and by the time I finished my slow, cautious approach I was shaking almost too much to make a cast. Fortunately my first cast was on the mark, and WHAM! The lunker stuck with a vengeance and was immediately airborne—an image for-ever burned in my brain.

To me a genuinely "small" stream is one you gotta wade fish, or at most can sneak a canoe down when water levels are good. On these modest waters, a "big" smallie is 18 inches and is truly a treasure, the angling equivalent of a 20-incher on larger water.

Finding Big-Fish Creeks

Finding the best small waters isn't nearly as easy as targeting popular big-name rivers. Often little known and little fished, these gems are only found by diligent investigation and exploration. The challenge of discovering "secret" hotspots is a major reason I love small-water smallmouthing.

One type of stream to check out are tributaries of big name-smallmouth lakes or rivers. Overshadowed by the nearby glamour waters, tributary streams of popu-lar smallmouth destinations often receive little pressure, yet support fine fish. Inaccessible sections of small waterways also have excellent potential. For example, rivers too small to easily canoe, with brushy banks that limit walking, often have lightly fished areas away from road access points. Difficult-to-float whitewater streams are also good candidates for big bronzebacks. These streams often have slower flowing (and little-fished) stretches tucked among the rapids.

Also, look for small sections of good smallmouth habitat hidden in otherwise unproductive water. Some streams are predominantly sandy or marshy, but have isolated stretches with rocky substrates and good depths. These hidden rocky areas can hold some genuine lunkers, simply because no one knows about them. I once caught a red-eyed beauty of nearly 21 inches and 5 pounds on a short, rocky sec-tion of stream bounded by miles of marshy (and bassless) water. One friend's piece of piscatorial paradise is a half-mile of deep, rocky water tucked away in an other-wise sandy, barren creek. Of course, it's unlikely anyone will lead you to these honey holes; it's up to you to find your own.

Small Water Habitat

On a typical creek, the best big-fish spots are pools at least 4 feet deep with good rock or wood cover. Often only one or two pools per mile have enough depth and cover to attract the biggest specimens. Besides logs and boulders, a small depres-sion (hole) in a pool is also a favored location for bigger smallmouth. In stream

A small creek, a 5-wt rod and 18 inches of bronze—it's easy to understand why Tim is smiling.

sections lacking cover, a small depression only a couple feet long and a foot deeper than the rest of the pool can hold a big fish.

Sneaky approaches are particularly critical on small waters. Splashing while you're wading invariably alarms big fish. Tromping along the bank of a pool you intend to fish does the same thing. Quietly ease up to a spot, keeping as far away as possible. And where the terrain necessitates getting close to the target, lower your silhouette by casting from one knee.

High Times and Low Waters

Many creeks get low and clear during summer. In these exposed environments, larger fish can disappear with the morning dew. But just as the dew returns when the sun sets, so do the hefties. No matter where you fish earlier in the day, plan to be on a prime pool in the evening. Low-light fishing is pretty good everywhere, but on creeks it's absolutely superb for big fish.

Besides summer evenings, spring can be another trophy time for creek bronze. On tributaries of productive lakes and big rivers, early season can be the big-fish period of the year. Larger fish from the main waterway move into these waters every spring and spend several weeks spawning. Some states have closed spring seasons to protect spawning fish, but many others do not. Targeting these spawning tributaries during March, April or May often means the biggest fish of the year.

I address some of the biological implications of fishing during the spawn in the "Smallmouth Though the Seasons" chapter. Here I want to make a larger point about small stream conservation. All smallmouth populations can be easily degraded by greed or thoughtlessness, but small streams are uniquely fragile. Not only can their diminutive watersheds be easily destroyed by bad land-use practices, but the fish populations themselves are also extremely fragile. Even the best creeks support only a few big fish per mile. And it takes them many years to reach heavyweight size. It's absolutely true that each fish is a rare treasure not quickly or easily replaced. Catch-and-release makes good sense everywhere; on our smaller waters it is absolutely essential.

12

Difficult Water Conditions

The glum looks said it all. The spin boys loading up obviously hadn't had a good day, and their response to my "how'd ya do, fellas?" confirmed it. The two complained that the heavy rains had "totally messed up the river." After a day of hard fishing they'd only caught a couple smallies. Perhaps it was just as well they drove away before learning that the fly fishers I guided had a fine time. Floating the same roily river where they fizzled, we managed to hook up with almost two dozen fish.

Now don't misunderstand. I'm not saying I always catch throngs of bronze no matter how lousy the conditions. High water, strong currents and dirty water can all be hair-pullers for the river angler. And rivers can certainly deal us these bad hands. Many agricultural streams muddy easily and often, and even rivers with forested watersheds become torrents after heavy rains. I've fished a lot of rivers that were in very foul moods and have developed some ways to deal with these tough conditions.

One thing I've learned is that smallmouth bass are a lot like people; they like stability in their lives and just like us, river smallies are able to adapt to a variety of situations once things have stabilized. Rapidly rising river levels or quickly muddying water can initially turn the fish off. But once the high water or turbidity has been around a few days, smallmouth generally adjust and develop a feeding pattern.

Secondly, every river is different—an obvious observation that's often forgotten. The smallies in Stream X may pile up at creek mouths when it rains, while in next-door River Y the creek mouths are as barren as the Dead Sea. It's always helpful to know a river before you fish it, but when water conditions are poor, intimate knowledge of a particular section of river is especially valuable.

Of course, these observations are just the beginning. Here's a short course on beating tough conditions, trial by trial.

Fighting Fast Water

Strong current is often deceiving. If the water hasn't risen or muddied too much, the river might appear much like it was before the rain. However, a closer inspection indicates the water is really cruising. In fact, depending upon a river's gradient and bank shape, a rise of only a few inches can double its current velocity. Now, wading and craft control are much more troublesome. Plus the fish will invariably have shifted their locations to avoid the strong current. Instead of feeding in head-of-pool areas or holding in open pools, smallmouth will move to more protected zones.

During the first day or so of a strong current period, when you can almost see the river rising before your eyes, smallies are particularly likely to hunker down and dramatically reduce their activity level, so fishing will be mighty tough. Fortunately, this initial period doesn't last long. Soon some fish will move into protected lies and start feeding again. These high-water locations are often bank eddies, shoreline cover (such as trees, bushes and grass) and large eddies downstream of big boulders or islands. The bass there can certainly be caught, but they're probably hanging tight to their slack-water sanctuaries, so won't pursue your fly very far.

At this time, your primary goal is to get the offering as close to the fish as possible. And no question, getting a fly down to bottom-hugging bronzebacks is tough in stiff current. A fast-sinking wet-tip line and a short leader is one good way to scrape bottom. Use a fly with 1/50th-ounce or 1/60th-ounce eyes. Another way to do the job is to use a heavy fly on a floating line with a long leader. Using a 1/32nd or sometimes a 1/24th-ounce fly on an 11-foot leader, you can bounce bottom in 4 feet of water yet still detect strikes.

When flows are slow I'm a big fan of with-the-current retrieves, but in strong current conditions I often work subsurface flies against the flow. Instead of letting your offering be swept quickly downstream, an against-the-current retrieve allows you to hold the fly right in front of an inactive fish.

Float-and-Fly Plus In-Their-Face

You can coax bottom-hugging, inactive smallmouth in strong current by combining two techniques discussed in the "Subsurface Smallmouthing" chapter: the Float-and-Fly and the In-Their-Face technique. Here's how it works: the Float-and-Fly is essentially suspending your fly below a large strike indicator buoyant enough to hold the fly at a precise depth. In this case, your target depth is right near bottom. The big indicator enables you to both control the fly and detect even the lightest strikes.

Using a floating line and a long, small-diameter (3 x) leader to cut through the current, try a fly tied with 1/30th or even 1/24th-ounce barbell eyes and add an indicator large enough to suspend this fly. Even a heavy fly won't suspend directly below the indicator in a strong flow, so start with about 6 feet between fly and indicator to fish 4 feet of water. Increase that length (by moving the indicator) until the fly occasionally hangs on the bottom.

Now for the In-Their-Face part: from an upstream casting position, put the fly about 10 feet above (upstream) of the target area. Allow the fly to settle (while keeping a tight line), then begin animating your offering with small twitches of the rod tip. You want the fly to dart a few inches forward (upstream) then settle back, while it remains in the same area near bottom. If you don't get a take in 15 seconds, feed out about 3 more feet of line so the fly is pulled downstream. Repeat the procedure until you've thoroughly covered the target zone. And beware of powerful bronze. The Float-and-Fly, plus In-Their-Face will entice surprising numbers of big fish, and they'll use the fast current to their advantage to give you the fight of your life.

If you're fishing from a boat, you can use a variation of this ultra-slow vertical presentation to fish right around your anchored craft, if the water is at least 4 feet deep and relatively turbid. By fishing your fly suspended below an indicator almost directly below the rod tip, you can meticulously fish both sides and the back of the boat. Don't work the fly excessively. A slow up-and-down rod-tip motion of only 6 inches is best. Purists might not regard this technique as true fly fishing, but I've seen plenty of folks who hooked an 18-incher right next to the craft quickly change their minds.

Fishing the flooded tributary mouth (in foreground) these on-foot fishers found a concentration active fish.

Surmounting High Water

I'm talking about a real flood, the kind of heavy flow that puts a river at least 2 feet above normal. This level of water often makes a river nearly unrecognizable; the pools, riffles, boulders and other reference points you know so well are now nowhere to be found. And for anglers toiling in this adversity, the fish also seem to have disappeared in the rising tide.

But wait a minute. High water smallmouthing can actually be darned good, if you can adapt to the new conditions. Years back, as folks down in Missouri sand-bagged against the mighty Mississippi's onslaught, I was bagging the smallies upriver in Minnesota. Though the upper Miss' wasn't quite in flood stage, it was up a solid 4 feet even in late July. After other smallie fans abandoned the river to its flooded fate, I persevered until I found an effective game plan. And hallelujah! Once I found the right locations and techniques, I was rewarded with day after day of tremendous high-water fishing. Out of that surging flow came dozens of high-jumping 17- to 19-inch "blackbacks" (those high-water smallies were really dark). And this was no fluke. Plenty of times since, I've experienced excellent angling even when the rivers were flooding.

High Water Locations

Just as with strong current fishing, targeting proper locations is a key to high-water success. Except now the fish may be in places that didn't even have water a few days earlier. Flooded bank vegetation and wood should be among your high-water targets, especially where the current is slow or moderate. Various minnow species often move into these flooded areas to feed, with smallmouth close behind. Eddies on inside bends and below islands seldom get a second glance from smallies if the bottom is sandy or depths are shallow, but now they're deep and slack enough to hold resting and feeding fish. Tributary mouths can also be real bonanzas for high-water bronzebacks. Almost any type of incoming creek carrying an increased flow, even normally dry drainage ditches, culverts and tile outlets, if they have running water, can draw various forage species to feed on the incoming nutrients, with the predators close behind.

A key to any high-water strategy is to quickly sort through the 99% of the water that's unproductive and find the productive 1%. If the river has good tributaries, this part of your strategy is relatively easy. Float a 10- to 12-mile section that has numerous incoming creeks (if the high water hasn't

> **HIGH WATER LOCATIONS:**
>
> 1. Flooded Bank Vegetation and Wood
>
> 2. Eddies on the Inside Bends
>
> 3. Eddies Below Islands
>
> 4. Tributary Mouths

created unsafe boating conditions) and you should find a few that hold fish. Quietly anchor and thoroughly work each tributary. Here, a good bow anchor is essential, and you may also need a stern anchor to keep the craft from being buffeted in the current. If you're on foot, you can get in on the tributary fun by "road fishing" them: identify those accessible by road and drive from one to another.

Finding fish-holding eddies, banks or flooded vegetation might not be quite as easy. Many flooded banks won't be productive, so the angler must cover a lot of water to find those that do hold fish. Use your paddles, oars or motor to really slow your craft down so you can accurately work potential areas. Once you find an area with fish, it pays to quietly anchor right next to it so you can work it thoroughly. Often, several good fish will concentrate in a favored location, but will require a slow, diligent presentation.

ANCHORING TO FISH HIGH WATER

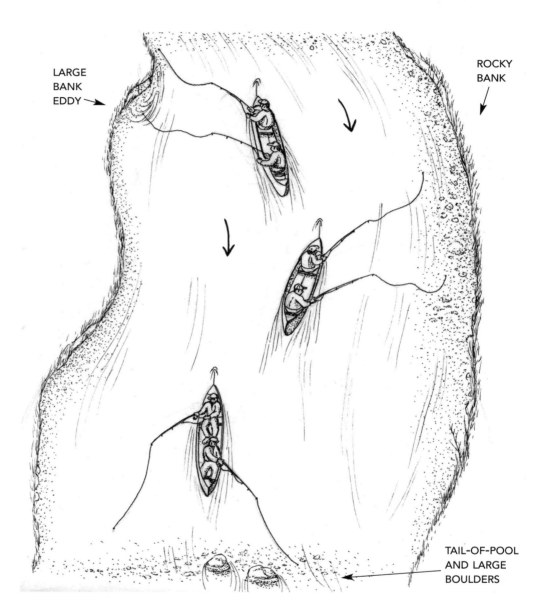

LARGE
BANK
EDDY →

ROCKY
BANK

TAIL-OF-POOL
AND LARGE
BOULDERS

Craft control in high water is difficult. One of the best ways to fish high
water is to anchor within casting range of each target location. Always tie
off directly to the bow or stern.

Drubbing Dirty Water

Dirty water is the third angling challenge. I'm not talking about water that's a little off-colored; I mean the stuff that looks like strong coffee with cream and makes most fly fishers shake their head in despair. Unfortunately, plenty of rivers around the country have low visibility for several days after a heavy rain. This can mean frustrating fishing, but some smallies can be suckered in even the dirtiest water.

If the water level or current speed isn't significantly higher than normal, the fish in a turbid river will be in their usual haunts: the same pools, current breaks, eddies, boulders and wood where feeding or resting fish hold during clearer conditions. During the first day or two of turbidity, smallmouth will be less active. However, as the low visibility continues, the fish's feeding increases.

Slow Flashy Flies

The most effective dirty water strategy is to cover prime areas thoroughly and meticulously with high-visibility flies. Bright colors like chartreuse, orange, and white are most visible in turbid water, and so is black. Sometimes a combination of these is best, such as a large-profile black-and-chartreuse fly. And choose your locations wisely. By skipping low-percentage locations and focusing on only the very best spots in the river, you'll have time to really work these key zones. This is an ultra-slow, highly focused strategy. Repeatedly bring the fly slowly along the bottom through the same area; you can often produce strikes where just a cast or two would draw a blank.

But cheer up, you impatient types. Here's a faster-paced approach—take your dirty water smallies off the top. Yup, you heard right. Though few fly fishers realize it, after low visibility has persisted for several days, noisy topwaters can be surprisingly effective. Working big poppers along slow-water banks and wood cover is one of my favorite techniques in dirty water. A moderately noisy topwater is easily noticed, and by working it slowly the fish have plenty of time to be tempted.

Winning In Weedy Water

Aquatic vegetation is generally associated with largemouth, but a number of smallmouth rivers also become quite weedy in summer. It's almost impossible to work heavy vegetation with conventional techniques and standard flies, but by modifying your tactics you can fish productively and enjoyably even in pretty thick stuff.

Most riverine vegetation grows in clumps, with the stems or leaves trailing downstream in the current. Fortunately, smallmouth seldom go deep into thick

Lots of rain often means dirty water. This murky-water fish was caught by working a noisy popper along a slow current bank.

weeds. Instead, they tend to lie at the outside and downstream edges of the clumps. So fishing them is an especially visual activity that requires good polarized glasses and reasonably clear water to identify the weed openings. Accurate casting is also a must.

The Pocket Drop

One weedy water technique I like is the Pocket Drop. The idea is to cast past openings (pockets) in the weeds and then maneuver the fly across the surface into the pocket, where you let it fall on a tight line. If the current is significant, you must anticipate the fly's downstream drift by casting across and upstream of the targeted pocket. Various weed-guard-equipped, slow-sinking patterns will work for the Pocket Drop. Two of my favorites are the Flash Dancer with its bright fluttering wings and the Spinner Fly with its flashing blades; they both elicit powerful strikes. Where river current is slow, you can also Pocket-Drop a weedless popper. Again, accurate casts are critical because you want to drop the fly right into the middle of the opening. Two or three pops are all you'll get before the fly drifts off target. Often that's enough.

Low Fertility Waters

Some rivers have extremely low alkalinity. Draining bogs and other low-nutrient soils, these often dark-stained "soft water" streams can only support low densities of fish. However, by targeting a few locations in those streams, fishing can still be surprisingly good. Since almost all the smallmouth will be concentrated in runs, rapids and at the heads of pools, keying in on current is your strategy.

I regularly fish a half-dozen low fertility "blackwater" rivers. By floating a long section of river (sometimes 12 miles) I can hit a bunch of smallmouth concentrations in a day, often picking up 2 to 4 fish per spot.

I work the fishy current areas hard and fast (often staying only 15 or 20 minutes per spot). Then by using the electric motor option on my Smallmouth Angler canoe I quickly cruise down to the next hotspot. Many streams only have one or two productive locations per mile, so getting through the barren water quickly is essential.

TEN TIPS FOR DIFFICULT CONDITIONS

1. **EVERY RIVER IS DIFFERENT.** Knowing your particular river really pays off in difficult conditions.

2. **IN FAST WATER, CAST FROM UPSTREAM.** Work a subsurface fly against the current to keep it In-Their-Face near bottom.

3. **TO GET DOWN IN FAST WATER** with floating line, you need a 1/30 to 1/24th-ounce fly.

4. **FOR STRONG CURRENT OR DEEP WATER,** use a fast-sinking, sparsely-tied pattern, like a Synthetic Streamer.

5. **FOR STRONG CURRENT USE A HEAVIER ROD.** An 8-wt is best for fast water and big fish.

6. **WHEN HIGH OR DIRTY WATER MAKES FISH INACTIVE,** use flies that have plenty of action when retrieved ultra-slowly (such as rabbit-strip patterns).

7. **FOR DIRTY WATER USE BRIGHT OR BLACK.** Bright colors like chartreuse, orange and white are most visible in turbid water, and so is black. A combination like black and chartreuse can be a killer.

8. **AFTER A FEW DAYS OF DIRTY WATER,** try a topwater worked slowly.

9. **IN WEEDY WATER, DO THE POCKET DROP.** Use a weed-guard-equipped slow-sinking fly, or in slow current try a weedless popper.

10. **TARGETING THE BEST LOCATIONS IS KEY** for most difficult conditions, especially high water or low fertility water

13

Lake Fishing: Shoreline Tactics

Here's a fly rodding frontier. Hundreds of thousands of acres of stillwater offer great smallmouth potential, but at this time only a few fly anglers are taking advantage of it. While a few lakes here and there have been "discovered" by fly rodders, a vast amount of water sees nary a fly line all year. New England lakes, mid-South impoundments, western reservoirs, and thousands of glacier-scoured gems in the northern US and Canada all hold great promise and big smallmouth.

Certainly the obstacles, such as the need for a boat, sometimes substantial winds, deep-holding fish, and perhaps the sheer size of the water, are real challenges for the fly fisher. But approached the right way and at the right time, lake fishing can be almost heaven.

Consider the famed Boundary Waters Canoe Area and Quetico Park along the Minnesota/Ontario border. It is 1,000 rugged lakes surrounded by two million acres of designated wilderness, where only canoes can be used. For years, I've fished and guided in this maze of water and woods. Armed only with an 8-wt and a spirit of adventure, even clients nearly 70 years old have caught massive smallies and impressive pike. More importantly, they had the time of their lives and many became devoted lake fly fishers.

It's the same for the lodge trips to Canadian lakes that I host. Many fly anglers who sign up for these trips have little lake fishing experience. Nevertheless, nearly everyone catches nice smallies (and other species) and has an all-around great time. Ditto for Great Lakes fly rodding. Though Erie, Michigan, Huron and the other great lakes are millions of acres, an increasing number of fly rodders are successfully pursuing bronzebacks in the shallow bays of these mega waters.

The allure of lakes is multi-faceted, and big fish are just one of its many attributes. But, of course, just showing up at a lake with a few flies and high hopes won't lead to much. Lake environments are radically different than rivers. Many warm-water rivers have barely 24 inches of visibility, while some lakes have clarity of 24 feet. Some streams seldom exceed 4 feet; on many lakes 40-foot depths are common. On small waterways, summer smallies are often confined to just a few square yards of pool; some stillwater bronzebacks have vast hunting zones encompassing many acres.

But not to worry. A river-oriented fly fisher can surmount these challenges simply by targeting stillwater smallies when they're shallow and near the shoreline.

A testimony to the productiveness and enjoyment of lake smallmouthing.

WHY FISH LAKES?

BIG FISH
Lake smallies are often substantially larger than their riverine cousins, so 5, even 6-pound leviathans are possible.

STABLE WATER CONDITIONS
Lakes don't become raging torrents or muddy messes every time they receive heavy rainfall.

EASIER ANGLING
No need to wade or fight the current by canoe. A full-sized boat allows you to fish comfortably and effectively.

UNCROWDED WATERS
Some lakes, especially in the northern US and Canada, are nearly pristine, and smallmouth there are still overlooked by spin anglers.

SCENIC SETTINGS
Hundreds of northern lakes and even many large southern impoundments are rock-studded, forest-fringed beauties that please the eye and soothe the soul.

It's a Spring Fling

Without a doubt, spring is the easiest time for fly-flingers to score on lakes. Lasting at least 4 to 5 weeks, the middle pre-spawn period through the completion of the spawn offers willing smallies in the shallows. From the beginning of the period until the end, here's what you need to know:

Pre-Spawn

Once bays and other shallow areas in a lake warm into the low to mid-50s, pre-spawn smallmouth start feeding actively. This can occur by late March in southern zones and not until late May in northern latitudes. And remember, main lake temps can still be several degrees cooler during this time, so be sure to actually

SPRING LOCATIONS OF LAKE SMALLMOUTH

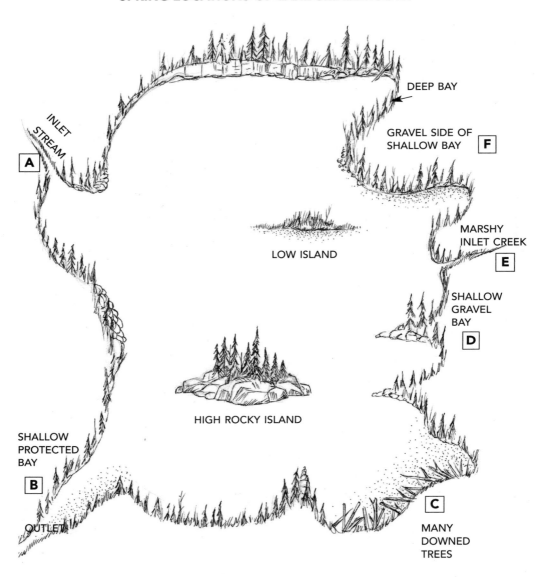

Lake Smallmouth Locations

Early Spring: A, B, C, E

Spawn: B, C, D, E, F

check the bays you're thinking of fishing. Also, north shore bays and shorelines often warm up first on large lakes.

Pre-spawn fish often relate to structure such as boulders, fallen trees and weeds in 5 to 8 feet of water. Though they're feeding, the smallmouth's sluggish metabolism requires a slow retrieve. The Clouser Minnow and Tim's Winter Minnow are good flies for this. However, if water temperatures drop after the fish have moved into the shallows, many smallmouths will temporarily slide deeper. Using a full-sink line and probing the 8- to 12-foot depths next to the shorelines that recently held bass is a productive cold-front technique.

Creek mouths also offer hot fishing in the spring. An incoming stream only a couple of degrees warmer than the lake itself will hold some fish if the stream mouth is at least a few feet deep. If minnows or other forage species are attracted to the creek, smallmouth numbers can be exceptional. These hot spots don't exist in every lake, but where they do, they are early-season magnets for smallies. The potential of creek mouths can be truly prodigious. There are scads of these warmwater magnets in the Boundary Waters Canoe Area, places where I've caught a half-dozen lunkers in as many casts. In fact, my wife caught her very first bronzebacks at one such spot. Her first was an 18-incher, the next two even larger. Talk about getting spoiled; I had a hard time convincing her that smallmouth don't all come this large.

Spawn Period

As temps in the shallows climb towards 60 degrees, more and more fish will gravitate towards gravel-bottomed bays and shorelines. Even if nests aren't yet visible, both sexes will be near their future spawning sites, likely in slightly deeper water. These waiting-to-spawn fish can also be caught, provided you get a fly near them. Working 5 to 8 feet deep with a sink-tip line is an excellent way to score at this time. In some of my favorite lakes, the late pre-spawn period offers the best big-fish catches of the year. Sometimes it seems that nearly all the fish that strike are over 15 inches.

Once spring smallies start fanning out nests, fishing becomes an exciting visual affair. While in many rivers nests are impossible to see, in lakes plenty of beds are visible, at least in calm water and bright light. Wood cover, even just a small piece of it, is a big draw for nesting bronze. While these "wood beds" can be difficult to detect and fish, they're worth it, because these are the sites the biggest males commonly choose. And remember that barring drastic changes in lake levels, smallmouth spawn in the same places year after year. So once you find fish, the following springs will likely see them at the same location.

The "Smallmouth Through the Seasons" chapter describes spawn fishing in detail. However, one thing not mentioned in that chapter is the phenomenon of deep-water spawning in lakes. With the proliferation of water-filtering zebra mussels in the Great Lakes and other bodies of water, some areas have seen a dramatic increase in water clarity. Now some smallies in places such as Lake Erie and Lake Michigan are building nests in 10 to 15 feet of water. Unlike in most lakes in North America, in these ultra-clear habitats the biggest bronze can be surprisingly deep.

Even if you can't see any beds this deep, targeting boulders using a sink-tip line and a rabbit bugger-type fly can still pay off handsomely. If you can make out the outline of a big rock, try casting to each side of it. And make sure you allow the line to sink to the bottom before slowly twitching the fly past the target.

For the more typical spawners in shallow water, very quiet slow-moving topwaters are dynamite when the surface is flat. Small foam and hair divers twitched over the nest are excellent. And sometimes a slow-moving Sneaky Pete is just what the doctor ordered. Subtle topwaters like this really outperform others as the spawn progresses and the males become less aggressive.

Summer In the Shallows

Once the glory days of spring are over, lake smallmouthing becomes trickier. When the spawn is complete, smallies on many lakes shift deeper down shorelines and points or to offshore humps and shoals. To find shallow smallies now, fly rodders have to carefully choose when and where to angle. Fortunately, on most lakes the low-light periods of mornings, evenings and rainy days still offer some fish cruising the shallows. Heavy concentrations of big bronze might no longer be available, but you can still have mighty fine mid-summer fishing, and sometimes right on the surface.

Early and Late

Many summer mornings I've started laying out a popper on the lake before sunrise and have been rewarded with two hours of superb angling. And it's nearly as good during the last two hours of the day. Even shorelines that offer nothing but babies during midday can hold dandies during these early and late periods.

This early and late dictum is well known, but it always surprises me how many don't heed it. So often, while staying on lakes I see guys heading out to fish just as I'm coming in for a late breakfast. Then around 6 PM as I'm preparing to go out again, I watch the same fellas who went out at 8 AM return. They seldom have more than sunburns and few small fry to show for their 10 hours of effort. On the other hand, my 2-times-2 hours almost always produces action. I might like to believe greater piscatorial prowess is the reason for my success, but it's simply that I fish when the smallmouth are shallow and willing.

Even in mid-July, this early morning fishing was productive.

Low Visibility Conditions

While smallmouthing in summer shallows is mostly an early, late (and night) affair, midday can be good if the light is low or the water stained. I've seen the shoreline bite hold up all day even on gin-clear lakes because of dark and rainy weather. Some folks hate fishing in the rain, but summer smallies love it. If you're on a clear lake be sure to pack your rain suit and hope for an all-day drizzle.

You can also target stained lakes during the summer. While many smallmouth lakes have secchi disk readings of 10 feet or greater, those heavily stained by bog drainage or algal blooms have clarity readings of only a few feet. State or provincial Fisheries Department reports often include the lake's secchi disk reading. If it has low visibility (5 feet or less), some smallies likely remain shallow during midday and there can be good shoreline fishing nearly all summer long. I've even had consistent sunny-day topwater fishing in late August on stained lakes.

Heavy algae blooms in the summer occur most often on more developed lakes where agricultural, municipal or residential activity puts extra nutrients into the water. Dark stain (due to bog or marsh drainage) is most common on smaller or shallow bodies of water. However, smaller is relative. I know of several thousand-acre lakes that are heavily stained because their incoming rivers drain extensive bog lands. These lakes don't necessarily have high numbers of fish because of their low alkalinity, but the smallmouth stay shallow all season long.

Location, Location, Location

Naturally, not all summer shorelines are productive. Those isolated bays and shallow shores that held so many spawning fish earlier in the season are now likely devoid of bigger specimens. During the summer, cover-laden shorelines adjacent to deeper water are the places to try. Fast-sloping banks dropping off into the lake's main basin are prime, particularly those with lots of cobble and large downed trees. In northern lakes, shorelines with aquatic vegetation, such as bulrushes, lily pads or coontail are also worth investigating, especially if the lake has few or no largemouth.

Summer weeds can be remarkably productive. Across the Canadian Shield (the vast geologic zone that includes much of Canada and the northern tier states) many lakes are deep, rocky and infertile—"oligotrophic" in biologist's parlance. Aquatic vegetation is very limited in these waters and largemouth are few. In these lakes, even small patches of submergent vegetation only 10 or 20 feet in diameter can attract smallies. On calm, sunny days you can spot weed beds even several feet below the surface by cruising slowly along shorelines and over reefs. Fishing the edges and the tops of this vegetation can produce excellent catches even during the August doldrums.

Rocky points extending into deep water are also excellent summer locations. In these situations, fish will often be on the very top of the point at dawn and dusk, and move deeper down the point's sides when light increases. And if you do get out there during low-light periods, don't hesitate to try a topwater. Standard poppers can be terrific, but that little "prop fly," Dan's Buzz Bomb, is often even better. There's something about that little buzzing sound that drives lake smallies wild.

If you draw a blank on the surface, switch to a subsurface "search pattern." You're hunting for active fish, so the fly doesn't need to scrape bottom and it can be worked rather quickly. A lightweight Deceiver, Marabou Streamer or a Clouser Minnow are good search flies. A foam or hair diver fished on a sink-tip line is also great for this work. Allow the line to first sink several feet then retrieve with 18-inch strips. A slight pause between strips causes the fly to rise and often produces a hard wallop.

Lake Tackle Tips

Lake fishing often calls for a substantial rod, sometimes up to a 9-weight, to punch through wind and to attain the distances required. However, in dead calm mornings and evenings a good caster can have high drama with just a 5 or 6-wt. Don't expect one of these lighter sticks to match the versatility of an 8-wt, but where fish run smaller and when conditions are optimum, gearing down is both possible and enjoyable.

Flies and Leaders

Many of the same patterns that are fine river flies are also good lake offerings. However, the best color schemes for lake smallmouthing are often different from what you might use in rivers, mainly because of the clarity of lakes and the preponderance of lake forage such as ciscos, shad, smelt or shiners. The best lake flies are often those with some bright whites and silvers blended into them. But this is a generalized color concept; color choices vary from lake to lake and even day to day.

No matter what fly you use, don't reduce its effectiveness by using too short or heavy a leader. As a rule, bass aren't leader-shy, but in the ultra-clear and bright conditions of many lakes, increasing leader length and/or reducing its diameter is a wise idea. When using floating line, I like to keep the leader at least 10 feet and preferably 11 feet long. And even with sinking line I use at least a 6-foot leader unless I'm using a floating fly. It's the same for leader diameter. For clear water away from heavy wood or weeds, I'll use the thinnest diameter 6-lb. test leader material I can find. For snaggier conditions I'll use a small diameter 8-lb. leader.

A float tube isn't practical on every lake, but along uncrowded, wind-protected shorelines, this can be a enjoyable way to fish smallies.

Watercraft and Wading

When you think of lake fishing, images of a large modern bass boat probably come to mind. Actually, there are many other ways to access shoreline smallies. So consider all the possibilities before selecting your transportation method.

Wade Fishing

While many lake shores are too deep or distant to fish on foot, others are very wadable. I love sneaking around Great Lakes bays in only my waders, not just for the quietness and simplicity of it, but also because it's a good way to catch fish. By choosing fishing sites carefully and working the water very thoroughly, the on-foot angler can have a great time, too. Small, protected spawning bays are wade-fishing hotspots in the spring and early summer. Later in the summer, large rock or gravel points extending out into the lake have good wading potential. And stream mouths bring in nutrients that attract smallmouth, making them productive all season. Riprapped shorelines are also good, especially early in the morning.

Float Tubes

Your smallest watercraft option is a float tube. It won't handle wind and it won't get you far down the shore, but for working a half-mile of sheltered lakeshore, a tube is an enjoyable and productive way to fish. And a float tube has a unique advantage: you can collapse it and tote it in a pack or carry it inflated on your back, which means you can launch almost anywhere. I've hiked float tubes miles through the woods to many remote smallmouth lakes. I've carried them into "no motor" lakes in state parks and launched them off big boats into the Great Lakes. An energetic and enterprising angler will find many places to use a float tube far from official boat landings. But no matter where you tube, always be sure to wear a life jacket.

Small Watercraft

There are several kinds of small watercraft you can use for near-shore lake fishing. My favorite is a canoe. I've spent thousands of hours fishing and guiding on wilderness lakes with this lightweight, yet sturdy craft. If the lake or bay you intend to fish is reasonably wind-protected and not full of high-speed motorboats, a canoe can put you on fish. However, you need to recognize the skinny craft's limitations: First of all, they're slow! Traveling to a spot just two miles down the lake takes a long time, either by paddle or electric motor. Second, equipped with just bench seats, a canoe isn't very comfortable and your low position makes casting more difficult. And lastly, unless you anchor or the stern person devotes all their time to craft control, a canoe quickly gets out of position. So a custom-rigged canoe such as my "Smallmouth Angler" (with its comfy seats, oars, rod holders, easy anchor system, casting apron and other fishing features) is best for lake fishing.

Another possibility is a kayak. I enjoy kayaking big water and have also rigged my 17-foot sea kayak for fishing. This includes an anchor system, rod holder and tackle bag. The boat's spray skirt allows you to handle substantial waves and serves as a good casting apron. For more protected waters, a sit-on-top kayak is yet another option. A solo angler who doesn't need to fish far from the launch site can use even a smaller craft. A one-person pontoon boat will work, if you rig it with an anchor and you avoid windy conditions.

Larger Boats

Of course, to traverse larger, windier waters you'll need something with an outboard motor. Nowadays, it's fashionable for the average crankbaiter to ape the tournament celebrities by getting an electronics-laden boat with enormous horsepower that costs a fortune. But huge, expensive machines aren't always necessary to successfully fish lakes; more modest craft will also do. A 14- or 15-foot aluminum

Vee-bottom boat equipped with just a 15 or 20 horsepower motor is fine. These smaller, no frills "tin boats" (as they're sometimes called) are lightweight and easily launched and trailered, durable enough to take plenty of abuse, large enough to accommodate two fly rodders and, perhaps most importantly, are quite inexpensive (especially if you get a used one).

Of course, to reach distant offshore islands and reefs, to cross large open water or safely fish in heavy swells on a windy day, an 18 foot Vee-hull with at least 50 horses is a smart idea. The next chapter covers open water/offshore lake angling. Here, I'm focusing on more-protected near-shore waters.

The key component won't be how fast you can blast down the lake, but rather how well you can control the craft while fishing. A good anchor system is essential for working a spot thoroughly. For bank shooting a bow-mounted trolling motor is best, but a transom-mounted electric will also work with practice. Oars, too, can work well for positioning a lighter boat; two anglers can take turns, one rowing while the other works the shoreline.

Boat Fishing Tips

No matter what type of boat you employ, make the effort to approach your targets quietly. While smallies in deeper or choppy water seldom give a hoot how much noise you make, these same fish are more shy when they're cruising calm-water shallows. A roaring motor or banging on the boat will frighten bank bass. You can also minimize spooked fish by making longer casts. A stealthy float-tube fisher can sometimes sneak right up to his quarry, but in higher-profile watercraft it's better to cast at least 45 feet.

Another sticky issue while boat fishing is line management. My customized canoe has a specialized apron that keeps the loose line from tangling in your feet. In a boat you can try a couple other ways to manage your line. If you can safely stand while casting, you can use a large stripping basket. Another possibility is to wear smooth footwear (or go barefoot) and completely clear the floor around your feet, so loose fly line has fewer things to attach to.

Lake fly fishing is surely a different scene than wading a stream. But mastering big water is well worth the effort. The challenges may be large, but so are the rewards.

14

Lake Fishing: Open Water Methods

I'll never forget it: over 21 inches of beautiful bronze framed against the setting sun. I was fishing a reef far from shore, but as soon as the bruiser hit it streaked towards the surface and shot skyward. Fishing open water with few visual cues isn't for everyone, but smallies like that Lake Michigan lunker can make a convert out of even the most devout stream fan. And just like the fly-rodders who have discovered offshore saltwater fishing, those who learn the tricks of open-water smallmouthing really can experience some exceptional angling.

In thousands of lakes across the Canadian Shield, vast areas throughout the Great Lakes and in hundreds of reservoirs, big smallies spend much of their summers on offshore shoals, reefs and humps. Sure, you may be able to find them in the shoreline shallows early in the season, but as the spawn ends they move to deeper lairs. Some may be too deep to comfortably fly fish (over 25 feet) but many of these open-water smallmouth reside in more fly-friendly depths of 10 to 20 feet.

In these locations, fly anglers with motors, depth finders and sinking lines can connect with the truly outstanding specimens of the smallmouth clan. Fish exceeding 5 pounds, perhaps even breaking the 6-pound mark, are possible. And because they have never seen a fly before, off-shore bronzebacks are very susceptible to our feathered creations. Besides the allure of giant bronze, offshore angling is a compelling challenge in itself; the skills needed are different than for shallow water, and mastering them is rewarding. So if you're looking for new challenges along with big fish, it's time to head for big water.

Lake Boats

To connect with offshore bronze, the first thing a fly angler needs is a boat. If you only fish big waters a few times a year, hiring a guide makes the most sense economically. However, if you want to become an offshore regular, you'll want your own craft. Naturally, you'll need more boat than what's okay for river fishing, but an adequate offshore craft doesn't have to be nearly as big or pricey as what many hardware-chuckers envision.

Across the Canadian Shield, lakes even thousands of acres in size are often quite protected due to a multitude of islands and points. South of the Canadian Shield, there are numerous smaller lakes that also aren't unduly windswept. Even many southern reservoirs, though they're miles long, are relatively narrow and sheltered by trees. Sixteen- and 17-foot boats powered by 20- to 40-horsepower outboards have been safely used on these type of waters for decades. You won't fly down the lake with a 25-horse motor, but it's enough power to get you where you want to go and, more importantly, safely get you through 3-foot swells when needed.

Of course, to roam the very biggest waters like the Great Lakes and huge western reservoirs, a 18-foot (or larger) boat with at least a 75-horse motor is in order. New, these rigs cost serious dollars, but you can purchase a used one for much less. Most larger boats have front carpeted decks, but the most basic aluminum models don't. If you install a deck and a couple fly rod holders in them, they're fine for fly fishing.

Anchor Essentials

You also need a good anchor system. Tournament-type bassin' boys using the "gun and run" method fish so quickly that they seldom anchor. Instead, they use their bow-mounted electric motor to temporarily hover in position. A good electric motor is fine for covering water, but you'll need an anchor to thoroughly work a concentration of fish, or to stay in position when wind and waves buffet the boat. So don't skimp on your anchor. First make sure you have plenty of anchor rope— to hold in 25 feet of water you need twice that length (50 feet of rope or more). Also consider getting at least two anchors. When variable winds cause the boat to pendulum-swing on the bow anchor, putting out a second anchor off the stern will keep you in place.

A 15-pound mushroom head will hold most boats if the wind isn't too strong. But a bigger boat or stronger waves may require a 20-pounder. For a lighter boat and less wind, a 10-pound, 3-pronged "river anchor" might work. The big advantage of using a light anchor is the ease of bringing it in. If your anchor is too tiring to use often, you won't, and your fishing will suffer.

On this clear lake, cloudy weather produced good fishing even during midday.

Seeking Structure and Smallmouth

Maps and Electronics

A major challenge of offshore angling is finding the smallmouth, so good maps and a depth finder are important. Pinpointing prime summer habitat (especially reefs and humps) is best done by first identifying them on a detailed lake map, then actually finding them electronically. Increasingly, lake features on maps are being marked with Global Positioning System (GPS) coordinates. In theory, this means a GPS-owning angler can simply motor out to a reef's coordinates. However, being able to identify a reef's edges, various depths and bottom substrates requires the accurate reading of a depth finder. Although electronic depth finders are of limited value on rivers and along lakeshores, they're extremely beneficial for mid-lake angling. Learn to get the most out of your depth finder; it will pay off with more fish on the line.

Finding Structure Without Electronics

While depth finders are best for finding deeper structure, I've found and fished dozens of mid-lake humps without 'em. Before the availability of small portable depth finders, many years of fishing the Boundary Waters Canoe Area Wilderness taught me how to find offshore humps with just polarized sun glasses. At midday during calm, sunny conditions, cruise slowly across the lake looking for different-colored water ahead of you. In many clear lakes, structure 12 to 14 feet below the surface will look browner than the dark blue of deep water. To keep from losing the spot (easy to do when the light declines or the surface becomes choppy) put out a little marker buoy. You can use a large white bobber anchored with a dacron cord and 1-ounce sinker. In a wilderness area like the BWCA, you can use a short section of birch log as your float. Just make sure to remove your buoys when you leave the lake.

Offshore Locations

Fly fishing without a shoreline, lily pad, current break or boulder in sight takes some getting used to. Instead of above-water or surface targets, an offshore angler is looking for subsurface structure that may only be visible on a depth-finder screen. On many lakes these will be reefs, humps, deep-water points, and bluff banks. Both reefs and humps are rises in the bottom surrounded by deeper water, but reefs can often be quite large, extending hundreds of yards and many acres. Humps, on the other hand, are generally much smaller, sort of tiny underwater islands, sometimes barely 20 feet across.

Deep-water points, are just that—rocky points that extend well out into the lake and gradually taper off into deep water. In limestone reservoirs, another potential summer location can be "bluff banks." These are steep, stone shorelines that quickly drop into deep water, and because of the nature of limestone, these bluffs have fractured and eroded below the surface into a staircase structure, offering deep-water habitat only a few yards away from shore.

Of course, finding and fishing just one of these locations is no guarantee you'll contact fish. To be more assured of success, you need to know of several potential hotspots. This is why taking the time to learn the lake (or a portion of a big lake) is so important. A fast-paced crankbaiter can cover lots of water, picking up scattered fish as he moves. In contrast, a deep water fly rodder fishes much more slowly, so our method is most effective when we can pinpoint concentrations of smallmouth. To do this you need to be able to identify the bottom material using lake maps and depth finder readings. You're looking for substrates much like the ones smallies favor in shallow areas. Fist-to-head sized rubble is excellent, and if a few boulders are scattered among the smaller rock, so much the better. Gravel reefs can also be good, and even a little sand is okay if some weed growth has developed on it. The worst substrates are large unbroken slabs or shelves of flat rock.

SUMMARY LOCATIONS OF LAKE SMALLMOUTH

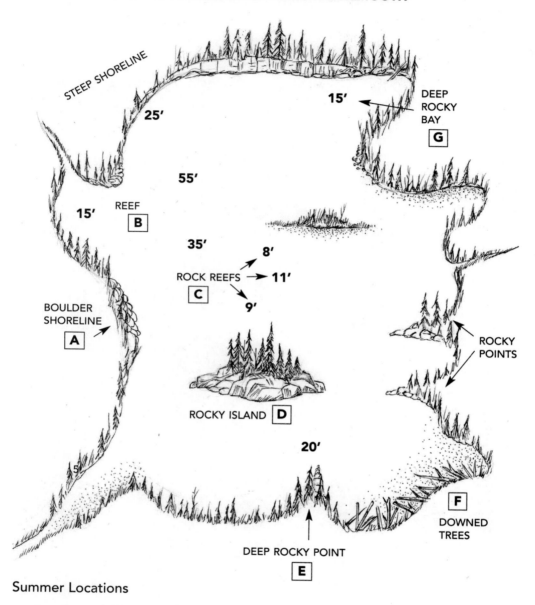

Summer Locations

    Low light: A, D, E, F

    Mid-day: B, C, E, G

A shallow reef 300 yards from shore held this dandy. A Hare Leech on a sink-tip fooled it.

The Milk Run

By carefully noting exactly where and what time of day you find fish, you can develop what traditional lake anglers used to call a "milk run." You start at a specific location (perhaps the top of a point if it's earlier in the morning), exhaust that spot and move on (maybe to a slightly deeper reef), then fish another spot, and later in the day you hit your deep-water honey hole. By having 4 or 5 (or more) proven locations to fish on any given day, you're likely to find some, perhaps many, willing mouths.

Schooling Smallies and Wolf Packs

I know deep-water fly fishers who hook dozens of smallies in day, including plenty over 16 inches. And it's not because they are chronically lucky or are experts who can catch hordes of lunkers anywhere. A big reason for their success is the fact that mid-lake smallmouth often school up. An extremely abundant food source, such as large schools of roving shiners, ciscoes or shad can prompt the smallies to concentrate in a small area. These schooling smallmouth can number in the dozens or even hundreds, so you can have phenomenal catches if you can stay in contact with the often-moving school.

Surprisingly, in other lakes a lack, rather than an abundance, of food causes smallmouth to form hunting packs. In some extremely oligrotrophic (infertile) northern lakes, forage is always low, so smallmouth adapt by hunting as a group of 3 to about a dozen fish. This helps smallmouth capture more of the lake's limited forage because a fleeing bait fish may escape one or two of the pack, but not all of them. These roaming "wolf packs" often travel the same circuit repeatedly hunting over a reef or along a shoreline. So if you figure out what time of the day a small pack or large school of smallmouth is likely to be at a given location, it can be a bonanza. Keep careful records of both where and when you catch fish. Over several trips you can often discover a pattern that will pay off in future fishing.

Deep Water Tackle

Sinking Lines

Of course, finding the fish accomplishes only half your mission. To actually hook deep-water bronze, you gotta get the fly down to them. Once you're fishing deeper than 9 or 10 feet, you'll need a full-sinking line. And to really get deep quickly, an offshore angler needs an extra-fast-sinking line. Most of the major line manufacturers market an ultra-heavy line with a sink rate of 6 to 8 inches per second (ips). With one of these super sinking lines you can get a fly down 15 to 20 feet in only half a minute (or even a little quicker with a moderately heavy fly). However, the fastest sink rate isn't always best. Casting a super-heavy line takes some getting used to, and a quick-sinking fly isn't always the most attractive to the fish. Especially when fishing 10 to 12 feet deep, a line with just a 3- to 4-ips sink rate is often better. Your fly will take a little longer to reach the fish, but when it's fished slower with longer pauses, it won't sink below the strike zone so quickly.

I keep two 8-wt rods (or at least two reels) rigged with two different lines. This way I can work the tops of shallower humps or points with the slower-sinking line, then quickly switch to the faster-sinking outfit for the deeper water.

Shooting Heads

If most of the locations you're targeting are extremely deep (20 feet or more), a "shooting taper" line may better than a standard line. There are shooting tapers (also called shooting heads) that sink at an incredible 10 ips. Shooting heads often come in 30-foot lengths and are designed to be attached to a very thin shooting (running) line with a loop-to-loop connection. Many casters have trouble with their timing when switching to a shooting head, because it requires a very different casting stroke than standard floating lines. However, perseverance usually pays off, and many of those that stick with shooting heads become big fans of them. They find they can quickly cast great distances, even in substantial winds.

A growing cadre of experienced fly casters are using shooting heads for much of their lake angling. Because you can "shoot" such a large amount of line on the forward stroke, 70-foot casts become relatively easy. By using a floating line and a couple different sinking heads, these lake fishing hotshots can really cover the water column. I wouldn't recommend a shooting head for the casual lake angler, but if you intend to spend a lot of time on still water, give these lines a serious trial.

Weighted Flies

For deep water, one fly feature that deserves special consideration is its weight. If you want to get down really quickly and/or keep your offering directly on the bottom, a moderately weighted fly is best (1/50th-ounce eyes or 15 wraps of .030 wire). And use about a 7-foot untapered fluorocarbon leader (fluorocarbon sinks better than mono). If you want to fish close to, but not directly on the bottom, choose a lightweight or even unweighted fly. The light fly won't sink as quickly, so you can retrieve it reasonably slowly just above the bottom without hanging up. And if you want the fly to ride a little higher than the line, try a completely unweighted pattern on an 8-foot tapered monofilament leader. Rigged this way, a Lefty's Deceiver or Shenk's Streamer tied without lead wrap can be worked effectively over various substrates. Part 2 of this book, "Flies for Smallmouth," also lists a number of effective lake patterns.

Open-Water Techniques

The Countdown Method

Sometimes hopping a fly along the lake bottom is the best way to score with deep-water fish, especially when the smallies are eating a lot of crayfish. For minnow-chasing bronze, however, working the fly a couple feet off bottom is more effective. A just-above-bottom fly is more visible to the fish, plus it isn't nearly as likely to snag as a bottom-dragging fly. To stay just above bottom use the Countdown method.

If you know the sink rate of your fly and the depth you're casting into, it's easy to do the Countdown. For instance, if the water is 12 feet deep and your fly sinks 6 inches per second, it will take 20 seconds to reach 10 feet. You can count off the seconds or use a wristwatch to time the descent. With the Countdown, like most deep water fly fishing tactics, patience is critical. If you start your retrieve before the fly reaches the prime strike zone, you'll dramatically reduce your hookups.

Top First, Then Deeper

The "Top First, Then Deeper" approach has long been a popular and productive lake technique. It means fishing the shallower portions of humps, points, shorelines or other structure first (which is also the easier and more fun water to fish), then moving deeper. The logic is simple and sound. Shallower smallies are most likely to be actively feeding, and are most easily disturbed by boat noise or other angler activity. By quietly positioning the craft in deeper water and casting towards the shallower zone you can target the active fish without alarming them. Then after thoroughly fishing the top of the hump, you shift your attention to the deeper sides of the structure.

Upwind Anchoring

Midday offshore smallmouthing often means contending with a 10- to 20-MPH wind. One way to use this wind to your advantage is by always anchoring upwind of the target zone. This gives you both better boat control and easier with-the-wind casting. Quietly drop anchor and play out the rope so the boat comes to a stop about 30 feet from the edge of the target. After working the upwind edge of the spot, pull up anchor, let the boat drift farther onto the target zone and re-anchor. Repeat this procedure until you've covered the entire area.

Be Smart, Be Safe

The final item that's indispensable for lake fishing is a healthy measure of common sense. Especially when venturing far from the landing, be very conscious of the weather. Get a local, up-to-the minute forecast before going out and also pay close attention to any weather changes while you're on the water. If conditions are poor before launching, don't go out at all. If the weather turns sour while you're out, go to shore. Being safe is always the smart move. A wise open-water angler will fish an alternative destination, like a small lake or stream, on those windy days.

15

Smallmouth Conservation

It's been an exciting time. When a friend and I started The Smallmouth Alliance in 1988 we could only dream that there would be so many conservation advances over the next 17 years. We wanted a better future for our smallmouth fisheries, but there were few concrete reasons to be optimistic then. Back in the '80s smallmouth faced increasing angling pressure, but the species was afforded very little protection by state or provincial regulations, and only a limited number of anglers practiced voluntary release. Smallmouth sizes had dramatically declined on many waters and it seemed little was being done to reverse that direction.

The two of us were determined to change this situation and improve small-mouth fishing. Drawing inspiration from Trout Unlimited, we founded The Smallmouth Alliance (TSA) as an explicit fisheries conservation organization.

Smallmouth Angling Regulations

As The Smallmouth Alliance's first president and conservation strategist, I believed promoting catch-and-release regulations and ethics was the easiest way a small group could start to improve our smallmouth fisheries. The first victory came quickly when our fledgling force proposed and won reduced harvest regulations on nearly 80 miles of Minnesota rivers. And that was just the beginning. In state after state in the 1990's, newly emboldened fisheries managers started to protect various smallmouth lakes and rivers with better angling regulations. The Smallmouth Alliance worked hard for better regs in the Midwestern states where it had a presence, while local clubs and ad hoc groups in other states did likewise. The results of this new-found enthusiasm for smallmouth conservation were striking. In less than 15 years, several hundred bodies of waters across the continent received new smallmouth regulations.

ATTENTION ANGLERS

CATCH & RELEASE AREA
All largemouth & smallmouth bass
caught in posted area must be
immediately released alive.

Iowa Department of Natural Resources

While numerous waters, like this section of an Iowa stream, are now protected by C&R regs, many others still suffer from heavy angler kill.

On many waters, these new protections have meant significant, sometimes even dramatic, improvements. For example, when a short section of Iowa's Maquoketa River went from the old statewide 12-inch minimum size regs to 100% catch and release, the number of larger fish skyrocketed. After no-kill regs were in place 3 years, fisheries personnel recorded 40 smallmouth over 15 inches in a stream section where only 5 fish this large had been counted previously. A stunning 8-fold increase. Anglers went from only hooking the rare fish over 15 inches to catching dozens a season. Results were equally impressive on Wisconsin's Pallette Lake. Fished down for many years, Pallette Lake had an average smallmouth size of only 9 inches. After several years of being protected by high minimum size rules, average smallmouth size soared to 14 inches. In some places, protective regulations were not as effective (due to poor compliance or negative environmental factors). But overall, they're a huge boon to smallmouth.

The Catch and Release Ethic

As important as these regulatory advances were in the '90s, another factor was even more central to our improved fisheries—the voluntary release ethic that took hold. All the efforts of progressive fishing writers and conservation groups like The Smallmouth Alliance to educate anglers on the value of recycling smallmouth really started to bear fruit in the past decade. While most North American waters still have outdated regs that allow the heavy kill of smallies, actual harvest has become quite low in many areas. Instead of routinely killing the bigger fish they catch, now most serious smallmouth anglers release virtually all their fish, and even many casual anglers release the smallies they land. This has led to a steady improvement in fish sizes. Certainly not everywhere, but in many waters, this growing release ethic has been a godsend for our fragile smallmouth populations.

Research and Habitat Improvement

Another positive development is all the smallmouth research completed in recent years. While it's often not readily apparent to anglers, a scientific understanding of a species' life cycle is critical for the long-term management of that fishery. Because so many more anglers started to take smallies seriously, research biologists felt they could spend more time and money studying smallmouth. Recent studies have revealed many things about the species' spawning and wintering requirements, seasonal movements, growth rates and other critical characteristics.

Now even habitat improvement is finally being addressed. Though it's still in its infancy compared to the efforts on behalf of trout, a little smallmouth habitat work is starting. So far this is mostly bank stabilization (such as riprapping or planting streamside vegetation) and dam removal. These habitat efforts have impacted only a tiny fraction of the smallmouth waters that need improvement, but they're a very important start and point the way forward.

New Respect

Perhaps the most important development of all in the past 15 years is the respect smallmouth have garnered from anglers, fishing groups, angling professionals and agency personnel. In the past, smallmouth were often treated as a second-class species, today they are increasingly respected as an important sportfish deserving of protection and proper management. No longer do fisheries departments dismiss smallmouth as not worthy of attention. Of

Electrofishing is the best way fisheries departments have to monitor smallmouth populations. Biologists also use angler diaries to survey fish.

course, this growing respect is a marvelous thing for the fish and our fishing. Just as trout are highly respected and hence diligently cared for, increased respect for smallmouth means we can now tackle some of the serious threats that face our fisheries.

Threats to the Fishery

Sure it's great that catch and release has boosted fish sizes in some places, but the habitat on many smallmouth waters continues to suffer. Dams have destroyed many miles of once-prime smallmouth water. Intensive agriculture has ruined much more. In just the Midwest, over 5,000 miles of once-productive streams support few smallmouth due to the massive flooding, heavy siltation and pollution from fertilizers and pesticides caused by unregulated agriculture. Coal mining in the East continues to poison some streams with toxic acidity. In the West, massive irrigation projects increasingly drain away the very life-blood of our rivers. And of course, across much of the smallmouth's range, exploding residential development degrades our waters.

Another growing threat is the proliferation of exotic species. Bighead carp, silver carp, round gobies, eurasian ruffe and quagga mussels are just some foreign species that have recently invaded North American smallmouth waters. Some of these are already having big impacts on native fisheries, and it may get much worse. It will require strong measures by anglers to mitigate the negative effects of these invaders.

Impacting or intensifying all of these environmental problems is Global Climate Change. The industrial world spewing ever-greater amounts of greenhouse gasses into the atmosphere is inexorably altering our climate. Not only are glaciers retreating across the planet, but right here in North America increasingly erratic weather means more violent floods, more intense droughts and heat waves—ever more strain on already pressured water resources.

And despite our success at promoting catch and release in certain areas, there are many waters where angler harvest is still pervasive and severely limits the fisheries. In these waters, few smallmouth ever survive to 14 inches. Efforts to improve these angler-degraded fisheries have a long way to go.

There's even the less-serious, yet still quite vexing issue of the recreational threats to quality fishing. In places, heavy recreational use of our streams makes angling increasingly difficult or unappealing. Jet Skis, hordes of paddlers, competitive (tournament) anglers and other user groups are all vying with us for the same relatively small amounts of water. These conflicts could be addressed by rational and fair user regulations, but that won't happen without a strong and concerted effort on our part.

Conservation Solutions

Smallmouth anglers now have a great opportunity to improve and protect their fishing. While there have been some excellent advances on behalf of smallmouth in recent years, it would be a huge mistake if we took the short-sighted view and didn't do anything more. The threats mentioned to healthy fisheries and to the future of our sport are real and will only get worse if anglers don't organize and act. Just as those who love trout made enormous strides in protecting and enhancing coldwater resources, we can and should do likewise for our beloved smallmouth. And there are plenty of practical things we could do right now.

A Dam Shame

Think if we removed just 20% of the thousands of small dams marring our smallmouth streams? Even "lowhead" dams just 5 feet high block essential movements of fish on many rivers by cutting the smallmouth off from spawning areas or halting winter migration. Just as bad, dams have turned thousands miles of once-prime riverine habitat into stagnant silt-laden basins, fit only for carp and bullheads. Removing these old dams would almost instantly give us a "new" river. A stream that's long been diminished by these concrete obstructions can quickly be restored to a smallmouth-producing waterway again.

And some dams are already coming down. TU and other trout groups are doing it on coldwater streams. Environmental and river conservation groups are working to remove dams on warmwater rivers. So dam-busting smallmouth anglers would have plenty of allies. And we have the most to gain, since healthy, free-flowing streams are the lifeblood of our sport. I think it's high time smallmouth fans got involved in the dam removal campaign in a major way. Nature isn't creating any new rivers, but we can breathe new life back into degraded ones.

Stopping Bank Robbery

Here's another instance where enhancing degraded waters would pay off in big ways for us and the fish. Portions of many human-impacted streams have severely eroded banks, leading to wide, shallow channels and silty substrates, which in turn means few fish. So anything that reduces bank erosion means better habitat and better fishing. On livestock-impacted waterways, protecting the banks by fencing pays big dividends. Armoring with rock (riprapping) is another way to prevent bank erosion and create instant smallmouth habitat. Conservation projects that create just a 20-foot-wide greenbelt buffer strip are extremely beneficial for banks abused by agriculture, industry or residential development.

Smallies are an ideal catch-and-release species. They are easy to hold and unhook, and virtually all lip-hooked smallmouth live to fight another day.

In-Stream Efforts

For over 100 years, trout anglers have been successfully restoring and improving trout streams with in-stream habitat work. These efforts take many forms, such as scouring out channels, creating pools and installing wood or rock structures for the fish to hide under or behind. Very little in-stream work has ever been completed on smallmouth streams. This is partly because many smallie waters are bigger than trout creeks, so the projects have to be larger. However, the primary reason so little in-stream work has ever been done for Micropterus dolomieui is because smallmouth anglers have been too complacent and unorganized to champion these projects. I believe many small warmwater streams could benefit tremendously from well-executed habitat projects. Protecting banks, deepening pools and increasing instream cover would likely lead to real increases in bigger bronze in small, shallow streams.

Organization Is Key

This leads me the main point of this chapter—organization. In the world of conservation, ideas, dreams and goals only bear fruit when there is an organization that can turn them into reality.

Trout conservation is a clear example of this. Because of Trout Unlimited, North American trout fishing is pretty darn good. Without TU it would be much worse. It's just that simple. Certainly, plenty of individuals and other groups have also contributed to coldwater conservation, but TU is by far the leading force, because it is a powerful national group with explicit conservation goals and a long-term commitment to those goals.

Our smallmouth fisheries are also in serious need of a strong national organization. Sure, small autonomous local clubs can score limited conservation victories. After all, The Smallmouth Alliance is essentially a loose collection of local clubs, and it's had successes in winning better regs. And I strongly urge everyone to get active in their local groups as one important way to help the smallmouth cause.

However, after nearly 20 years in the fisheries conservation field I'm firmly convinced that we need something more—a strong, national group. This is the only way we can take advantage of larger conservation opportunities. Removing dams, stopping invasive species, fighting destructive development projects, garnering the support needed for habitat improvement projects—these are just a few of the major issues that require a national organization with lots of clout and expertise. Hunters have understood the need for strong national groups for decades, and effective groups like Ducks Unlimited, Pheasants Forever, the Ruffed Grouse Society and the National Wild Turkey Federation each have tens or hundreds of thousands of members.

Nearly 3 million anglers fish for smallmouth. If 10% joined a smallmouth group, that would be 300,000 members. Even if just 1% supported it, that would be a 30,000-strong organization, plenty to be a respected and effective national voice for smallies across their range.

The Time Is Now

Passionate and far-sighted fly fishers built TU. I believe it's time fly fishers again step forward and lend their special passion, talents and expertise to help build a national smallmouth conservation organization. Trout Unlimited would be a fine model for us, with its huge network of active local chapters, strong state councils, and a committed national leadership and effective national staff. I'd love to be part of such an organization for smallmouth. What about you?

Smallmouth Bass—The Facts of Life

The reason some folks aren't concerned about conserving smallmouth fisheries is because they know so little about the species' life cycle or biological requirements. Here are a few "facts of life" you can provide your buddy, Uncle Joe or whoever you feel needs a little education on how fragile smallmouth populations are, plus a few tips on proper handling.

1. Smallmouth Are Slow Growing!

In many waters, it takes them 12 years to attain just 18 inches and 14 or 15 years to make 20 inches. That's a growth rate of only a few ounces a year.

2. Nearly all Artificial-Caught Smallies Survive!

Close to 100% of lip- and mouth-hooked bass live. In contrast, a substantial percentage of smallmouth that are throat (gut) hooked while using live bait die from the hook wound or from the hook left in the throat where it blocks food passage. Therefore, by using artificial baits we can catch and release smallmouth many times over their long life span.

3. Going Barbless

Although bass that are lip-hooked with barbed hooks rarely die, going barbless does make unhooking quicker and easier—good for both the fisher and fish. Barbless wounds also cause less tissue damage, which may allow fish to resume feeding and growing quicker. Barbless subsurface flies result in only a small reduction in fish landed. And using barbless topwaters in river current actually gives you a 10 to 20% increase in fish landed.

4. Play Away

"Play fish quickly" is an axiom that has little relevance with black bass, since those species rarely develop the muscle fatigue that causes them to lose swimming ability. Large trout and Esox (pike and muskie) can become so exhausted they can't remain upright, but not the hardy bass clan. Time out of the water is the real issue. A minute or so to get a measurement and quick photo is fine, but then it's time to slide 'em back into the water.

5. Tricky Unhooking

Gill-hooked fish often sustain their worst injuries during unhooking. To reduce gill injuries, remove the hook via the rear of the gills, rather than through the mouth. First, immediately take the pressure off the hook (and gill) by relaxing pressure on the leader. Next, lift up the gill plate so the hook placement can be easily seen and targeted from the back of the gills. Now very carefully grasp the bend of the hook with a forceps and pull the fly (hook) away from the gill rakers and out the rear of the gills (or turn the hook so the fly can safely be pushed back out the mouth). Make sure the hook point never touches a gill. Once the fly has been pulled out from the rear, snip the leader, pull the leader out the mouth and retie the fly.

6. Spawning Is Tough!

Weather, high water, erosion and nest predation can all lead to reproductive failure. A late spring or cool, rainy summer often means no young smallmouth survive that year. On some rivers, only one year in five produces a good spawn. Compounding the difficulty, on some waters it takes smallmouth over six years to reach sexual maturity.

7. Bigger Is Better

Larger smallmouth are particularly important to the reproductive cycle, and this is one reason they should always be released. Smallmouth populations with large numbers of males over 15 inches have higher reproductive success. Larger (older) males seem to choose better nesting sites and defend their nests better than smaller and less-experienced males. Big fish may also spawn earlier and deeper, both tactics that boost their offspring's odds of survival.

8. Safeguarding the Spawn

On rivers and lakes where adequate spawning habitat is very limited, but spawn fishing is heavy, even 100% release fishing can seriously hurt smallmouth reproduction. This is because it takes a released male at least 30 minutes to recover enough to start protecting his nest again, often enough time for predators to devour his offspring. One solution to this problem could be a rotating spring season. Each spring, half of a lake's spawning bays (or different sections of a river) would be closed to all fishing and the other half open to catch-and-release angling. This would provide unmolested spawning every other year, likely plenty enough to ensure good reproductive replacement.

Of course, removing males from their nests for prolonged periods (like what happens during early summer tournaments) means 100% loss of those nests.

9. Bigger Is Natural

Natural or "climax" smallmouth populations (where angler kill hasn't unnaturally altered the size structure) are often composed of a high percentage of large fish. In many climax populations, at least 30% (one out of three) of the total smallmouth exceed 15 inches. In contrast, in waters where angler harvest is pervasive, often fewer than 5% (one out of twenty) of the fish exceed 15 inches.

10. Winters Are Tough

In northern latitudes, smallmouth eat very little for several months during the winter. This "winter starvation period" is especially difficult for young-of-year fish, who die over winter if they haven't attained enough weight during their first summer. Some winters, entire "year classes" of fish are lost during the winter starvation period. Cool summers or prolonged high water are the primary reasons for these losses.

SMALLMOUTH ALLIANCE PRINCIPLES

Here are the original principles of The Smallmouth Alliance we drafted 16 years ago. I believe they're still very relevant today.

1. TSA is committed to seeing our smallmouth waters treated as priceless and fragile natural resources.

2. TSA supports practices, policies and legislation that protect and improve the water quality and habitat of our smallmouth watersheds, including land use and management practices that inhibit environmental degradation from agriculture and industrial pollution, watershed siltation and unchecked urban sprawl.

3. TSA works for and supports fishing regulations that protect and improve both the size and number of smallmouth. We recognize the need for reduced angler harvest of our better-sized smallmouth as a key way to improve fish sizes, and we support special angling regulations that realize the benefits of reduced harvest or catch-and-release angling.

4. TSA understands the need for smallmouth anglers to be directly involved with the protection and improvement of their sport, and is committed to providing an organizational structure that encourages member involvement and activism.

Smallmouth creeks are great no matter what you catch in them.
Include an 18-incher and you have a place to treasure.

Preparing to launch. A beautiful, uncrowded river and hungry fish,
all the fixings for a great angling adventure.

21 inches of pure power, combined with a strong flow, made this angler happy to have an 8-wt.

A Midwest pasture creek. A good 5-wt outfit, sturdy set of legs, careful approaches and you're all set.

Stopping to wade, cast and take in the sights on a Mid-South river.

Working riprap on a big river. Accurate casts are required, beagles are optional.

The author with five and a quarter pounds of November smallmouth.
Late season is often prime time for the heavyweights.

The Sneak Technique isn't just for trout. When smallmouth streams
get low and clear like this one, cautious approaches are in order.

The golden days of fall. Smallmouth fans should never hang up their rods when the leaves turn.

Bank shooting by kayak. Various watercraft can be used for lakeshore smallmouthing if winds aren't strong.

Warm weather, big fish, pretty scenery—summer floats are pure joy.

Tim with a friend.

Barely 300 yards from a town, yet a beautiful wooded corridor means quiet undisturbed fishing.

Evening bronze. Twenty-inchers like this one are suckers for low-light topwatering.

Fighting a fish in the current break near a rapids. Concentrated fish and careful wading below waterfalls and rapids means fast action.

Want to try lake smallmouthing? How about by float tube along a quiet shoreline in the springtime? Just one of many grand ways to fish smallies.

Glorious fall! Solitude, a feast for the eyes and sometimes smallies pushing 21 inches.

Bronze-laden rivers flowing into lakes are common in Canada and great places to fish.

Target shooting in a boulder field—topwaters or subsurface, it's a gratifying way to fish smallies.

A little rain, a lot of fish. Rain doesn't always produce five-pounders, but when the water is clear, cloudy wet weather can be awesome.

Evening on a smallmouth stream truly is a magical time.

On shallow streams where fish are scattered, keep moving and
quickly cover water.

Part II

Flies for Smallmouth

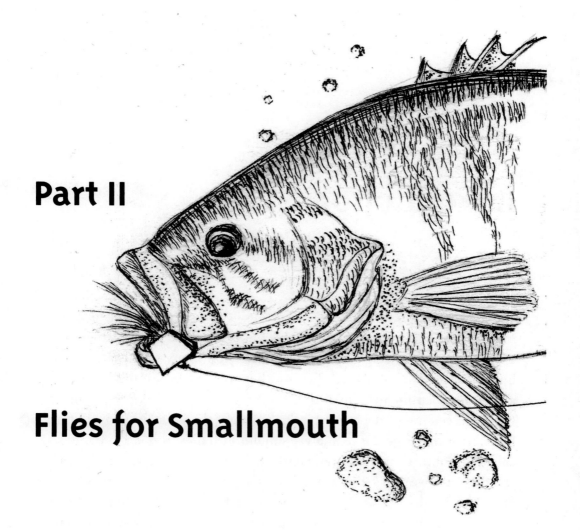

Introduction

While this section of the book offers you 40 good flies to consider, more importantly, it is intended to help you understand the general characteristics that go into effective smallmouth flies. Too many warmwater pattern books simply list individual flies and how to tie them, but offer nothing about the scientific principles that should guide the tier (or user). In contrast, this section of the book does much more than just list some patterns I like. Its primary goal is to analyze smallmouth flies from a more theoretical standpoint. If anglers understand what generic fly features appeal to smallmouth, we will be in a much better position to buy or tie effective flies. This is why I strongly recommend reading the "What Makes a Good Fly?" chapter before the pattern chapters. Once you learn how to judge smallmouth flies based on sound biological principles, rather than traditional fly dogma, it is relatively easy to turn that knowledge into productive patterns.

16

History of Smallmouth Flies

Now is a heady time to be a smallmouth aficionado. Besides increasing numbers of great places to fish and qualitative advances in tackle and techniques, there is a recent explosion of fly tying innovation for the species. The past decade has brought a dramatic increase in fly tiers enthusiastically creating new patterns, modifying old ones and experimenting with new materials for smallmouth flies.

Smallmouth fly fishing is actually centuries old, yet still in its formative stages, because for much of its history it was overshadowed by trout fishing and spin angling. While the trout universe has dozens of well-known patterns going back generations, there are still only a modest number of smallmouth flies with widespread or long-standing popularity. Flies, tackle and techniques that will someday be smallmouth classics are still being created and debated, and our sport is a new fishing frontier.

200 Years of Smallmouthing

Some folks were avidly pursuing smallies over 200 years ago. Robert Hunter's 1785 account of the popularity of fly fishing for smallmouth in the rivers around Montreal is one of the earliest records of smallmouthing in North America. The pursuit of Micropterus dolomieui since then is a story of periods of enthusiasm and progress interspersed with times our sport was neglected or overshadowed.

In the 18th century, smallmouth weren't popular among most American fly fishers, partially because angling influentials of the period lived along the Atlantic

19TH CENTURY SMALLMOUTHING

By the time James Henshall wrote *Book of the Black Bass* in 1881, scenes like this were increasing on smallmouth streams. And yes, many of the well-to-do gents of the day really did dress up to fish.

seaboard in places like Boston, New York City and Philadelphia. Smallmouth were not native to the Atlantic watersheds, but brook trout were abundant. So naturally, 18th and early 19th century fly fishing luminaries sang the praises of their next-door trout, rather than the more distant bass. And most of these early East Coast elites, striving to emulate the English aristocracy, viewed trout and salmon as the only "refined" species worthy of attention. "Coarse fish" like bass were okay for eating, but not fish to write about. And alas, early fishing records and literature reflect this bias. Compared to the voluminous literature on early trout fishing, records of early smallmouth angling are quite sketchy and seldom offer a description of the patterns used. So we can only speculate on what they tied on their leaders.

Fortunately, 100 years later much more began to be written about smallmouth and the flies used for them. In 1881, James Henshall wrote the popular *Book of the Black Basses,* containing his still-famous "inch for inch, pound for pound, the gamest fish that swims" ode to the species. This book also delved into the nitty-gritty of bassing, including patterns and specific rods to use (he favored 9- to 11-footers).

The Early Bronze Age

By the beginning of the 20th century, fly fishing for bronzebacks was really gathering steam, especially in the Midwest. By the 1920s in states like Ohio, Indiana, Missouri and my birthplace, Iowa, catching smallmouth on flies was common. Trout were limited in these areas, but there were smallmouth streams aplenty. Just as importantly, spin tackle didn't yet exist and the heavy plugs required for bait casting outfits were too big for stream smallmouth. If you wanted to do more than soak bait under your pole, the fly rod was the way to go. These practical midwesterners may not have seen fly fishing as a grand art form, as did eastern trout anglers, but they pursued the species with determination.

THREE HISTORIC FLIES

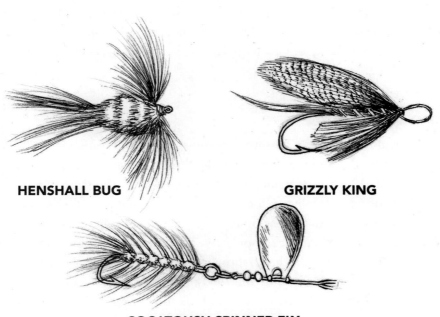

HENSHALL BUG

GRIZZLY KING

COCATOUSH SPINNER FLY

Three popular smallmouth flies from past eras. The Grizzly King, a large wet fly, and the Henshall Bug, a deerhair topwater, are from the 19th century. The Cockatush Spinner-Fly is from the mid-20th century. All three caught fish, but were hard to cast or fish with.

Before this time, many bass patterns had been colorful, oversized versions of trout wet flies, often with large feather wings and names like the Coachman and the Grizzly King, which were generally dabbled and skated on or near the surface. Fortunately, the surface flies created after 1900 were more effective. The earliest "hair bugs" interested the fish, but their bushy profiles made them difficult to cast. More user-friendly topwaters were produced when cork came on the scene. By 1915 a number of manufacturers were selling cork poppers, all under the general category of "bass bugs." And by 1930, dozens of companies were selling large quantities of both cork and hair bugs.

While the 1920s and 30s might be primarily remembered for prohibition and the Great Depression, it was also the first golden age of smallmouth fly fishing. Smallmouth were now well-established in the Atlantic drainages, so the species was available from Maine south through Virginia and all the way west to Minnesota and Arkansas. Meanwhile, brook trout were dramatically declining due to logging, farming and overfishing. So for many fly anglers in the '20s and '30s, bronzebacks were the reliable, close-to-home catch. This widespread availability, combined with the enormous popularity of bass bugs, led to plenty of anglers enjoying topwater smallmouthing.

Time of Decline

This heyday didn't last long, for several reasons. When spin fishing made its debut after World War II, those practical folks who flung flies because that's all that was available quickly discarded the long rod. The '40s and '50s also saw a decline in the productivity of many smallmouth rivers, due to increased agriculture, industrialization and damning. And a new immigrant, the brown trout, contributed to the postwar decline in the smallie's popularity. Tolerating warmer and siltier conditions than brook trout, the hardy brown was widely introduced and quickly regarded as an excellent catch. By the 1960s, the transition was nearly complete: most of the fly fishers who remained went back to viewing their sport as a purely trout thing, and those who pursued bronze forgot about flies and fixated on the latest spinners and plugs.

However, a few smallie fans didn't jump on either of these bandwagons. Here and there across the smallmouth's range there were independent souls who knew a good thing when they hooked it. Trout fly fishers may have scorned them and the spin boys may have thought them daft, but a core of individuals quietly continued to fly fish for smallmouth in the '50s, '60s and '70s, right up to the sport's renaissance in the 1980s.

While smallmouth-on-the-fly never completely died, direct links to its early days were largely lost during this long period when interest was low. Whereas descriptions of early trout fishing and the patterns used have been carefully detailed and passed down from generation to generation, few fly anglers today are familiar with the early smallmouthing.

Shaking Off Dogma

In a sport that prides itself on its long historical roots, it's unfortunate that many are unaware of the smallmouth chapter of fly fishing's past. I find it satisfying to know that over a century ago anglers already appreciated the sporting characteristics of smallmouth. James Henshall's book and other writings of the late 19th century touted "black bass" as impressive sportfish in an era when most anglers thought of fish as simply free fillets.

But forgetting our historical roots isn't all bad, for this might help free us from the dogma of the past. I believe the biggest problem with the smallmouth flies of a century ago was that tiers, viewing the world through trout-colored glasses, created what were essentially big trout flies for smallmouth. The larger sizes and bright colors at least made the flies noticeable to smallies, and if a spinner blade was attached to the fly it added more attraction. But the relatively stiff wings and lack of long tails made poor patterns with little undulation or action. (And adding a substantial spinner blade made them horrific to cast, as I can personally attest from my boyhood experiences in the 1960s.)

Conversely, the early cork topwaters were much more bronzeback-appropriate because they had largemouth and smallmouth bass origins, rather than trout roots. Many of the "bugs" created for smallmouth long ago were actually pretty good, precisely because the tiers weren't simply trying to copy what worked for another species. And today, the most effective and exciting smallmouth flies are created by folks who focus on the specific needs and habits of smallmouth.

Sadly, fly fishing still suffers from some stifling traditions. Even today, a few fly anglers won't consider warmwater fishing because it's not what their mentors introduced them to 30 years ago. And I still see lifeless forage replicas in smallmouth fly boxes, testimony to a misguided match-the-hatch notion. Our sport was hindered a century ago by concepts that didn't respect the smallmouth as a distinct species. Let's not fall into that trap again. Instead, let's learn all we can about the unique complexities of the smallie, and use this to create the best flies and fishing for the finest fish in fresh water.

The foam popper in this fish's mouth is lighter and more durable than old materials. The Blockhead's flat face also "pops" better than other shapes.

17

What Makes a Good Fly?

Which flies do smallmouth like? If we could just get inside a smallie's head, we'd have The Answer. We can't, of course, but we do know some important things about the species: The smallmouth is a curious, opportunistic predator. It's highly adept at capturing large, quickly-fleeing prey like minnows and crayfish, and it targets whatever is most available and offers the most calories. Smallies often live in low-visibility environments, they are attracted to highly noticeable or unusual prey, and only infrequently exhibit super selectivity. Thus, Micropterus dolomieui generally responds much better to larger flies, brighter colors, exaggerated motions, and unusual sounds than to diminutive natural-looking prey imitations.

In contrast, the trout is a very different critter. Most trout live in clear water, eat lots of slow-moving prey, and can be quite selective when they focus on specific insect hatches. So many flies that catch trout are duplications of specific aquatic or terestrial insects. These flies usually look much the same in the water as they do in a fly box. When warmwater fly fishing became popular, many tried to use rigid forage duplications for smallmouth, too, with poor results. This kind of match-the-forage approach for smallmouth takes us down the wrong path.

Mimic-the-Motion, not Match-the-Hatch

For smallmouthing, it doesn't matter whether a fly looks to the human eye like any particular smallmouth food. What appeals to smallmouth is a fly that mimics the motion of its prey, and often exaggerates that motion. And many times they're also attracted to even more-unusual features—colors or sounds not found in nature. For instance, my all-time best topwater is a yellow foam blockhead popper. Its color, shape and sound resemble no living organism, yet it's caught thousands of hefty smallmouth in hundreds of settings over many years.

CRAYFISH IMITATION   **HOLSCHLAG HACKLE FLY**

Two "crayfish" patterns: one for the fish, the other for the angler. While the carefully crafted imitation on the left appeals to our eye, its stiff materials make it unattractive to smallmouth. In contrast, the Holschlag Hackle Fly's body, tail and legs all create fish-appealing action.

Sure, we might call a fly "Fred's Frisky Frog" or "Larry's 'Lectric Leech." Such fanciful names are part of the colorful tradition that helps make our sport so enjoyable. But smallmouth fly names are often arbitrary, and the fish don't care what we call 'em. I have two nearly identical patterns on my desk tied by different tiers; one is called a "leech," the other a "minnow." I doubt the fish can tell which is which. But smallmouth love 'em both because their flexible tails undulate enticingly underwater.

Smallmouth only care how a fly acts when it's wet and in motion, not what it looks like dry and motionless in a box. Still today, I see flies tied to be exact visual replicas of almost any supposed smallmouth food—crayfish, hellgrammites, grasshoppers, frogs, mice, etc. These rigid duplications catch mostly anglers, rather than fish. An exquisitely-crafted crayfish with intricate pinchers, legs, eyes and antennae may be oh-so-pretty on display, but doesn't move in the water like the lively animal it intends to copy. For this reason, I water-test all my flies, rejecting stiff, lifeless creations.

Key Criteria

The biggest danger of focusing on how a fly appeals to the human eye is that this leads us to neglect far more important criteria. How *heavy* a fly is (or how deep it goes), how it *performs in current*, how much *motion* it has, *type of action, visibility, sound* and even its *castability* are all far more critical than how it looks in the fly box.

To focus on the fly qualities that matter most to smallmouth, *we need a standardized system to accurately describe our flies.* With the broad array of warmwater patterns that have been and are being created, a new fly description system is essential. A complete and accurate fly description would tell producers and consumers (tiers and buyers) what they are actually getting and how the fly will perform in the water. In the next chapter I offer just such a description system, but first let's get a clear understanding of the primary features that make a smallmouth fly productive.

Top Five Smallmouth Fly Features

1. Size Matters

Fly fishers with trout backgrounds tend to use flies too dinky for smallies. Those coming from bass baitcasting traditions try to sling stuff that's too big. This demonstrates how easy it is to be dogmatic about fly size. Don't fall into this common trap; instead choose offerings appropriate for the actual conditions encountered that day. For example, if you're a poor caster, if the water is extremely clear or if the average fish size is quite small, then smaller is better.

Conversely, if stream visibility is less than 4 feet or the fish are very active (and you're a good caster) larger flies are probably the way to go. This is especially true if you want to catch more big bronze. Naturally, there are scientific reasons why bigger is often better. Since larger flies are more visible at greater distances, an offering 3 inches long is more noticed by the fish than something only half that length. And from the fish's perspective, it usually requires less energy to capture one large meal than a half-dozen tiny morsels. Especially if smaller offerings aren't producing the way you would like, don't hesitate to go larger. Even flies 4 inches long can be surprisingly easy to cast if they are thin-profiled, and they're good baits for lunkers as well as modest-sized bronzebacks.

2. Color Coordination

While many trout flies attempt to duplicate the subtle hues of the "naturals," many effective artificial lures for bass sport exceptionally bright finishes, often in totally unnatural shades. The reason a gaudy color like chartreuse is so good is simply because the fish can see it better. A smallie often has to find your fly in a low visibility environment, plus your offering is going by quickly and it has to compete with an abundance of real food. A fly that stands out often receives more attention (and more strikes) than a drab creation. Some of the most visible colors are white, yellow, chartreuse, orange, black, and metallic gold and silver.

Color placement is also important. Certain colors on certain areas of the fly seem to be the best triggers. Some red or orange on the head or eyes is an old color scheme that still has merit. Belly color can also significantly influence a subsurface fly's effectiveness. White, of course, is popular when the forage is minnow-based, and a gold or orange belly often works well when crayfish are the predominant food source. A newer color strategy is the use of red hooks. Perhaps reminding the fish of blood, red hooks sometimes increase your strike rate.

3. Sound and Fury

Under most conditions, all the bass species detect sounds or vibrations from many yards away. And while they're regarded as sight feeders, it's likely small-mouth often first detect the prey by using their lateral line and inner ears. The role of sound is especially obvious when you make a popper "pop" and fish suddenly become very interested. Fish that wouldn't give a quietly drifting surface fly a second glance will come from significant distances to investigate the odd noise created by a popper or bug.

Because we don't have a lateral line, it's hard for humans to understand what a fish detects with that organ. In the past, this handicap has kept most fly tiers from giving much consideration to the vibrations/sounds made by subsurface flies. We only used sound/vibration inadvertently, as with the large deer hair heads on some patterns, which likely produce an acoustic signature noticeable to fish. But now tiers are taking sound more seriously, some even trying to incorporate rattles in their flies. I believe there will be much more experimentation with fly sound in the future.

4. Why Weight?

Here's another overlooked fly feature. Anglers often use, buy and even tie flies without knowing how much they weigh. This is a big mistake, because with a floating line, fly weight will determine how close to the bottom you can fish, how fast the fly will sink, how fast you can retrieve, how easily you can cast, and even how much you'll snag up. Depth, current speed and the buoyancy of the fly's material must all be considered when deciding how much weight to use. Obviously, you'll need a lot more weight to stay on bottom in 4 feet of moderate current than in 3 feet of slack water. Yet I regularly see guys trying to use the same weight fly no matter what the situation.

Besides the total weight of the fly, *how* it sinks is important, too. A weight-in-the-body fly sinks horizontally, and will sink slower than one tied "weight forward" that dives head first. In the new fly description system I propose in the following chapter, every fly's weight and weight-placement is clearly listed.

5. The Action Faction

Undoubtedly, the motion or action of a fly is its most critical attribute. If a subsurface fly doesn't produce an attractive motion, you're out of luck. In fly tying, the easiest place to create lots of movement is in the tail of our creations. (That's why stiff crayfish and hellgrammite duplications without flexible tails are usually so poor.) The 6 most common materials that create enticing tail action are marabou, rabbit strips, long bucktail, synthetic hair, long feathers and thin silicon strands. Even with slow retrieves, all of these materials produce good to excellent undulation. The majority of effective patterns include one or more of these materials in their tail.

Patterns that have a pronounced side-to-side wobble or an up-and-down hopping motion also appeal to fish. And when you combine plenty of tail undulation with side-to-side action or up-and-down motion, you likely have a terrific fly.

Supernormal Stimuli

To better understand the role of size, sound, color and motion in smallmouth flies, a key concept is what I call Supernormal Stimuli. These are simply greater-than-normal characteristics that trigger responses in predators. In the piscene realm, a larger-than-life stimulus might be the extreme wobbling action of a crankbait or the powerful acoustic signature of a plug. In fly fishing, it might be exaggerated tail undulation, hopping motion or extra-noticeable eyes. If we can learn what a key stimulus is for a given situation, then intensify or exaggerate it, we can often get the fish to take a strong interest in our offering. The fish might even be more excited by our enhanced artificial than their natural prey.

Lest you think this "supernormal" concept is a new idea, consider the classic book *Animal Behavior*. Written by the scientist John Alcock, the book delves into what triggers a response by various predator species, including birds and bass. In the book, there is a picture of a bass bombarded by numerous lures. The caption reads: "The welter of lures surrounding a black bass indicates the lengths to which lure makers will go hoping to stumble on what attracts a bass. If this could be determined scientifically, then a supernormal lure could be designed that might stimulate the fish into biting every time."

This was writtten 40 years ago! Back then many lure manufacturers already understood (at least partially) that incorporating supernormal characteristics into a lure often triggered a strike response. Nowadays, lure manufacturers clearly understand that adding larger-than-life features to their products is essential. These can be anything from the loud banging of steel shot to holographic eyes, potent scents, fizzing bubbles or a myriad of other exaggerated characteristics.

It's time fly tiers also more consciously recognize how important Supernormal Stimuli is in our creations. For example, the Flash Dancer, with its extremely bright wing, and the Holschlag Hackle Fly, with its highly visible yellow legs, are perfect examples of sinking patterns with exaggerated trigger characteristics. And the ultra-noisy Big Blockhead popper is a supernormal topwater. The following box describes some situations where Supernormal Stimuli are the key to success.

WHEN SUPERNORMAL IS BEST

LOW VISIBILITY
Dirty water or very low light, whatever the reasons, when the fish can't see much, an extra-large, bright or loud fly offers a much better target than a small, drab or quiet one.

FORAGE ABUNDANCE
When smallmouth have an abundance of food available, you gotta impress 'em with something that stands out from the crowd. Forage abundance is common in August. It also occurs where high-reproducing forage species (like rusty crayfish) are present. And sometimes there's extra forage because smallmouth numbers are low due to poor spawning (likely caused by chronic flooding over many springs).

FORAGE SCARCITY
Too little forage means hungry fish. Lots of flies will produce in this situation, but something big and gaudy will catch more, simply because it gets noticed more quickly.

ACTIVE/AGGRESSIVE FISH
When smallmouth are aggressively feeding, an enhanced offering invariably catches more because more fish see and hear it.

Subtle Simulations

After such an effusive endorsement of Supernormal Stimuli, you may think I jazz up all my flies. Not true. Sometimes more-subdued presentations really are better. I call these low-key patterns Subtle Simulations. These flies aren't exact imitations, but generally they are smaller and incorporate more natural hues. Though most effective smallmouth flies have some sort of exaggerated characteristic, the strike triggers of Subtle Simulations are less obvious. To our eye (and perhaps to the fish, too) these patterns look more natural than those heavily loaded with supernormal stimuli. Small, quiet topwaters (like a small Sneaky Pete or Skipping Minnow) and subtle bottom patterns (like a small woolly bugger or Tim's Tube Tail) fit in this category. The following box describes when to use Subtle Simulations.

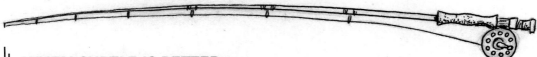

WHEN SUBTLE IS BETTER

HIGH VISIBILITY
When the water is clear and light intensity is high, fish can more easily detect a fake. Smaller, more natural-colored offerings don't seem as fraudulent.

HEAVILY PRESSURED WATERS
Heavy angling pressure can make fish more wary and acclimate them to artificial baits. Subtle offerings don't raise their suspicions as much.

SINGLE FOOD FOCUS
Sometimes smallmouth key in on a certain size or species of minnow. For example, when early summer fish are only eating small shad, a fly that closely matches the shad's size, shape and color will likely do best. And on occasion smallies focus on insect hatches and are looking for flies approximating those bugs.

COLD FRONT/FALLING WATER TEMPERATURE
A sharp cold front and falling water temperature can put smallies in a heavy funk, especially in lakes, but even in rivers. There's no magic answer to this situation, but subtle patterns fished slow and deep have the best potential if the water remains clear.

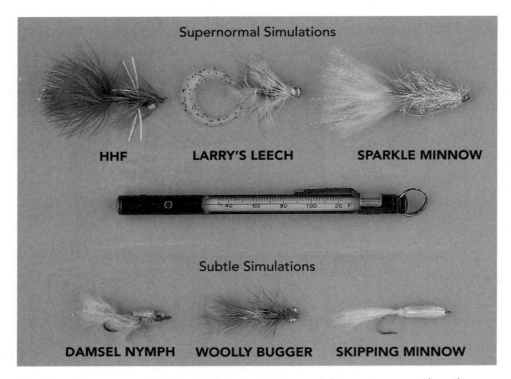

The three Supernormal flies on the top project a much larger presence than the smaller Subtle patterns on the bottom. The Holschlag Hackle Fly has protruding yellow legs and bright orange eyes, the tail on the Larry's Leech generates considerable wobble, and the Sparkle Minnow's body definitely sparkles.

Four More Features

There are four other features I always consider when judging a fly. These features are not quite as critical as the top 5 (size, weight, color, sound and action) but they are still pretty darn important.

1. Durability

You can have the most appealing pattern in the world, but if its fragile material or design makes the fly so delicate it falls apart after just a fish or two, then it's not much good. One way to check a pattern's durability is the finger test. If you can easily pull it apart or break its tail, fins, claws or other protrusions, it likely won't hold up under the normal wear and tear of fishing, or will crumble from a few impacts with a boulder or the bottom.

2. Castability

Can you cast it? Some warmwater flies look great, but are so bulky or heavy that only a few experts can comfortably cast them. Be particularly leery of large rabbit-strip patterns and those with extra-heavy metal eyes. Rabbit fur absorbs and holds lots of water, so large "leech" flies can easily become too heavy to cast well. Flies with 1/24th-ounce or heavier metal heads can be just as bad. A friend once knocked himself out throwing 1/20th-ounce of lead. Fishing alone in a boat, he whacked himself sharply in the back of the head on a forward cast and found himself sprawled flat on the deck sporting a large goose egg. To avoid ending up with flies in your box that are too big to throw, be very realistic about your casting ability.

3. Versatility

Some flies are only effective in an extremely narrow range of conditions. These patterns don't make my list of favorite flies. Sure, I have specialty patterns stowed away for those unusual occasions when they are the hot ticket. But I don't tote them around in the fly boxes I use regularly. And that's my advice to everyone. Don't clutter your everyday boxes with specialized patterns you rarely need. On an average outing, two dozen flies drawn from the Top Twenty list in various sizes, weights and colors will be far more valuable than 100 specialty patterns.

4. Hooking Ability

You can't catch 'em if you can't hook 'em. Yet I regularly see flies that do a poor job of hooking smallmouth. Years ago this was primarily because hooks were too dull. Nowadays it's often because the hook gap is too small. The problem is that folks think they don't have to consider the distance between the fly's body and the hook point if they use an extremely sharp hook. In fact, too small a hook gap will significantly reduce the number of fish you hook and land, no matter how sharp the point. For both topwaters and harder-bodied subsurface flies, the hook gap should be at least 5/16th of an inch.

How to Choose the Right Fly

Choosing an appropriate fly for a specific situation can be challenging. And I won't pretend there's a foolproof system for picking the best pattern on your first attempt. However, if you start by considering the 10 factors listed in the following chart, fly selection will be much faster and easier than the rookie's method of randomly trying everything in the fly box. This method should help you decide whether to start with a topwater or subsurface offering, how much weight the fly should have, its size and maybe even its color scheme.

FACTORS TO CONSIDER WHEN CHOOSING FLIES

SEASON
Early Spring, Spawn, Early Summer, Mid/Late Summer, Fall, Late Fall/Winter

WEATHER
Warming, Stable, Falling Temperature, Bright Sunshine, Cloudy/Rainy

WATER TEMPERATURE
Below 52, 52–56, 56–60, 61–72, Above 72

WATER CLARITY
Ultra-Clear, Clear, Moderately Clear, Dark Stain, Turbid, Very Turbid

WATER DEPTH
Shallow (under 30 inches), Moderate (2½ to 4½ feet), Deep (over 4½ feet)

CURRENT SPEED
Slack Water, Slow, Moderate Current, Fast Flow

SNAGS
Open Water/Clean Bottom, Weeds, Broken Rock, Sunken Logs

FISHING PRESSURE
Very Light, Moderate, Heavy

FORAGE ABUNDANCE
Low, Moderate, High, Very High

FORAGE TYPE
Varied Forage, Primarily Minnows or Crawfish

SMALLMOUTH DENSITY
Low, Moderate, Abundant

For a detailed discussion of each of these factors, see Part 1 of this book, "Smallmouth Fly Fishing Techniques." It explains smallmouth behavior in each season, temperature, water condition, etc., with instruction on specific fishing techniques and flies to use in each instance.

18

A New Fly Description

It's darn confusing. Quaint critter names like "Billy's Leech" and "Dancing Minnow" give us almost no clue about the characteristics of the fly we may be thinking of buying or using. And trying to squeeze the growing multitude of sub-surface smallmouth flies into the old trout categories of nymph, streamer and wet fly is just as useless. While these fly designations may make sense for insect-eating species, they don't for smallmouth and other piscavore (fish-eating) species.

Even the old trout fly method of listing the hook size to help describe a fly has only limited value for warmwater flies. I use the same #2 hook to tie various flies, but depending on the pattern, fly size and profile I want that day, the completed flies are significantly different in size. The hook is the same, but what's presented to the fish is entirely different. And this hook size business is getting more confusing by the day. I have a #10 hook in front of me that's the same size as another company's #2 (though a #10 is supposed to be four sizes smaller). This nonsensical sizing system is only one example of why we desperately need a new system to describe and categorize warmwater flies.

Let's look at it historically. Smallmouth, indeed, warmwater fly fishing as a whole has come of age. It is no longer the illegitimate offspring of trout fishing. Our sport has developed many unique aspects in the past 20 years, just as saltwater fly fishing has. Most of today's smallmouth flies have little in common with trout patterns, and trying to fit them into the trout fly description system isn't working. Instead, if a rational and comprehensive description system was standardized, just think how user-friendly both fly tying and buying would be. With the archaic system we now have, a fly buyer gets little useful information. From the descriptions in catalogues and fly promotions, it's often impossible to determine even the size of the product (its length) or its weight, how deep it goes or its action. Frankly, how

many other product lines could get by offering such a paltry amount of information to their prospective customers?

A Better Fly Description

As a fly tier, buyer and user, I think a truly useful description of any smallmouth fly
should include the following information:

TYPE OF FLY: I divide all smallmouth flies into two types, based on the
Supernormal Stimuli and Subtle Simulation concepts of smallmouth-triggering
characteristics. (These are discussed fully in the "What makes a Good Fly?" chapter.) Thus, is it a "Supernormal" fly, like a noisy topwater or a subsurface fly with a
wildly undulating tail or swimming legs? Or is it a "Subtle" fly, like a quiet topwater or a small natural-hued subsurface fly?

DEPTH: Is it a topwater, or a shallow-runner, or is it best fished mid-depth or
near the bottom?

ACTION: What does it primarily do in the water? For topwaters, does it pop,
dive, buzz, slide, dart, or is it a dry fly? For subsurface flies, does it undulate, hop,
swim, wiggle, or have other distinctive motion?

WEIGHT: If it's weighted, how heavy is it? The ounces in the head or the number
and size of lead wraps in the body.

PROFILE: Its overall shape—bushy, bulky or sleek.

COLOR: The primary colors of head, body and tail, or belly and back.

BODY MATERIAL: Its primary composition—cork, foam, chenille, hair, etc.

TAIL MATERIAL: Marabou, rabbit strip, hair, feather, silicon, etc.

EXTRAS: Any extra features not already listed—legs, wing, rattles, large eyes, etc.

LENGTH: Total length of the fly in inches.

HOOK DIMENSIONS: The hook shank length (hook eye to bend) and the hook
gap (point-to-shank distance).

If a new standardized fly description included all this information, here's how it might work for some common smallmouth flies:

CLOUSER MINNOW

TYPE: Supernormal
DEPTH: Bottom
ACTION: Swimming
WEIGHT: 1/60 to 1/30 oz.
PROFILE: Sleek

COLOR: Various, belly and back
BODY: Long bucktail
TAIL: (Same)
EXTRAS: Orange eyes
LENGTH: 3 1/2"
HOOK: 7/8" shank, 1/2" gap

SNEAKY PETE

TYPE: Subtle
DEPTH: Topwater
ACTION: Slider
WEIGHT: (not applicable)
PROFILE: Sleek

COLOR: Chartreuse
BODY: Cork
TAIL: Short hair
EXTRAS: Long legs
LENGTH: 2"
HOOK: 7/8" shank, 9/16" gap

HOLSCHLAG HACKLE FLY

TYPE: Supernormal
DEPTH: Bottom
ACTION: Hopping
WEIGHT: 1/50 oz.
PROFILE: Bushy

COLOR: Brown body and tail
BODY: Chenille and Hackle
TAIL: Marabou
EXTRAS: Yellow legs, Orange eyes
LENGTH: 2 1/2"
HOOK: 7/8" shank, 1/2" gap

Sure, listing all this information makes a substantial description, but I think it certainly beats the confusion we have now. And if the description is always listed in the same order it could be shortened to this:

HOLSCHLAG HACKLE FLY: Supernormal, Bottom, Hopping, 1/50 oz., Bushy, Brown body and tail, Chenille/Hackle body, Marabou tail, Yellow legs, Orange eyes, 2 1/2", 7/8" shank, 1/2" gap

---

Consider how much information this method provides. Even without a photo you know that the Holschlag Hackle Fly uses Supernormal Stimuli, hops along the bottom, has a 1/50th-ounce head, has a bushy profile, is mostly brown with a chenille body and marabou tail, has yellow legs and orange eyes and is 2 1/2 inches long. And with a photo of the fly, an experienced tier could make one. The hook dimensions tell you what size and type hook to use, and the shaft length subtracted from the total fly length gives you the tail size.

Thus, even with no other advice on where or how to use this fly, you know a lot about it and would be in a good position to decide if you wanted to buy it, tie it or try it. A pretty nifty deal!

Perhaps my description method will stimulate others to come up with a better system to describe flies. That would be great. My idea is only one attempt, and there's plenty of influential people in the fly industry who could likely develop an accurate way to describe non-trout flies. But so far they haven't. In the meantime, why not try this method?

As just one guy in the wide world of fly fishing, I can't change the way the whole industry describes warmwater flies. But you can! You can by thinking clearly about what qualities are important in a fly. You can use more accurate and complete descriptions when you talk about or tie flies. And start expecting better information from those who promote and sell flies. Why buy or try a fly without getting all the key facts about it?

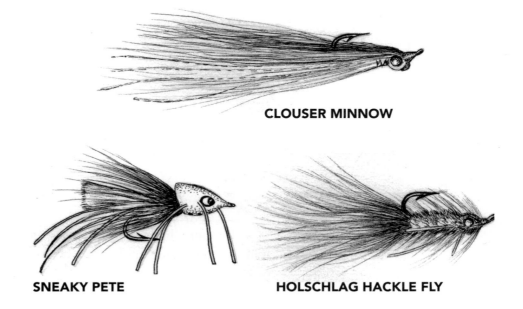

CLOUSER MINNOW

SNEAKY PETE

HOLSCHLAG HACKLE FLY

Topwater Categories

POPPER DIVER BUZZER

SLIDER DARTER DRY FLY

There are dozens of different smallmouth topwaters and more being created daily. But most fall into one of these six major categories.

Topwater Categories

Some overly ambitious writers and fly tiers divide surface patterns into a dozen or more categories. Chuggers, poppers, sliders, divers, darters, skippers, bullet heads, flat-faced, hair bugs, etc.—the list is nearly endless. It's also confusing and redundant. Instead, I put topwaters in two broad groups: Supernormal (noisy) and Subtle (quiet). Supernormal topwaters include poppers, divers and buzzers. The Subtle topwaters are the sliders, darters and dry flies.

Supernormal (Noisy) Topwaters

POPPERS: Whether they're flat-faced or concave, whether made of cork, wood, foam or deer hair, all of these are intended to make "popping" sounds when twitched. This is the largest category of surface flies. Depending on the their size and design, poppers can be productive in a wide array of situations. A small style like Tim's Micro Popper makes only a tiny "pop," while some like the Big Blockhead can really call 'em up with their loud sounds.

DIVERS: Both hair and foam divers also "pop," but aren't as loud as poppers, because they have convex (pointed) faces. This shape also makes them dive down a few inches when rapidly retrieved, and the dive produces an enticing bubble trail.

BUZZERS: This third category of noisy topwaters is by far the smallest. Nevertheless, buzzers are important because these propeller-equipped flies produce a very different type of sound that is sometimes just what the smallies crave.

Subtle (Quiet) Topwaters

SLIDERS: These are like shy cousins of the divers. With their extremely pointed faces, they make very little noise and "slide" just under the surface when retrieved. Especially productive in shallow, clear water, sliders attract fish with their motion, legs and small bubble trail.

DARTERS: This is a less-defined category of quiet surface flies. I put all sleek-profiled topwaters in the darter category. By twitching the rod tip and other manipulations, you can make these flies dart or skitter on the surface. Since they make so little noise, their biggest attribute is their erratic action. Like all quiet surface offerings, darters are generally best in clear, flat water or when smallmouth are actively chasing minnows on the surface.

DRY FLIES: In most situations, this is the least effective type of surface fly. But on those special occasions when bronzebacks are feeding with gusto on an insect hatch, a hefty dry fly is just the ticket. And once in a while, a large dry skated on the surface will interest smallies even when there is no hatch. (The "Topwater Techniques" chapter in Part 1 of this book explains how to "skate" dry flies.)

Even Montana trout guides love to catch smallies.

TOP TWENTY FLIES

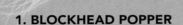

1. BLOCKHEAD POPPER

2. FOAM ROUNDHEAD

3. TIM'S MICRO POPPER

4. FOAM DIVER

5. DAN'S BUZZ BOMB

6. SNEAKY PETE

7. SKIPPING MINNOW

9. FLASH DANCER

8. SHENK'S STEAMER

10. SYNTHETIC STREAMER

TOP TWENTY FLIES

12. WHITETAIL HARE

11. MARABOU STREAMER

13. BUSHY BUGGER

14. LEFTY'S DECEIVER

15. SPARKLE MINNOW

Strike Indicators

(L)

(M)

(S)

16. CLOUSER MINNOW

17. HOLSCHLAG HACKLE FLY

19. HARE LEECH

18. TIM'S TUBE TAIL

20. TIM'S HITAIL CRAW

TWENTY MORE FLIES

21. PENCIL POPPER

22. HOT LIPS

23. TURCK'S TARANTULA

24. TAP'S BUG

25. BIG BLOCKHEAD

26. BALSA MINNOW

27. MURRAY'S HELLGRAMMITE

28. LARRY'S LEECH

29. ZONKER

30. F.C. SHINER

TWENTY MORE FLIES

31. TIM'S WINTER MINNOW

32. MCCRAWFISH

33. GIRDLE BUG

34. SPIDER FLY

35. SPINNER FLY

36. WOOLHEAD GOBY

37. FUR BALL

38. GEIBE'S DAMSEL FLY

39. DAN'S ARTICULATION

40. RECEDING HARE WORM

The underwater world of smallmouth. One of these spawning fish is attacking a crayfish that got too close to its nest.

A summer pool, the Crayfish Hop and a Holschlag Hackle Fly is a deadly combination, as this porkster attests.

The "Park and Wade" on a small stream. On-foot casting and covering water by craft—the best of both worlds?

Hooked up on a small stream.

Fishing below a rapids is great anywhere. On a wilderness Canadian river, it's a special treat.

19

Top Twenty Smallmouth Flies

Why these twenty flies? With hundreds of flies out there, how do you choose just twenty? Picking these patterns wasn't actually as hard as I thought it would be. I simply asked myself, "What flies would I choose if I could fish with just twenty patterns for the rest of my life?" The flies would have to cover a broad array of water and weather conditions and diverse angling situations, so variety and versatility were key. This is the selection I came up with.

From noisy topwaters to quiet bottom-bouncers, this diverse group of flies thoroughly covers the water column, and also the wildly different water clarity, current speeds and fish activity levels an angler is likely to encounter in smallmouthing. Plus, many of the subsurface patterns are versatile enough to use in a variety of situations, once you learn to use them proficiently.

Naturally, my selection won't match someone else's list of favorite flies. For each angling situation, several different flies may be equally productive. Hence, different people coming up with different lists. And of course, those who fish in only a few places or a narrow range of conditions will not need such a broad selection. So don't assume every one of these 20 flies will fit your particular needs. Instead, view this selection as a guide to which patterns to try under different conditions.

My selection of top flies is definitely not just a match-the-forage list. Instead, many of these patterns are designed to accentuate distinguishing motions, colors or features of smallmouth prey. This follows the Supernormal Stimuli concept explained in the "What Makes a Good Fly?" chapter. Others in this selection are Subtle Simulations, lower-key patterns containing less-obvious strike triggers.

Topwater Picks

Since everyone loves surface fishing, let's start with topwaters. Over a lifetime of fishing and research, I've found that of all the different topwaters just 3 types—poppers, divers and sliders—will cover about 85% of all surface-fishing situations. An angler with a couple different sizes of each of these 3 types is ready for most occasions. The Top Twenty list includes 3 poppers, a diver and a slider, plus a buzzer and a darter to cover even more situations. (In the next chapter, "Twenty More Favorite Flies," you'll find more topwaters, including even a dry fly.)

1. BLOCKHEAD POPPER

HOOK: Shank $^7/_8$", Gap $^5/_{16}$"
TAIL: Marabou
SKIRT: Red Hackle
BODY: Hard Foam
EYES: Hollow Plastic
TOTAL LENGTH: 2 $^3/_8$"

Don't let this fly's unusual rectangular shape fool you; foam "blockheads" are extraordinary fish producers. A few friends and I have been refining them for 15 years. Blockheads have hooked tens of thousands of big smallies, including some of the very largest fish my clients and I have ever landed. This pattern is unrivaled in rivers and excellent in still water, too. Its unique shape allows it to "pop" and ride better in strong current than virtually any other design. Add its always-quivering marabou tail, its extreme durability and light weight, and you have my all-time favorite topwater.

A standard popper presentation is usually best with the blockhead. Let the fly sit for several seconds then give it a modest "pop." If that doesn't generate a strike, repeat the pop every three seconds. "Tim's Top Presentations" in the "Topwater Techniques" chapter describes this and other presentations in detail.

Blockheads, like all the foam topwaters listed in this book, are cut from relatively hard blocks of closed-cell foam of various colors. This means that not only is the finished fly extremely light, it is also much more durable than cork or deer hair, the color is permanent and the foam can be cut to almost any shape. However, it's not easy for the casual tier to produce good foam heads. Accurately cutting the material is best done with power tools; using a razor blade is possible, but difficult. Tiemco 8089 hooks in sizes 12 and 10 (similar to standard #4 and #2) are excellent for this and many other listed topwaters.

With spring water temps near 60 degrees, this 20-incher was eager for a topwater

2. FOAM ROUNDHEAD

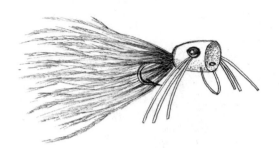

HOOK: Shank 7/8", Gap 1/2"
TAIL: Marabou
SKIRT: Red Hackle
BODY: Hard Foam
LEGS: Silicon
EYES: Painted
WEEDGUARD: Hard Mason
TOTAL LENGTH: 3"

Here's another great topwater. Because it's a cup-faced popper, its sound is slightly different than a flat-face, so fish sometimes prefer it over the blockhead. It also has silicon legs, which makes it good for lakes and slow-current rivers where the legs can splay out. Made of foam, it's more durable than traditional cork. Its nifty front weed-guard (secured just to the fly's head) lets you work the Roundhead through wood and weeds with impunity. Best of all, this type of snag-guard doesn't reduce fish hook-ups like the traditional mono loop weedguards that cover the hook point do. In fact, many generic "bass bugs" that are commonly sold use such stiff loop snag-guards that they're nearly worthless, because most smallmouth can't hook themselves on them.

Multi-legged poppers like this are generally best when fished very slowly in slack water, so the quivering appendages can work their magic. In strong current the legs loose their effectiveness because they flatten against the body and tail. The legs also make the Foam Roundhead a great largemouth fly. Some fly fishing materials companies now offer pre-cut foam roundheads. With these, even a beginning tier can add the marabou tail, silicon legs, doll eyes and weed guard to create a functioning fly. And of course, concave roundheads made from old-fashioned cork are still good poppers.

3. TIM'S MICRO POPPER

HOOK: Shank 5/8", Gap 5/16"
TAIL: Marabou
SKIRT: Red Hackle
BODY: Hard Foam
EYES: Painted
TOTAL LENGTH: 2"

This is a dinky fly that packs a big wallop. A very small, round-bodied concave-faced foam popper, the Micro is so light it can be cast on a 4-wt rod, yet catches 20-

inch bronzebacks. It produces just a modest "pop," so it's great for shallow, clear water where a larger, noisier popper might alarm the fish. My Micro Popper is outstanding on smaller streams in the evening, and it can also be good when fish are rising to mayflies or other hatches.

The castability advantages of this foam topwater can't be exaggerated. Because beginning fly fishers can cast it all day long, they keep their fly in the water much more than they would with a larger popper, which means they catch a lot more fish. Even good casters will love the Micro. Though 60-foot distant targets may be too far to comfortably reach with a standard-size offering, they're easy to hit with this little popper. One way I've improved the tiny popper concept is to use a long marabou tail (this gives it extra action and makes the fly appear larger than it is). Also, I tie it on a short-shank large-gap hook. (Typical "panfish"-size poppers use such tiny hooks they're nearly worthless for smallmouth; Tim's Micro Popper hooks smallies excellently.) A size 6 Mustad 3366 hook has the right dimensions for this little fly.

4. FOAM OR HAIR DIVER

HOOK: Shank $7/8$", Gap $1/2$"
TAIL: Rabbit Strips
SKIRT: Hackle
BODY: Hard Foam or Deer Hair
EYES: Hollow Plastic
WEEDGUARD: Hard Mason
TOTAL LENGTH: 3"

Hair Divers are fine flies. Variations of the Dahlberg Diver are fun to tie if you're handy with deer hair, and they catch plenty of smallies. But fishing with a deerhair topwater requires extra effort, because even if you dress it regularly with floatant, its buoyancy isn't consistent and it ultimately becomes waterlogged and sinks. My foam diver doesn't require any waterproofing and never gets waterlogged, plus it's more durable. However, both varieties of divers are excellent in lakes and rivers, especially when water clarity is moderate to quite clear.

A diver can be fished either on top or as a subsurface offering. On a floating line it's a topwater, on a sink-tip or full-sinking line it's an excellent shallow to medium-depth fly. You can use it to fish just over submerged wood and weeds, by letting a sink-tip line pull the diver down several feet, then working the fly with strips and pauses. The "yo-yo" (up-and-down) action of the floating diver on a sinking line often drives fish wild—not only smallies but also largemouth, spotted bass and all the Esox species (pike, pickerel and muskie).

5. DAN'S BUZZ BOMB

HOOK: Shank 1³/₄", Gap ¹/₂"
TAIL: Marabou, Flashabou
PROPELLER: Metal
BODY: Hard Foam
EYES: Painted
TOTAL LENGTH: 3³/₄"

This little prop fly really draws smallies to the top. Refined by Dan Johnson, it's one of the few propeller-equipped flies I've ever seen that actually attracts fish, yet is castable. The Buzz Bomb can be cast with a 7-wt rod, but is easier on an 8-wt. It's soft buzzing sound is totally different than any noise made by a popper or diver, and sometimes it's just what the smallies want.

Dan's Buzz Bomb produces best when the surface is calm. Usually the best technique is to make it buzz with sharp 1- to 2-foot line strips with 3-second pauses between sputters. Once in a while, the fish prefer a more steady buzz or sputter retrieve. Always be willing to experiment to see which type of presentation the fish want that day. Smallmouth chasing minnows near the surface are often suckers for Dan's Buzz Bomb. Working the buzzer along lakeshores in the morning can be phenomenally effective. I've had great mornings when nearly every cast seemed to produce a smack from a shoreline-cruising bronzeback.

To make the Buzz Bomb, you need to cut and sand the body to the proper shape. And open the size 2 Daiichi 7X hook with a forceps to create a sufficient hook gap.

6. SNEAKY PETE

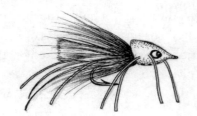

HOOK: Shank ⁷⁄₈", Gap ⁹⁄₁₆"
TAIL: Floss, Hackle
BODY: Cork Painted
LEGS: Silicon
EYES: Painted
TOTAL LENGTH: 2"

Here's a quiet slider that generates loud praise among smallmouth fans. While it's only mediocre in deeper or low-visibility waters, on shallow, clear streams and calm lakeshores the Sneaky Pete is tops. Its sharply pointed nose produces little noise, but with 12- to 18-inch line strips, the fly "slides" just under the surface, leaving a slight bubble trail. These appealing bubbles, combined with long trailing legs, make Pete superb for smallies in clear water. The fly is especially good when a summer dry spell leaves a stream unusually low and clear. Working it along shoreline cover during mornings and evenings, you can catch scads of smallies.

7. SKIPPING MINNOW

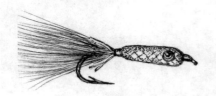

HOOK: Shank 1¹⁄₄", Gap ¹⁄₂"
TAIL: Short Marabou
BODY: Mylar, Soft Foam
EYES: Small Hollow Plastic
TOTAL LENGTH: 2"

Definitely the quietest topwater of this selection, this Mylar-bodied darter is good for extremely clear flat water or shallow water. It can also be excellent when fish are chasing minnows on the surface. Since the fly neither makes noise nor has any quivering legs, the attraction is its darting or skipping action, which you create by twitching the rod tip. For extremely shallow water, just slight twitches are often enough; over deeper water, more animation is better.

Because it is sleek and quite buoyant, the Skipping Minnow is very quiet and rides high on the surface. It is not an effective fly for stained water or a choppy surface, but under the right conditions it is both a good producer and a fun fly to fish.

A more-elongated version of this fly is the Dahlberg Floating Minnow, which calls for hand-painting and then epoxying the Mylar body. A Mylar minnow can also be used subsurface on a sinking line.

Subsurface Picks

I said before that choosing the Top Twenty wasn't difficult. Not quite true. Because some subsurface flies (like the rabbit-strip "leeches") have literally dozens of variations, choosing specific ones required some serious head-scratching. But after the dander cleared, I think the final 13 subsurface picks represent a mighty fine selection. This baker's dozen thoroughly covers the situations most anglers will encounter over the course of a season.

I divide subsurface flies into 3 broad categories based on the depth they're intended to be fished—shallow, mid-depth, and deep (bottom-bouncers). But many patterns in this selection can also be fished in more than one part of the water column if they're tied with different weight or fished on a different line.

Alas, a smallmouth pattern's name generally tells you little about how the fly actually performs in the water. There are literally hundreds of flies with "leech," "crawfish" or "minnow" in their names, and even more called "streamers." So don't give much consideration to these words in a fly's name when choosing which to try. Instead, use the specific description of each pattern as your guide.

Twitching a black Shenk's Streamer slowly through a bank eddy fooled this 18-incher.

Shallow Runners

8. SHENK'S STREAMER

HOOK: Shank 1 1/8", Gap 7/16"
WEIGHT: 18 wraps .020
TAIL: Marabou, Flashabou
BODY: Dubbed Rabbit
TOTAL LENGTH: 2 1/4"

Here's a slow-sinking shallow-running pattern that drives smallies wild. The original Shenk's White Streamer was mostly intended for trout. Over the years, I've tied much larger "bassified" versions in various colors for big smallies, but my favorite colors are still all black and all white. The Shenk's has a marabou tail and a dubbed hair body, usually rabbit hair nowadays. The secret of this fly's effectiveness is its darting action. It darts because the body is fatter in the front than the rear, and the limited amount of lead wrap in the fly keeps it light.

Because the pattern has such unusual side-to-side motion, it often brings strikes from savvy fish that ignore conventional offerings. Allowed to sink 2 or 3 feet, it can be twitched back slowly on a floating line in slow current. To get the fly down deeper or to use it in stronger current, a sink-tip line is best. The Shenk's Streamer is effective from the spawn to the early fall period.

Though this is a great pattern, it takes expertise to tie it well, dubbing large quantities of loose fur, then carefully trimming it. For the casual user, buying Shenk's Streamers is the smartest route.

9. FLASH DANCER

HOOK: Shank 1 3/8", Gap 9/16"
WEIGHT: 12 wraps .030
TAIL: Red Marabou
BODY: White Chenille
WING: Gold Flashabou
HEAD: Deerhair
TOTAL LENGTH: 2 1/2"

A blast to fish and a great producer. Who wouldn't like such a fly? The Flash Dancer is a streamer pattern that generates almost blinding brightness with its huge Flashabou wing. It was created years ago by TV celebrity Larry Dahlberg when he was a smallmouth guide. With its light weight and deerhair head, the Flash Dancer is a slow sinker that is best fished shallow to mid-depth.

It's a summer pattern that works well in slow current and moderately clear water. Extra-limp Flashabou is used to produce proper turbulence of the wing.

The Flash Dancer is fished with 2-foot pulls interspersed with short pauses, and smallies will hit the fly both on the forward pull and when the fly falls during the pause. Keep a close eye on the gold wing to spot the falling strikes. In clear water, many strikes will be seen before they are felt.

The way I like to fish the Flash Dancer is to cast it up and across-stream in slow current, working it back with the flow until it's downstream of me. Like trout, some smallies will wait until the fly changes direction on the downstream swing before they strike.

10. SYNTHETIC STREAMER

HOOK: Shank 1", Gap ½"
WEIGHT: 3 Brass Cones
BACK: Olive Synthetic Hair
BELLY: Pearl Synthetic Hair
EYES: Large Plastic
TOTAL LENGTH: 3¼"

This pattern is like two different flies. It can be fished fast and shallow in rivers and lakes, or it can be modified to plummet like a stone to work very deep water. It uses sparse amounts of synthetic hair (marketed by Umpqua as "Wing n Flash"). This gives it a flashy semi-transparent look that's especially effective in clear water.

With little other weight besides its hook and large epoxied-on eyes, it's light enough to be fished as a shallow-runner for minnow-chasing smallies near the surface. On the other hand, Mark Hoffmeyer of Minnesota makes it a deep runner by sliding two or three heavy brass cones unto the hook shank This way, you can get it down nearly 6 feet on a floating line, and more on a sink-tip. As an added bonus, the cones can be left loose on the shank to create a clanking sound. If you don't want the noise, just use a little epoxy to weld them together.

11. MARABOU STREAMER

HOOK: Shank $^7/_8$", Gap $^7/_{16}$"
WEIGHT: 10 to 14 wraps .030
TAIL: Marabou
BODY: Chenille
WING: Marabou
TOTAL LENGTH: 2 $^1/_2$"

A simple pattern with trout roots, the venerable Marabou Streamer also has bronze appeal. Its quivering, undulating wing and tail give it enticing action even when retrieved slowly. The Marabou Streamer is effective in a wide variety of colors. A chartreuse one with a black body is excellent in stained water. An all-brown model is often good during the mid- to late-summer crayfish season. A mostly white one with a little silver Flashabou in the wing can be a hot ticket for lake fishing or in rivers where smallies commonly target minnows.

Lightly weighted, the Marabou Streamer can be worked shallow for active fish around riffles, runs and head of pools. With more wraps of lead, it's good as a mid-depth offering in deeper pools and runs.

Using good flies is only part of the fishing equation. Taking a Smallmouth School and receiving on-the-water instruction, as these anglers are doing, is a good way to increase your skills.

Mid-Depth

12. WHITETAIL HARE

HOOK: Shank 1¹/8", Gap ⁷/16"
WEIGHT: ¹/50
TAIL: Rabbit Strip, Silver
    Flashabou
BODY: Palmered Rabbit
HEAD: Deerhair
EYES: Orange Barbell
TOTAL LENGTH: 2¹/4"

One of many rabbit-strip patterns, the Whitetail Hare's special attribute is its large deer-hair head. Pushing lots of water like the old Muddler Minnow, it no doubt produces a noticeable acoustic signature along with its enticing tail action. With 1/50th-ounce eyes, the Whitetail performs well as a mid-depth streamer on a floating line. It's a favorite of *Midwest Fly Fishing* publisher Tom Helgeson, who successfully uses it for steelhead and trout as well as smallmouth.

The Whitetail Hare is especially productive with the Minnow Swing retrieve (described in the "Subsurface Smallmouthing" chapter). It can also be effective worked directly against the current. Cast downstream into the tail of a pool and twitch the fly back slowly using rod-tip manipulation. Worked with short strips past boulders, around wood and over submergent vegetation, the Whitetail Hare brings up the fish. Its all-white hue is one of the most consistent subsurface color schemes. It is good in either clear or murky water from early summer through mid-fall.

13. BUSHY BUGGER

HOOK: Shank ³/4", Gap ¹/2"
WEIGHT: 9 wraps .030
TAIL: Marabou
BODY: Chenille, Large Hackle
TOTAL LENGTH: 1⁷/8"

The woolly bugger is so omnipresent in the world of fly fishing some folks feel almost embarrassed to tie or use this plain-Jane pattern. Not me. Buggers catch fish like the dickens and this small, bushy variant is a go-to fly when I need a subtle pattern for clear water or very inactive smallmouth. By using a very short-shank, wide-gap hook, extra marabou in the tail and a large neck hackle, you end up with a short but very fuzzy fly. Sometimes I also use a red hook, which at times seems to increase strikes. Used by bait fishers for a number of years, the red hook may remind the predators of blood and stimulate feeding.

A small or medium-sized woolly bugger in brown, black or olive is a mighty effective fly, especially in clear water and bright light. One of the best ways to fish it is to weight it lightly so it's slow sinking, then allow the fly to nearly reach bottom. This may take 8 to 10 seconds in 3 or 4 feet of water. But it's worth the wait. Worked back just a little faster than the current, a bushy bugger often tempts even the most sluggish fish.

14. LEFTY'S DECEIVER

HOOK: Shank 1", Gap ⅝"
WEIGHT: 12 wraps .030
TAIL: Brown Feathers-Gold
    Flashabou
WING: Gold Krystal Flash-
    Brown Bucktail-Peacock
    Herl
THROAT: White Marabou
EYES: Solid Plastic
TOTAL LENGTH: 4 to 4¾"

Developed by Lefty Kreh, the Deceiver is a saltwater pattern that warmwater species also crave. I originally started using big, bright Deceivers for pike many years ago. It's deadly for Esox, but in slightly smaller, less-gaudy versions it's great for big smallies, too.

Veteran fly tier Bob Giebe from Pennsylvania uses a large Deceiver to score some of his biggest bronzebacks from small streams. He sometimes uses a 5-inch one with white tail and belly and a brown back to entice lunker fish. A Deceiver this size might be a little large in a stream with mostly 12-inchers, but don't go much less than 4 inches long; any shorter diminishes the action of the feather tail.

This large-profiled pattern is especially productive during the late summer/early fall period when forage species are large and abundant. Because of its profile, a Deceiver performs well with a fast retrieve, so is a good "hunting pattern" (a highly noticeable fly used to cover lots of water quickly).

15. SPARKLE MINNOW

HOOK: Shank 1", Gap $^3/_8$"
WEIGHT: 12 wraps .030 plus
    Brass Bead
TAIL: Marabou, Krystal Flash
BODY: Dubbed Lite Brite
TOTAL LENGTH: 2$^1/_4$"

There are dozens of variations of this pattern using palmered Ice or Crystal Chenille in the body. This one is a little different. It uses dubbed Lite Brite material in the body, which makes it shaggy and extremely reflective. Greg Coffey of Illinois steered me to this pattern several years ago and it has been good in both lakes and rivers.

Coffey ties the Sparkle Minnow in many colors; I've had the best success with the all-white version and a sort of olive/brown color. All the varieties have a mostly marabou tail with a few strands of Krystal Flash, and are weighted with both a brass bead head and lead wrap. This makes the fly effective for mid-depth to near-bottom fishing. Like the Shenk's Streamer, there is a learning curve required to dub the material into this pattern.

Deep Runners

16. CLOUSER MINNOW

HOOK: Shank $^7/_8$", Gap $^1/_2$"
WEIGHT: $^1/_{50}$
BACK: Bucktail
BELLY: Bucktail, Flashabou,
    Krystal Flash
EYES: Orange Barbell
TOTAL LENGTH: 3$^1/_4$"

No question, this is one popular pattern. And not just because fly fishing legend Lefty Kreh started touting it many years ago. Even without the celebrity endorsement, Bob Clouser's creation would have gained notoriety as a proven producer for smallies and many other species. With its sleek weight-forward design and long hairs and fibers, it quickly plummets to the bottom, yet has plenty of appealing tail action.

Working a Clouser Minnow along the bottom is an effective technique during much of the year, including during the peak of the late summer crayfish season. Don't let the "minnow" in the name confuse you. Doing the Crayfish Hop with a crayfish-colored Clouser is superb.

Even a near-stationary retrieve does well at times. Where the flow is moderate, simply hold a lightly weighted fly against the current. Give it slight twitches every few seconds, letting it dart forward and back a foot or so, but always ending up in the same place. This In-Their-Face technique works especially well during early fall.

The pattern can be tied in various sizes, but those over 2 1/2 inches long have the best tail action. Color combinations are nearly limitless, though the "Baby Bass," and my "Albino" and "Golden Craw" colors are the most consistent for me. To obtain maximum flash and translucency, you can use Ultra Hair and other synthetic material.

17. HOLSCHLAG HACKLE FLY

HOOK: Shank 7/8", Gap 1/2"
WEIGHT: 1/50
TAIL: Marabou, Copper
    Flashabou
BODY: Chenille, Hackle
LEGS: Yellow Silicon
EYES: Orange Barbell
TOTAL LENGTH: 2 1/2"

I often call this "the best crayfish imitation I've ever used," to emphasize how different a crayfish imitation that fools humans is from one that catches fish. This bottom-bouncer has the woolly bugger's attractive brown marabou tail and bushy hackle body, but also a weight-forward design with bright orange eyes and, most importantly, contrasting yellow legs. This deadly combination often out-catches a plain woolly bugger 3 or 4 to one. The Holschlag Hackle Fly (HHF) has been one of my best subsurface patterns for over a decade, attracting big smallies like few other flies. The 1/50 ounce size is the most versatile, but I tie them from 1/60th to 1/30th ounce to cover all situations.

The HHF is outstanding for doing the Crayfish Hop during the summer, and for spawning spring fish, too, especially if it's fished extra-slow. Other river species also like this fly; it has caught countless rock bass, walleyes, carp and channel catfish for my clients and I.

Hopping a gold Clouser Minnow along the bottom interested this summer smallie.

18. TIM'S TUBE TAIL

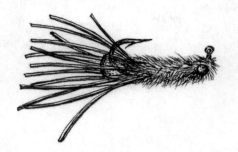

HOOK: Shank 1⅛", Gap ⁷/₁₆"
WEIGHT: ¹/₄₀
TAIL: Silicon Strands
BUTT: Orange Foam
BODY: Crystal Chenille
EYES: Barbell
TOTAL LENGTH: 2¼"

My version of the tube fly isn't much to look at, but this is an excellent get-it-down-in-front-of-their-noses pattern. Taking a cue from the spin fishers deadly tube jig, the tube tail incorporates weight-forward design with a chenille body, a silicon tail and a foam butt, all on a jig-style hook. This means the fly sort of spirals down as it sinks, and the buoyant piece of foam keeps the silicon-stranded tail riding upwards. The foam butt both reduces snagging and makes the fly more visible when its resting on the bottom.

Perhaps it's the odd hopping motion of the tube fly that attracts smallmouth, or maybe its waving silicon legs, or a combination of these. Whatever its appeal, working this pattern deep and down along the bottom puts fish on the line. Especially when a sharp cold front or cold rain has knocked down the water temps, inch the Tube Tail along the bottom a foot or so, then let it rest several seconds. Strikes may be very light, so stay alert.

19. HARE LEECH

HOOK: Shank 1", Gap ½"
WEIGHT: ¹/₄₀
TAIL: Rabbit Strip
TAIL GUARD: Mono Loop
BODY: Palmered Rabbit strip
EYES: Barbell
TOTAL LENGTH: 3"

Pure bunny power. An all-rabbit-fur fly means all-over undulation that even Marilyn Monroe couldn't generate. There are dozens of patterns that incorporate a rabbit-strip tail along with extra accouterments like silicon legs and Flashabou strands. The Hare Leech is much simpler and easier to tie. It uses just one long black rabbit strip palmered up to the barbell eyes, plus a short chartreuse "butt" strip. Other colors also work, but this black-and-chartreuse combo is especially reliable in moderately stained water.

The Hare Leech is outstanding for inactive summer smallies. By hopping the fly ever-so-slowly along the bottom, you keep it near the fish for a longer period, and even when at rest the rabbit fur still pulsates in a slight current. This fly also fascinates many other species; I've caught dozens of nice-sized walleyes by hopping a yellow leech through stream pools and outside bends.

20. TIM'S HITAIL CRAW

HOOK: Shank 1", Gap 1/2"
WEIGHT: 1/40
PINCERS: Small Rabbit Strips
BUTT: Orange Foam
BODY: Ice Chenille, Hackle
EYES: Brass Barbell
TOTAL LENGTH: 2 1/4"

I discount a lot of imitations because they're stiff and lifeless, but if a fake craw appeals to the smallies, I'm all for it. This one does. It uses a jig hook with the barbell eyes tied right at the hook eye. This unusual hook and weight configuration means the fly almost always rides head-down and tail-up. Even if buffeting currents and rough substrates temporarily turn the fly on its side, the piece of foam in the rear still keeps the tail riding high (hence its name).

This unique high-tail design makes the fly a highly visible target even in low-visibility water, and keeps the small rabbit-strip pincers continuously waving in even the slightest current. The foam piece in the rear also keeps the pincers splaying out, and its orange color increases visibility and strikes. Plus, this dandy fly's always-upriding hook seldom snags. I've kept the HiTail Craw close to the vest the past couple of years while testing it, and am now making it public. I think it will become a popular pattern.

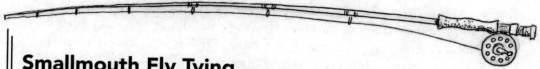

Smallmouth Fly Tying

For these Top Twenty flies and the Twenty More Favorite Flies in the next chapter, I have included the fly ingredients, but not full tying instructions. Instead, I focus on describing each fly and how to fish it, and mention any unusual tying requirements.

There are scores of books and videos that teach the basics of fly tying, and others that give step-by-step instructions to tie many common patterns. Obviously, the best fly tying books for the smallmouth fan are those heavy on warmwater information, rather than having a trout focus. Here are a few things to look for and things to avoid when tying (or buying) a smallmouth fly.

TIM'S TYING TIPS

1. LESS IS MORE
A beginning fly tier should start with just a few types of material, and become proficient with these before adding others. This limits the initial confusion and frustration of working with the vast array of ingredients now available. Just 5 old-fashioned materials—marabou, rayon chenille, rabbit strips, bucktail and chicken feathers (neck and saddle hackles)—will allow you to tie many patterns. Then by adding just 2 more materials—Ice Chenille and Flashabou—your tying possibilities increase to dozens of flies.

2. THE CURRENT TEST
Many patterns don't perform well in current, especially those with large protrusions like fins or pincers. The current catches these features, twisting the leader or making the fly spin or run off-center. Always carefully test a new pattern in moderate current to check its performance before tying or buying the fly in quantity.

3. MORE MARABOU (AND BUCKTAIL)
Tie extra material into your marabou and bucktail patterns. A little material is lost per fish caught, so starting with a little extra prevents the tail or wing getting too sparse too quickly. If you get too much marabou, you can easily tear some out with your fingers.

4. SMALL CLAWS ARE BETTER
Adding large pincers or claws to a crayfish pattern is generally counterproductive. Crayfish pincers are weapons, so smallmouth prefer to avoid large-clawed craws and dine on those with less-formidable pincers.

5. HEAVIER THREAD

Different patterns call for different types of thread, but as a rule, most flies will last longer with kevlar thread or a heavier nylon. And to really bullet-proof your wraps, lightly coat them with epoxy.

6. RECORD YOUR WEIGHT

It's easy to get confused about how much weight you've incorporated into a fly. Was it 16 wraps of .020 or 16 of .030? It's a big difference, and will affect the fly's action and sink rate. Don't guess or try to keep it all in your head; keep careful written records of the weight used in each fly.

7. SUPERNORMAL EXPERIMENTATION

Because various Supernormal Stimuli attract smallmouth, figuring out which exaggerated features appeal to the fish is in the tier's interest. Some types of Supernormal Stimuli have not yet been discovered or clearly understood, so the adventurous tier would do well to experiment.

8. CRAFTY CRITTER TYING

Fine fly craftsmanship, incorporating anatomically correct ears, fins, spots, antennae or feet into flies, can be a satisfying art in itself. And beautiful flies are an enjoyable part of our sport. Just remember that anglers and fly tiers, not smallmouth, are the true fans of this pursuit.

20

Twenty More Favorite Flies: Specialized and Local Patterns

Delve into the world of smallmouth flies and you find hundreds of different patterns, with dozens more created each year. However, on closer examination many of these (despite their different names) are very similar to one another. For instance, flies with rabbit-strip tails are exceedingly popular. I quickly found over 40 different bunny-tailed flies while researching this book, but not more than 7 or 8 of them were significantly different from each other. It's much the same for woolly bugger variations. So many different ones, yet most are alike. And don't get me going about all the crayfish imitations I found. It seems that over half the tiers on the continent have a personal crawdad creation (never mind that many of these flies catch very few fish).

So how to separate the best from all the rest? Frankly, its not easy, since there is no "Better Fly Bureau" where patterns that actually catch fish can be registered or certified. Often you gotta do it the old-fashioned way. Take 'em out, tie 'em on, and see what the fish think of 'em.

Here, I've selected another 20 patterns that are worthy of your consideration. Some of these aren't as versatile or consistently productive as my Top Twenty picks, but in certain locales and under specialized conditions they're excellent. Taken as a whole, they also display the great diversity and creativity that has been part of warmwater fly tying in recent decades.

Topwaters

21. PENCIL POPPER

HOOK: Shank 1 1/4", Gap 3/8"
TAIL: Krystal Flash
BODY: Painted Balsa
EYES: Painted
TOTAL LENGTH: 1 7/8"

This popular thin-profiled topwater has been around for decades. A particularly well-made one I like is from Oklahoma guide Larry Clark. It's good in clear water because it pops quietly, and also darts or dances on the surface when you twitch it. The pencil popper is also a killer for surface-feeding white bass.

Clark puts an elaborate and durable finish on his poppers; others get by with just a single coat of paint. And don't make the mistake of using too big a body on pencil poppers. Longer ones may have a little better action, but bodies 1 1/8 inches or less are much easier to cast.

22. HOT LIPS

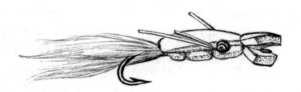

HOOK: Shank 1", Gap 1/2"
TAIL: Marabou
BODY: Foam Strips
LEGS: Yellow Silicon
TOTAL LENGTH: 2 1/4"

Strips of soft foam can be shaped into all sorts of patterns, including this 2-lipped popper. Fly tier Curt Nordrum produces this excellent one by tying the two strips of foam to the hook shank and incorporating two sets of silicon legs and a sparse marabou tail. A light wire hook allows the fly to float better. The Hot Lips is pretty good in rivers as well as lakes. I like the Hot Lips for evening fishing on moderately clear rivers.

The soft foam used for this fly isn't nearly as durable as the hard foam used for blockhead poppers, but foam strips are easy for the average tier to work with because they can be cut with common tools like scissors and razor blades.

23. TURCK'S TARANTULA

HOOK:Tiemco 5266 size 6
TAIL: Pheasant Tippets
BODY: Hare's Mask Rabbit Fur
WING: Black and White Calf Tail
HEAD: Trimmed Deerhair
LEGS: White Rubber
TOTAL LENGTH: 3/4"

This is a trout pattern most places, but on small, clear New York streams guide Ray Utlich has good success with it on smallmouth. Sort of a large-profiled dry fly, the tarantula can be skated, dragged or twitched so it interests smallies. The white protruding legs significantly increase its visibility and give the fly extra fish-appealing action, without adding bulk. It's easy to cast, even on a 4-wt rod.

With a small split shot a foot above the Tarantula, it also has good potential as a tiny subsurface fly in very clear water. Casting it upstream and working it back with slight twitches will produce a yo-yo action that can be very effective when fish are extra-finicky.

24. TAP'S BUG

HOOK: Shank 1", Gap 1/2"
TAIL: Marabou or Calf Tail
BODY: Deerhair
TOTAL LENGTH: 2 3/4"

With just deerhair in the body, and only a single material in the tail, this is one of the simplest hair bugs to tie. Yet its wide, flat face produces great "pops" that are highly appealing to fish. Tap's Bug was developed by the legendary writer H.G. "Tap" Tapply decades ago, and it's still equally effective for both smallies and bigmouth. Multi-colored bodies like the one shown can be fun to tie, but seldom catch more than single-colored bugs. Though I prefer marabou tails for their extra action, the original Tap's Bug incorporated a stiff deerhair tail for greater durability.

Besides dressing it with a floatant, another way to keep a hair bug floating high is to tightly pack each bunch of deerhair against the previous bunch after you spin it on. If you want a glittery bug, you can add a few strands of Flashabou into each bunch of deerhair you spin on the hook.

25. BIG BLOCKHEAD

HOOK: Shank $^7/_8$", Gap $^1/_2$"
TAIL:Marabou
SKIRT: Red Hackle
BODY: Hard Foam
EYES: Hollow Plastic
WEEDGUARD: Hard Mason
TOTAL LENGTH: 3"

Another of my beloved hard foam creations, this noisy bad boy really makes a pop and calls up fish even when the water is turbid or the surface is choppy. It's my go-to topwater for low visibility water and where largemouth are also present. And this is a favorite of many of my guiding clients who are gunning for trophy-sized fish.

The Big Blockhead is lighter and easier to cast than many standard-sized cork poppers, yet its large, flat face can make huge "pops." The open-hook weedguard is another advantage, making it especially good around wood or weeds.

Yup, it's a largemouth. The smallie's cousin loves the Big Blockhead popper, too. And the fly's well-designed weedguard comes in handy when fishing in cover.

26. BALSA MINNOW

HOOK: Shank 1¼", Gap ⁷/₁₆"
WEIGHT: None
TAIL: Short Sparse Krystal Flash
BODY: Glitter Painted Balsa
TOTAL LENGTH: 1⁷/₈"

Really a topwater/shallow runner combo, the Balsa Minnow is not considered a legitimate fly by some traditionalists. However, it casts reasonably well on a 6-weight and has a great fish-appealing wobble. Carved out of lightweight wood, this banana-shaped creation is essentially a tiny shallow-running crankbait. Because it runs only an inch or two deep on a floating line, it is good as a quiet darting topwater, especially for fish chasing baitfish near the surface. With split-shot or a sinking line, it will dig deeper.

Some crankbait-type lures are made from a thick strip of foam bent into a banana shape. These foam varieties are harder to lift off the water and aren't as durable as the Balsa Minnow, but may be easier for the average person to produce.

Subsurface

27. MURRAY'S HELLGRAMMITE

HOOK: Shank 1⅛", Gap ⅜"
WEIGHT: 14 wraps .020
TAIL: Black Ostrich Herl
BODY: Black Chenille, Soft Hackle
FEELERS: Silicon
TOTAL LENGTH: 3¾"

On clear eastern streams with lots of fish, this handsome creation by Virginia fishing writer Harry Murray really does catch smallies when it's dead drifted. But it's often better when given a little extra animation, especially in less-clear water.

Murray uses ostrich herl for his tails; others find marabou equally effective. One advantage of ostrich herl is its stiffness, which reduces the tail's tendency to wrap around the hook bend. No matter what type of material you use, when you're fishing check the tails of all your flies regularly; a tangled or twisted tail will greatly diminish the effectiveness of any pattern.

28. LARRY'S LEECH

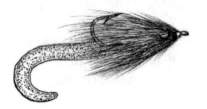

HOOK: Shank ⁷/₈", Gap ¹/₂"
WEIGHT: ¹/₄₀
TAIL:Rubber or Plastic
BODY: Palmered Rabbit
EYES: Orange Barbell
TOTAL LENGTH: 2 ¹/₂"

With a curved rubber (or plastic) tail similar to the jig fisher's grub, this old Larry Dahlberg pattern really quivers and vibrates when retrieved quickly against the current. The softest, thinnest tails have the best action, but can be torn off by fish. A chamois tail variation is more durable, but has less wobble. Rabbit fur is most often used in the body, but Ice Chenille is also productive. Using 1/40-ounce eyes keeps the fly down even with a quick retrieve.

Worked against the flow in deeper runs and rapids, a Larry's Leech can generate strikes galore, especially from smaller fish. Occasionally stopping the retrieve and letting the fly flutter in place can stimulate a strike. Many colors are good, depending on the conditions: basic black or purple is great for stained water, while white or chartreuse is better for clear water.

29. ZONKER

HOOK: Shank 1¹/₂", Gap ⁷/₁₆"
WEIGHT: Lead Body Strip
TAIL: Rabbit Strip, Mylar Strands
BODY: Rabbit Strip, Mylar
EYES: Painted
TOTAL LENGTH: 3"

The Zonker is extremely popular in some areas, and for good reason. It combines the great tail undulation of a rabbit strip with the flash of a Mylar body. It's weighted keel-shaped body makes the hook ride upright. Many color combinations are effective: A white fur strip and silver body are good during spring and early fall. Olive rabbit is often good in clear water, while a chartreuse strip and black body is a winner in stained water.

I know a West Virginia smallmouth aficionado, who, over several years, has landed nearly a dozen fish over 4 pounds on Zonkers by hopping them slowly along the bottom of deep pools. Of course, other patterns can also be used this way, but my West Virginia pen-pal is sold on the Zonker, since it has produced so well for him.

Working against the flow on the edge of fast water. This is a good summer tecnique with the F.C. Shiner or a Larry's Leech.

30. F.C. SHINER

HOOK: Shank 1⅛", Gap 7/16"
WEIGHT: 10 wraps .020
TAIL: White Ostrich Herl, Krystal
   Flash
BODY: Trimmed Cactus Chenille
EYES: Solid Plastic
TOTAL LENGTH: 2½"

Ed Story of Feather-Craft Tackle says this is his company's most popular small-mouth pattern. It's an easy-to-tie, Ice Bugger-type streamer. I use pearl Cactus Chenille for the body and trim the sides. This narrow profile and the F.C. Shiner's light weight both help the fly dart.

Because it is both bright and sleek, it's especially good for doing the Minnow Swing in quick-flowing streams during the summer and early fall. It is also productive where smallies or other species are pursuing shad. To better attract shad-feeding fish, add a little silver Flashabou to the tail.

31. TIM'S WINTER MINNOW

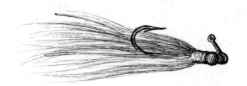

HOOK: Shank 1", Gap ½"
WEIGHT: ¹/₄₀
BACK: Brown Craft Fur, Gold
    and Chartreuse Flashabou
BELLY: White Craft Fur
EYES: Orange Barbell
TOTAL LENGTH: 3¼"

This is a favorite cold-water pattern of mine. Its mostly-craft-fur back and belly quivers even when it's nearly stationary. Its unique weight placement makes the Winter Minnow ride horizontally even at rest. The secret is using a jig hook and bending the hook eye back so it is directly over the barbell eyes. A white belly is best during late season; during early pre-spawn a chartreuse belly is sometimes better.

When the water is really cold (47 degrees or less), this fly suspended under a large strike indicator near the bottom is hard to beat. To fish reservoirs in late fall, I increase the weight to 1/30-ounce and I'll sometimes work it 10 feet deep. It takes 10 or 12 seconds to get down, and it must be fished very slowly. But for anglers with the patience required, suspending the Winter Minnow at bass-eye level is exceptionally effective when the fish are concentrated in cold water.

32. MCCRAWFISH

HOOK: Shank 1¼", Gap ³/₈"
WEIGHT: 15 wraps .030
TAIL/PINCERS: Long Marabou,
    Orange Marabou Tuft
BODY: Trimmed Marabou
ANTENNAE: Black Silicon
TOTAL LENGTH: 3"

A nice fuzzy crayfish imitation, this mostly marabou fly is tied by Midwest casting guru Bob Nasby. Its palmered, then trimmed and tapered marabou body gives it a fuzzy appearance, yet it's still soft. The long marabou fanning out at the rear and sides gives it great undulation, even with a slow retrieve. The long silicon antennae also produce good motion.

In darker colors, it's effective during the mid- and late-summer crayfish period. It's not tied "weight-forward," but by adding plenty of lead wrap you can still do the Crayfish Hop effectively with the McCrawfish.

33. GIRDLE BUG

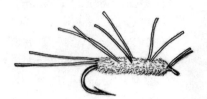

HOOK: Shank $3/4$", Gap $7/16$"
WEIGHT: 8 wraps .030
BODY: Yellow Chenille
LEGS: White Silicon
TOTAL LENGTH: $13/4$"

Originally tied as a stonefly nymph, this concoction of ten silicon legs and a chenille body also catches smallies in faster flows. The Girdle Bug is a fun-to-fish pattern in clear, shallow water because it can be sight-fished by drifting and lightly
twitching it through runs and fast-flowing pools. It can also be used with a strike
indicator if visibility is low.

This fly works best where there are high numbers of smaller fish. However, a
few folks also swear by the Girdle Bug's effectiveness on heavyweight bronzebacks.
They tie it in black or brown with no weight, add enough split shot on the leader to
get it down, and ever-so-slowly hop or twitch the Bug along the bottom. Pay
extremely close attention to your strike indicator with this technique.

34. SPIDER FLY

HOOK: Shank $7/8$", Gap $3/8$"
WEIGHT: 14 wraps .030
TAIL: Thin Silicon
BODY: Ice Chenille
COLLAR: Long Hackle
TOTAL LENGTH: $23/4$"

This fly features long, ultra-thin, yet durable, silicon strands in the tail (marketed
as "Tentacles" by the Montana Fly Company). Refined by Dan Johnson and I, the
Spider Fly wiggles and pulsates with the slowest retrieve or the least bit of current.
Twitched along the bottom, it's superb for inactive fish. For deeper water and
stronger current it can be tied with barbell eyes. With less weight and fished faster,
it's great for bank shooting.

An all-yellow Spider Fly is excellent for stained water. Last season, during a
long period when rivers were off-colored, my guiding clients consistently caught
big smallies on the yellow version. For clear conditions, silver-and-pumpkinseed or
white-and-pearl color combos are good. Because I've only used this pattern for two
seasons, I put it in the specialty category. But I think it will prove to be a consistent,
all-around smallmouth producer.

35. SPINNER FLY

HOOK: Shank ³/₄", Gap ⁹/₁₆"
WEIGHT: 15 wraps .020
BODY: Lead Wrap, Thread
WING: Yellow Bucktail
HEAD: Epoxy
EYES: Small Plastic
SPINNER: #00 Brass Indiana
    Blade, Swivel
TOTAL LENGTH: 2 ½"

Decades ago, warmwater fly-rodders regularly attached hefty spinner blades to bulky flies. This sleek modern creation, with a sparse bucktail wing and small rear blade, is much more castable than the 1930s models, yet it still attracts smallies. Larger blades are tougher to cast, but some hard-core spinner casters tie this fly with a #1 blade to get more flash and vibration. This version has a gold body and blade; some also have success using a white body and silver blade.

I like to fish the Spinner Fly with a pumping retrieve (raising and lowering the rod tip). The wide gap of a Kahle or Stinger hook offers the best hooking. You can adjust the fly's weight by varying the lead wrap in the hook shank.

36. WOOLHEAD GOBY

HOOK: Shank 1 ¹/₈", Gap ¹/₂"
WEIGHT: 10 Wraps .030
TAIL: 2 Saddle Hackles, Marabou,
    2 Furnace Hackles (on outside)
HEAD: Grey Wool (top colored
    brown with Art Marker)
EYES: Small Plastic
TOTAL LENGTH: 2 ½"

One of many patterns with a trimmed wool head, this one by Illinois tier Bob Long Jr. attempts to imitate the Round Goby, a small exotic bottom species spreading throughout the Great Lakes. In fact, this pattern likely reminds smallies of various bottom species, especially sculpins and darters. Its tail and body fins are mottled brown hackles and a little brown marabou is blended in between the head and tail. One good way to fish the Woolhead Goby is unweighted on a short (30-inch) leader and sink-tip line, using 12-inch strips and 2-second pauses.

37. FUR BALL

HOOK: Shank $3/4$", Gap $7/16$"
WEIGHT: 8 wraps .030
TAIL: SAAP Wing Fiber, Grizzly
    Hackle
BODY: SAAP Body Fur Wrapped
    and Trimmed
HEAD: Epoxy
EYES: Solid Plastic
TOTAL LENGTH: $2 1/4$"

This bulky streamer pushes a lot of water, but doesn't absorb much, so it's relatively easy to cast and works well as a search fly. Wisconsin fly shop owner Pat Ehlers ties the Fur Ball using synthetic SAAP Wing Fiber and Body Fur, which is durable and easy to work with. Ehlers likes a silver-and-grey one for Great Lakes smallies and an all-chartreuse model for stained and turbid rivers. Red-and-white is another good color combo.

38. GEIBE'S DAMSEL FLY

HOOK: Shank $7/8$", Gap $5/16$"
WEIGHT: $1/60$
TAIL: Marabou-Gold Krystal Flash
REAR LEGS: Marabou
BODY: Brown Chenille, Gold Wire
BELLY: Orange Swiss Straw
EYES: Unpainted Barbell
TOTAL LENGTH: $1 1/2$"

Here's a small, subtle simulation that's good when summer streams are running low and clear. Pennsylvania fly tier Bob Geibe calls it a Damsel Fly nymph, but it bears more resemblance to a small crayfish. This little fly is heavy enough so it gets down quick, and hopped slowly along the bottom with-the-current it looks like a tempting morsel. It uses light brown marabou for a small tail and side legs, and chenille in the body. Geibe also glues on a wing case using Swiss Straw, but this is an optional addition.

One reason the Damsel Fly out-produces many other small patterns is because it's tied heavier. Diminutive woolly buggers and rabbit strips can also be deadly in ultra-clear water if they're heavy enough to quickly reach bottom.

39. DAN'S ARTICULATION

HOOK: Shank $3/4$", Gap $7/16$"
TAIL: Icelandic Wool
WING: Icelandic Wool
EYES: Large Plastic
TOTAL LENGTH: 4"

Articulated (jointed) flies have been around a long time, but most of them have little action. This one sinks slowly and darts like the dickens when worked with sharp twitches and pronounced pauses. Originally created by Dan Johnson as a hot pike pattern, this Icelandic Wool creation in smaller sizes also catches plenty of smallies. Large plastic eyes add bulk (but little weight) in the head. The front part of the fly is tied on a #2 hook cut off before the bend; the rear of the fly is a small #4 hook joined to the front by 30-lb mono using a loop with an epoxy-coated knot.

A big reason this pattern produces good action is because it is so light. Unless a jointed fly has a crankbait-type lip, too much weight only diminishes its potential to dart or wobble. If you want to fish deeper, use a sink tip-line or a split shot on the leader at least 24 inches away from the fly. A wide range of colors are possible and productive. A mix of black, brown and orange is good during mid-summer, an all-white version is also effective year-round, and a black and chartreuse combo works well for stained water.

40. RECEDING HARE WORM

HOOK: Shank 1", Gap $1/2$"
WEIGHT: $1/50$
TAIL: Trimmed Rabbit Strip
BODY: Rabbit Fur, Several
    Flashabou Strands
EYES: Reflective Metallic
TOTAL LENGTH: $3 3/4$"

Here's a rabbit strip with a twist (actually a trim). Georgia Fly tier Craig Rendeau progressively trims the hair in the fur strip, so the tip of the tail is just skin. This gives it a tapered, skinny-tail appearance and a different tail movement than standard rabbit-strip patterns. It can be tied in various colors and using different metal eyes, and smallies love it.

In the middle of Minneapolis and two million people, yet plenty of smallies are just a cast away.

Love that lime. Streams with lots of limestone are both pleasing to
the eye and fertile fisheries.

Rafting West Virginia's New River. Great scenery, great fishing and great places to stop and wade.

This pretty and productive stream is near millions of people, and it's just one of hundreds of fine waterways available to the small-mouth angler.

Casting for bronze from a well-rigged canoe.

This rapids-laced river boils through a difficult-to-access gorge.
Just the kind of place Tim Holschlag loves.

Fine fish like this James River beauty are increasingly common in many Virginia waters.

Flies in the hat, tape on the fingers, bass in the hand.
Does life get any better?

Lots of great water all to yourself, a common occurance on many smallmouth streams.

Wet wading in July. Air temps are 80 and water nearly as warm. What's not to love about summer smallmouthing?

Dawn on a north country lake. Thousands of pristine Canadian lakes offer lakeshore camping and morning smallies.

Part III

100 Top
Smallmouth Destinations

These 100 premier smallmouth destinations are spread across the continent, offering almost everyone a fishing hotspot that's nearby.

21

100 Top Smallmouth Adventures

There are so many great places to fish smallies! North America is blessed with over two thousand streams and many more lakes that support smallmouth. That's literally tens of thousands of miles of flowing water and millions of acres of still water. Many of these places are in the species' historic range, but others are rivers and lakes where *Micropterus dolomieui* didn't exist decades ago. This expansion of smallmouth into new waters continues, with new hotspots created every year.

This means most of us have good smallmouth fishing close to home. And likely some of the 100 destinations described in this section aren't far from you. But don't overlook more-distant waters. Fly fishers routinely travel to far-away locales in pursuit of trout or saltwater species. I think it's time for more smallmouth fans to expand their horizons and cross a few state or provincial borders in their quest. Some distant hotspots will likely amaze you with their superlative fisheries as well as their beautiful and uncrowded settings.

Our smallmouth fisheries are exceedingly diverse—intimate overlooked creeks, beautiful easy-to-float streams, sprawling rivers, nearby urban reservoirs, pristine wilderness lakes and the mega-waters of the Great Lakes. These top 100 destinations are a sample of this variety, with an emphasis on fly-fishing-friendly locations. Many of our smallmouth rivers and streams are tailor-made for fly fishing, so they naturally make up the bulk of the 100 listed destinations. A number of deep, clear and crowded reservoirs have big bronze, but they are neither easy to fish nor places most fly fishers enjoy spending time, so you won't find them in the Top 100. But I have included some stillwater locations, primarily those that are relatively uncrowded, where the scenery is grand and the fish large and often shallow.

Great smallmouth waters come in wide variety of sizes and types, including hundreds of small, uncrowded gems like this one.

Planning a Trip

For each destination, I've tried to describe where the water is located, which river sections are best, fish sizes and abundance, seasonal variations, fly tips and local contacts. But you'll need more information to plan a trip to one of these waters, especially if it's a distant location. Foremost, you need a detailed map. Delorme's line of "Atlas and Gazetteer" maps for each state are excellent. For larger rivers and lakes, you can find specific maps that show even more helpful detail. In areas where smallmouth are popular, state or provincial fisheries personnel can be especially helpful as unbiased information sources. Unfortunately, in jurisdictions where smallies get little attention, fisheries employees may know little about the small-mouth fisheries in their areas. But even in these departments, if you're persistant you can often find an individual who has some information on the destination you're interested in.

Contacting local sources for up-to-the-minute information on water condi-tions, access sites and fish activity is equally crucial. Rivers are extremely dynamic. Flows change daily, and floods and droughts have major impacts on fish abun-dance and sizes. Even boat landings and other access sites change. What was true at the time of this writing may not be at a later date. Don't skip the pre-trip research; it pays off many fold.

You can start your research by checking out Fishery Department websites, which are listed in Appendix A in the back of this book. You should also check at the Smallmouth Angler.Com website for more destination information.

Fish Tales and Sizes

I hate the wild exaggerations that too often crop up in angling circles, especially when they come from commercial interests. Gross exaggerations of how big or how many fish can be caught cause people to invest time and money on trips they otherwise wouldn't have. Equally bad is the demoralization these tall tales can gen-erate. A magazine writer, a TV host or a shop owner says "a half-dozen 4-pounders a day" is the norm on a certain river. Sam and Sue fish it for several days and catch plenty of smallies, but none over 18 inches. Instead of enjoying their trip and being proud of their success, Sam and Sue think they're worthless anglers.

Fortunately, these wild tales aren't nearly as prevalent in fly fishing circles as they are in the rest of the angling world. But they do occasionally circulate, so I tried diligently not to let them creep into these descriptions. For a few locations, the magic 5-pound or 21-inch size is mentioned. And while these monsters are sometimes landed, I'm certainly not implying that they're everyday catches.

On most smallmouth waters, 2-pound (15- to 16-inch) fish are excellent specimens, and anything over 3 pounds (17 to 18 inches) is a true treasure. One big reason some folks seem to catch so many "4- and 5-pounders" is that they don't weigh the fish and assume (or hope) that their 18-inchers are really 4 pounds. In reality, a smallmouth must be a full 20 inches before it makes 4 pounds on many rivers. Only on select waters (primarily lakes) where the fish run unusually stout do 19-inchers routinely make the 4-pound mark. And frankly, tales of enormous 24-inch (or even longer) smallies should be greeted with extreme skepticism. An average-girth 24-inch bronzeback would be nearly 8 pounds—a size nonexistent in most waters and exceedingly rare everywhere else.

Big fish, big water and a happy angler. This scenario is common across the smallie's range.

Hiring a Guide

It's easy to see the merits of a guided trip, especially when it comes to fishing new or distant waters. You don't need your own boat. You don't need to learn the waters or figure out the best fishing techniques, and you don't even need to have appropriate tackle and flies. A good guide can provide all that and much more. A guided trip can truly be an unrivaled experience.

However, too many anglers don't get nearly as much out of their guided trip as they should because they fail to think seriously about what they want in a trip before booking a guide. This can lead to frustration and disappointment for both client and guide. Before you book a trip, stop and carefully consider what you value most in a fishing trip.

- Are you primarily interested in big fish?

- Is fast action/high numbers of fish more important?

- Do you only enjoy topwater fishing?

- Do you crave quiet, uncrowded waters?

- Are you looking for expert instruction?

- Do you primarily want to learn the local waters?

A single guided day probably cannot offer all of these. So it's up to you to decide what you want most from a trip, then make that clear to prospective guides. If fact, a serious dialog with the guide before you hire him or her is the most important part of trip planning. Ask the guide very specific questions and tell him what you and your fishing partner most desire. Find out what you should expect and what type of trips the guiding service offers. Some key questions to ask are:

- Type of waters? (Scenic? Residential? Congested?)

- Average catch rates and fish sizes? (Not just last year's best day)

- Type of fishing? (Working deep structure? Mostly topwatering?)

- Casting ability required?

You should also be as honest as possible about your abilities and limitations. Telling a prospective guide that you can't cast in wind or that a health condition prevents you from fishing for 8 full hours, for instance, may allow the guide to modify a trip to match your capabilities. Don't try to downplay your limitations; you may book a trip you're not suited for and set yourself up for a bad experience.

Lastly, find out something about the guide. How many years of smallmouth fishing experience does he or she have? How many years of smallmouth guiding? How much experience does the guide have on the waters you are going to fish? Good guides, of course, should have considerable knowledge of and experience with the species they target and the waters they guide on. They should also be happy to provide you with plenty of background information on themselves.

22

The Northeast

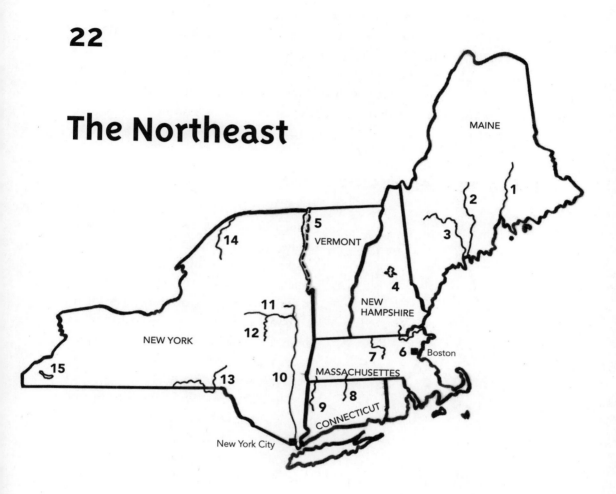

MAINE

1

2

3

5
VERMONT

14

4

NEW
HAMPSHIRE

11

12

7

6 Boston

NEW YORK

MASSACHUSETTES

15

13

10

9

8

CONNECTICUT

New York City

MAINE
1. Penobscot River
2. Kennebec River
3. Androscoggin River

NEW HAMPSHIRE
4. Squam Lake

VERMONT
5. Lake Champlain

MASSACHUSETTS
6. Merrimack River
7. Nashua River

CONNECTICUT
8. Connecticut River
9. Housatonic River

NEW YORK
10. Hudson River
11. Mohawk River
12. Schoharie Creek
13. Susquehanna River
14. Grass River
15. Chautauqua Lake

The Northeast

New York to Maine was historically the heart of the East's trout country, and a strong coldwater tradition still lingers in much of the region. So despite smallmouth being plentiful and widespread, angling pressure on them is often low. Sparsely populated Maine with its powerful trout and salmon tradition is particularly noted for its lightly fished, yet imposing bronzebacks. And even heavily populated New York has a plethora of lightly fished streams with high numbers of smallmouth.

1. Maine: Penobscot River

The Water: Its headwaters have long been popular brook trout territory and its lower reaches a top salmon destination. Only recently has the Penobscot's middle section gained a little notoriety for its tremendous smallmouth fishery. However, use is still low compared to popular rivers farther south. The beautiful and heavily forested Penobscot is a good-sized river that's best float-fished by a canoe or small boat.

The Fish: Some world-traveling fly rodders consider the Penobscot the best river in the east for mid-sized smallmouth. Due to local anglers' disinterest in eating bass, average fish size is excellent. Fifteen to 18-inchers are abundant from Medway down to the Veazie Dam, a distance of 60 miles.

Seasons, Flies, Special Tips: June spawning means fast topwater fishing, and catch rates of 30 to 45 fish are common. In summer surface action can be good, especially on cloudy days, but subsurface patterns like large marabou streamers and Deceivers are even more consistent. As excellent as the Penobscot is, some of its tributaries and connected lakes are nearly as good and see very little angling pressure. This includes the Sebec and Piscataquis rivers. Wood cover is a prime big fish location everywhere.

Access and Use: The middle Penobscot flows near Hwy. 2 much of the way, which affords several access points. Overall use is light, though several guide services regularly ply the river and a few individuals also float it.

2. Maine: Kennebec River

The upper river is mostly trout and land-locked salmon territory, but downstream of Solon smallies rule the Kennebec. In fact, there is excellent smallmouthing all the way down to Augusta. Highway 201 and other roads pass near the river, allowing easy access, but fishing pressure is only light to moderate. Two of the very best sections in this long section of river are from Madison to Skowhegan and from Waterville down to Augusta.

Floating is the best way to cover water, but by mid-summer parts of the river can also be waded. The Sandy River, a productive tributary that enters near Norridgewock, is even more wade-fishing-friendly. Like many Maine waters, average fish size on the Kennebec is excellent. A one-fish bag limit during the spawn helps protect fish during that vulnerable period.

Many Northeast rivers can be float-fished and others, like this one, can be successfully wade-fished, too.

3. Maine: Androscoggin River

The Water: An overlooked gem in southern Maine, the Androscoggin offers a huge amount of lightly fished smallmouth water. Beginning at Rumford (near the New Hampshire border), smallmouth become the primary species for the next 150 miles, all the way downstream to Brunswick.

The Fish: As in many Maine waters, fish sizes are excellent on the Androscoggin, with many 14- to 16-inchers and a fair shot at a 19. To help maintain this quality fishery, reduced harvest regs have been put in place on the river.

Seasons, Flies, Special Tips: Like many eastern rivers, the Androscoggin runs very clear, so early season (May and June) is often the easiest time to fish it . However, those with reasonable skills will also find superb mid-summer angling, including good low-light surface fishing. The early fall (September) bite is also excellent.

Upstream of Livermore Falls, fly fishers will find both big fish and high numbers in a manageable mid-sized waterway. Those looking for even more intimate waters should try the Nezinscot, a beautiful and bronze-filled tributary near Turner.

Access and Use: The lower river around Lewiston has plenty of fish, but is somewhat urban, with boat launches big enough for full-sized boats. Wilder stretches start upstream of Turner. Numerous canoe and walk-down accesses are available between Livermore Falls and Rumford Falls. Float fishing is easiest, but good waders can productively fish this upper stretch, too.

4. New Hampshire: Squam Lake

New Hampshire reservoirs are often noisy and crowded in the summer, but Squam near Holderness is different. Jet ski restrictions and other protections keeps Squam more pristine and less crowded than nearby lakes like Winnipesaukee. With 7,800 acres of rock-studded water, there are plenty of 13- to 17-inch smallmouth available, but you'll need at least a 14 foot Vee-bottom boat to reach them.

Shoreline fishing during the spawn (late May and early June) is outstanding. During July, morning top-watering is also superb, and those willing to employ a sinking line will find fine midday fishing by working a fly over deep weedbeds or rocky reefs in the 8- to 14-foot depths. **General info: Squam Lake Area Chamber of Commerce (603-968-4494).**

5. Vermont: Lake Champlain

Often called the "Sixth Great Lake" by its fans, 280,000-acre Lake Champlain along the Vermont/New York border is truly massive. But this nearly pristine mega-lake isn't just deep windswept water. Its numerous bays and islands create thousands of acres of prime bronze-back habitat that is sheltered and close to shore. Even small boats can access some of this protected water. One of these fishy areas is Malletts Bay, another is the Champlain Islands. There are several state parks and campgrounds on the islands that offer boat camping. On the New York side, Ausable Point offers a huge, shallow (and fish-filled) flat.

Smallmouth numbers and sizes are both impressive on Champlain; multi-dozen catches are common, and so are 18-inchers. In the weedy areas of bays, largemouth are also abundant. The spawn is prime time, but summer fishing in less than 8 feet of water is also remarkably good. Even popper fishing can be quite consistent on cloudy summer days.

6. Massachusetts: Merrimack River

Flowing out of New Hampshire into the northeast corner of Massachusetts, the Merrimack offers 50 miles of big river in the state before emptying into the Atlantic at Newburyport. The river flows through two older urban areas, Lowell and Lawerence, sites where the river has been dammed since the 19th century. The less urban areas of the river hold good numbers of smallmouth, including some larger fish.

Floating is the most viable way to fish the Merrimack. Numerous boat landings scattered along the river make trips of various lengths possible. Summer is prime time, though fall is a close second. Besides smallies and other warmwater species, a limited Atlantic Salmon run occurs on the Merrimack.

7. Massachusetts: Nashua River

The Water: With such an intense focus in the state's trout and saltwater fisheries, an outside observer might assume bronzebacks don't swim in Massachusetts waters. That's definitely not the case; the Nashua in the north central part of the state is a fine smallmouth river. A productive stretch on this mid-sized river is the 40 miles from the Wachusett Reservoir to the New Hampshire border.

The Fish: Don't expect many lunkers, but smallmouth numbers are good. The river is actually better known for its trout, which come from several stocked tributaries of the Nashua. Largemouth and chain pickerel are also available in slackwater areas.

Seasons, Flies, Special Tips: In the early season most angling interest is directed towards trout, but in summer warming temps cause trout to seek cooler water and the smallies to kick into high gear. A wide variety of flies appeal to the Nashua's smallmouth. Smaller woolly buggers and rabbit strip patterns will catch both bass and trout in the spring and early summer.

Access and Use: Hwy. 111 parallels much of the river and several other roads span it, offering many canoe and small boat access points. One good float starts at the mouth of the Nissitissett River. On-foot anglers can access the river in several places where the Nashua runs through the Harry Rich State Forest. Below the dam in East Pepperell is another popular wading site, especially for trout in the spring.

8. Connecticut: Connecticut River

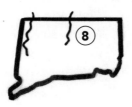

One of the Northeast's larger waterways, the Connecticut has been impacted by industrialism and other human activity for over 200 years. Fortunately, the smallies still hold their own and even prosper in the river. The 15-miles stretch from the Enfield Dam down to Hartford is some of the Connecticut's best water for fly fishing. It is shallow enough for on-foot folks to get in on the fun and big enough to float with a variety of watercraft.

The Connecticut may be the state's best river for large smallies. In the Hartford-to-Enfield stretch, most fish run 12 to 15 inches, but smallmouth over 18 inches are also caught, and smallmouth are found below Hartford, too. In the lowest reaches of the Connecticut closer to its terminus at the Atlantic Ocean, a wide array of both fresh and saltwater species are present at various times of the year.

9. Connecticut: Housatonic River

Near millions of people, this western Connecticut river still offers surprisingly

good fishing. The Housatonic from the Massachusetts line down to Gaylordsville commonly produces daily catch rates of 20 to 30 fish. Release rates are high due to residual PCB contamination, but growth rates are very slow and most smallmouth are in the 9- to 13-inch range. Fish over 17 inches are rare.

Topwater action kicks into high gear in July and extends into September. Significant insect hatches occur during this period, so large dry flies are often successful. Perhaps the most fly-fishing-friendly section is from Falls Village down to Kent. Both wading and canoe fishing are possible, and hefty brown trout are also occasionally caught by smallmouthers. Canoes can be rented in the 12-mile section between the Fall Village Dam and Bulls Bridge Dam.

10. New York: Hudson River

New York City

The Water: This river, steeped in history, offers two extremely different angling experiences. The lower Hudson, near New York City's multitudes, is a large tidal river big enough for bass boats, yet boasts an uncommonly good smallmouth and large mouth fishery. The much smaller upper river, flowing through the beautiful Adirondacks, is a float-fisher's dream. In total, this eastern New York river offers nearly 175 miles of fishing water.

The Fish: Both bass species are common in the lower Hudson below Catskill, with largemouth regularly breaking the 5-pound mark. The water-filtering zebra mussel has cleaned the once-dingy lower river, allowing the sight-feeding bass to significantly increase in numbers. Anadromous species such as striped bass and American shad are also available. The upper river above Corinth is the domain of bronzebacks, and while lunkers aren't common, the overall population is strong.

Seasons, Flies, Special Tips: Serious bassers believe fall is prime time on the lower river, because large concentrations of both species stage around the mouths of tributaries. On the upper river, summer is the prime time for fast-paced action. The tide is a big factor on the lower Hudson. Both incoming and outgoing tides are good, with active fish waiting at points to ambush prey. Mid-depth-running streamers like a Lefty's Deceiver are good for tidal fish. Upriver, small, quiet topwaters can be excellent, as well as an array of smaller subsurface patterns.

Access and Use: Numerous boat ramps between Poughkeepsie and Albany draw plenty of crankbaiters, but the river's large size still leaves room for long casts. Riffles and rocks in the river between Warrensburg down to Corinth means this section is seldom crowded with anglers. Landings are more limited on the upper river, but day floats with small craft can be easily organized.

11. New York: Mohawk River

New York City

The Water: Fifty years ago it was so polluted it supported few fish, but today it's one of New York's best s m a l l m o u t h rivers. This despite the fact that the lower Mohawk is also a barge route with a lock and dam system that harnesses 50 miles of the river. Flowing through Montgomery and Schenectady counties, the Mohawk is the Hudson River's major tributary.

The Fish: Smallmouth abundance in much of the Mohawk is admirable, and populations of hybrid tiger muskies are also excellent, along with lesser numbers of largemouth. Besides increasing numbers, fish sizes on the river have also been improving. Smallies over 14 inches are common and 3-foot tiger muskies are regular catches. Much of the river from St. Johnsville down to the city of Schenectady is prime smallmouth water.

Seasons, Flies, Special Tips: Skilled anglers do well on the Mohawk all summer long. Larger flies are best. Some of the best sections for smallmouth includes the one mile of river just upstream of Lock 8, the islands between lock 10 and 11, and the mouth of Schoharie Creek. The prettiest stretch, and one of the fishiest, is between lock 15 and 16.

Access and Use: With a series of 10 locks, the Mohawk is big enough for all manner of craft, so plenty of "bass boats" ply the river. Other craft are used, too, and even some on-foot fishing is possible, especially below the locks. Nine public boat landing are available from St. Johnsville to Schenectady. Launching is free, but the Mohawk River Barge Canal system operates the locks and charges a fee for boats passing through them. The "Lower Mohawk Fishing Guide" is a free pamphlet of the Department of Environmental Conservation. **DEC regional office: 607-652-7366.**

12. New York: Schoharie Creek

New York City

Larger than its name implies, the 25-mile lower Schoharie is really a medium-sized stream with big potential. A Mohawk River tributary in Montgomery and Schoharie counties, the Schoharie used to be sort of a local secret. Fortunately, since its been "discovered" in recent years, it continues to offer quality fishing. It holds strong numbers of smallies (along with a few walleyes) from Middleburgh all the way to its mouth.

Though it has few DEC canoe landings, the section downstream of Interstate 88 can be floated by small craft during much of the year. At the same time, the Schoharie is also a great wading stream over its entire course. In the lower reaches, plenty of fish can be found within a mile of the Hwy. 161 bridge. Lunkers are possible around Burtonsville and more good fishing can be had around the hamlet of Schoharie.

13. New York: Susquehanna River

New York City

Its hard to keep a good river down. The lower Susquehanna in Pennsylvania is one of the country's finest, and the upper river in New York is pretty impressive, too. From Windsor down to Owego, New York, the upper

Susquehanna is much smaller and less intimidating than the gigantic lower river. This part of the river loops along the NY/PA border, and 10 miles of this section is actually in Pennsylvania. Several miles of the river also flows through the urban center of Binghamton, where it is damned.

More scenic water is the 20-plus river miles above the city, where both wading and float fishing is easy and productive. Another nice section is downstream of Binghamton between Crest View Heights and Owego. New York's Susquehanna is mostly known for oodles of 12-inchers, but the occasional heavyweight is possible.

14. New York: Grass River

This St. Lawrence River tributary is practically unknown compared to the famous seaway, but the canoe-sized Grass River has its own attributes. This stream flows quietly through St. Lawrence County for over 40 miles, and its abundant smallmouth and muskies makes it a great combo water. In most places, the mighty muskie is hard to catch on fly tackle, but the Grass' manageable size makes "muskie on a fly" a viable option here. Muskies will be found in the river's bigger, deeper pools and larger bank eddies. A natural dark stain also means Grass River smallies aren't light-shy and midday fishing is good.

Just to the east of the Grass is another St. Lawrence River tributary, the Raquette. Another nice combo stream, the Raquette has lots of smallmouth, plus plenty of pike. The lower 10 miles of the Grass and Raquette are only a few miles apart, so if one river doesn't look fishable, you can easily move to the other one. Floating is the best way to fish both waterways.

15. New York: Chautauqua Lake

New York City

Not many "typical" lakes made this Top 100 list, and this southwestern New York lake isn't typical. The plentiful smallies in 13,000-acre Chautauqua are surprisingly overlooked because of the lake's popular muskie fishery and its proximity to the famous Lake Erie.

Excellent habitat combined with low pressure means some of the largest, fattest smallmouth in the region; 16- and 17-inchers are common and 5-pounders quite possible. The northern basin is deep, while the southern basin next to Jamestown is mostly under 14 feet.

Fly anglers competent in the lake fishing techniques described in Part 1 of this book will score in all seasons. However, spring and early summer is the easiest time to fly fish on Chautauqua. There are a dozen boat landings distributed around the lake, and anglers who rent a boat or who have their own can experience fine fishing, especially during midweek.

23

The East

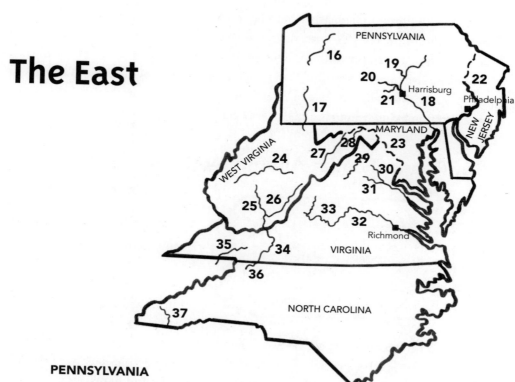

PENNSYLVANIA
16. Allegheny River
17. Monongahela River
18. Susquehanna River
19. Penns Creek
20. Juniata River
21. Buffalo Creek

NEW JERSEY
22. Delaware River

MARYLAND
23. Potomac River

WEST VIRGINIA
24. Elk River
25. New River
26. Greenbrier River
27. South Branch Potomac River
28. Cacapon River

VIRGINIA
29. South Fork Shenandoah River
30. Rappahannock River
31. Rapidan River
32. James River
33. Cowpasture River
34. New River
35. North Fork Holston River

NORTH CAROLINA
36. South Fork New River
37. Little Tennessee River

The East

It's an amazing amount of smallmouth water in such a small geographic zone. Pennsylvania, Maryland, the Virginias, New Jersey and North Carolina are only a small slice of North America, yet they hold hundreds of smallmouth rivers and creeks. With limestone substrates, good gradients and mild weather, smallies prosper in most of the region's waterways. A lingering harvest mentality still limits fish sizes on some rivers. But with so much productive water it's easy to catch plenty of mid-sized fish, and more protective regulations are improving sizes in more and more waters. Many of the region's rivers are also quite scenic and easily floatable by small craft, making fishing in the East especially enjoyable.

16. Pennsylvania: Allegheny River

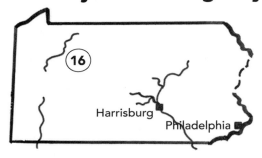

The Water: Overshadowed by more famous rivers, the Allegheny in western Pennsylvania doesn't get the attention or crowds that the East's glamour waterways do. There are 140 miles of quiet, productive water to savor. From the Kinzua Dam near Warren all the way down to East Brady in Armstrong County, the Allegheny is classic riffle, run and pool water. The 70 miles below East Brady also holds smallies, but is a commercial river with locks and dams.

The Fish: Veteran anglers say Allegheny smallmouth populations are the best they've been in decades. Because the cold water releases from the Kinzua dam and gravel dredging have been mitigated, 15- to 17-inchers are fairly abundant once again. The most lightly fished areas, such as near Kennerdell in Venango County, support fish over 20 inches.

Seasons, Flies, Special Tips: Early season often means strong flows and off-colored water on the Allegheny, so the late spring is the start of consistent fishing. Summer angling is also excellent. Float fishers can both work deeper water from the craft and also stop and fish head-of-pool areas on foot. Many local anglers regard fall (starting in early September) as the peak time for fast action.

Access and Use: Over 15 landings are spread along the upper river and roads parallel it in many sections, providing accesses for a multitude of different floats. The low flows of summer also offer plenty of on-foot opportunities. The 25 miles below Warren is a sparsely populated section of river. Another lightly used and very productive section is downstream of Franklin.

17. Pennsylvania: Monongahela River

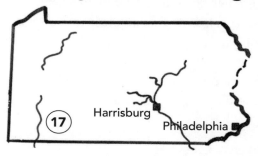

The Monongahela is a large river that flows out of West Virginia into southwestern Pennsylvania on its way to its merger with the Allegheny at Pittsburgh. Thirty years ago, the "Mon" was in sad shape, poisoned by acid mine drainage and other pollution. Happily, in recent decades improved water quality has led to a thriving smallmouth fishery. Nowadays, 15-inch plus fish are regular catches again.

Definitely not a wilderness waterway, the Monongahela flows through several urban centers and is dammed in 9 places. Numerous boat landings allow craft of various size to access the river. The least-developed stretch is upstream near the West Virginia border. Places to target include points created by incoming creeks, outside bends, water willow and other aquatic vegetation. A Buzz Bomb worked quickly over the top of vegetation is a good summer technique.

18. Pennsylvania: Susquehanna River

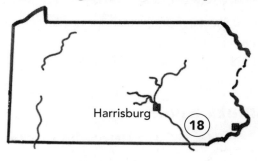

The Water: The Susquehanna is the East's most famous smallmouth river—for good reason. It's huge, over 440 miles long and hundreds of yards wide, and most of it is prime smallmouth habitat. The most popular area is the wide, but shallow and rock-laden lower river. From where the West Branch merges (near Sunbury) the Susquehanna is filled with islands, eddies and fish.

The Fish: The river is better than it was 20 years ago. Back then a harvest mentality kept fish sizes low; nowadays, better regs and an increasing catch-and-release ethic has brought back bigger bronze. Twenty-inchers are again possible and 15-inch fish are fairly common. Numbers of fish can be more outstanding than sizes.

Seasons, Flies, Special Tips: Smallmouth are caught on the lower river from April to December. And many lunker hunters regard the early and late seasons as the best times for big fish. Early spring means full-sized boats, heavy flows, bank-hugging bass, sink-tip lines, bright flies and big fish. Early winter fishing means targeting slack-water eddies, using ultra slow retrieves with patterns like Tim's Winter Minnow. In the summer, topwatering in the evening is excellent.

Access and Use: The Susquehanna is heavily fished during the summer, with large jet boats moving to and fro. Fortunately, the river's tremendous girth and many islands offer canoe and wading anglers places to fish undisturbed. The Harrisburg area has long been the focal point for lower river action. Other great areas are the islands around Halifax and those near Millersburg.

19. Pennsylvania: Penns Creek

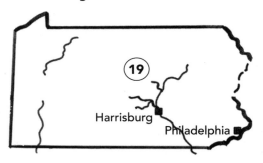

The Susquehanna in the center of the state has a myriad of productive tributaries, and Penns Creek in Snyder County is one of the best. The 20-plus-mile stretch from Hwy. 104 to the mouth is wade-fishing-friendly and yields surprisingly big fish, including the occa-sional lunker pushing 4 pounds. The upper creek in Union County is small water, but also holds some fish.

Rural Pennsylvania, like most highly populated states, has many small roads, but also many homes and private land. Be careful not to trespass when fishing or accessing the water, and abide by common-sense rules such as not driving onto private land, damaging fences, scaring livestock, walking on crops or littering.

20. Pennsylvania: Juniata River

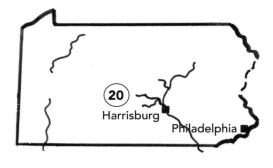

The Water: This river lives in the shadow of a celebrity. As a tributary of the Susquehanna, the Juniata doesn't get the attention it would have if it were located elsewhere. And that's good. This central PA river is prime water for the fly guy from Huntington all the way to its mouth.

The Fish: In the past, the Juniata had a reputation for high numbers of smaller fish and it still has those; there are spin fishers who rack up 50- and 60-fish days. In recent years, however, more smallies over 14 inches are also being caught, and even impressive fish over 4 pounds are again possible.

Seasons, Flies, Special Tips: Jonboat fishermen love the spring season because it allows them to fish from their craft and have good shots at big fish. When water levels are high in spring, a controlled drift while quickly working mid-river boulders and slicks is the prime method. By mid-summer much of the Juniata is low enough to be a wade fisher's paradise. Wide, shallow and rocky, it offers miles of wadable eddies and pocket water. One effective technique for these conditions is to use the Minnow Swing with a short leader, sink-tip line and a small streamer.

Access and Use: With boat landings distributed along its length, the Juniata provides plenty of access for the floater and wader alike. And while not as heavily used as the nearby Susquehanna, early summer activity on weekends can still be significant. Fortunately, during other times the Juniata can be quite tranquil. The 18 miles of river upstream of Lewiston is wide, shallow and the most scenic section, with several access sites.

21. Pennsylvania: Buffalo Creek

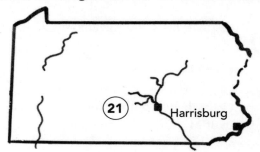

Some like to say that any Pennsylvania creek you can't step across has smallmouth bass. That may be a bit of an exaggeration, but the state certainly is loaded with smallie waters. One wonderful little waterway is Buffalo Creek, a Juniata tributary in Perry County near Newport. The lower 10 miles from Markelsville down to the mouth is prime wading water.

Small streams like the Buffalo can also be fished by the park-and-wade method, using small extra-light watercraft. Scout the stream first, to make sure it's not filled with so many blocking trees or shallow riffles that floating is impossible. Then only float when water levels are a little above normal, and never do more than 4 or 5 miles in a day. And travel very light so you're prepared to drag, lift or carry your craft around obstructions.

22. New Jersey: Delaware River

It's the East's only large, completely free-flowing river. Trout anglers revere its upper reaches, and the Delaware's beefy striped bass and American shad also draw a crowd when these salt species are running. American Shad, in contrast to the diminutive Gizzard and Threadfin Shad, reach a pound or more and provide fine sport when they ascend rivers to spawn. The Delaware's plentiful smallmouth are less noticed.

The Delaware where it flows through the Water Gap National Recreation Area has especially good smallmouth fishing. This scenic section of river is a big waterway running from Port Jervis down to Columbia. It offers numerous boat landings and other public access points for watercraft of various sizes and types. Mid-summer is a prime period here, with 25-fish days possible.

23. Maryland: Potomac River

The Water: This historic river flows through the political epicenter of the world. It's also one of the East's top bronzeback destinations. Once the Potomac rises above the tidal influences upstream of Washington DC, it is superb smallmouth habitat almost all the way to the merger of its north and south branches. The Potomac is a wide, shallow river, making up much of Maryland's southern border, in places 200 yards wide and barely a foot deep.

The Fish: In recent decades, floods have temporarily reduced the Potomac's overall numbers of fish, but generally the river has bounced back quickly. An abundance of habitat, including aquatic vegetation, means an abundance of smallmouth. It has a well-deserved reputation as a Mecca for 12- to 16-inchers. The section below the mouth of the Shenandoah down to Seneca is especially good.

Seasons, Flies, Special Tips: Like on most eastern waterways, summer is the hot time for high numbers and easy fishing, while spring and fall offer the best chances for the biggest specimens. With the Potomac's abundant submergent grass beds, the most productive summer technique is topwatering over the vegetation. In open water scenarios, a Hare Leech worked past boulders or around drop offs is a sure bet.

Access and Use: With its good reputation, numerous boat landings and proximity to millions of people, the Potomac gets plenty of use. But the river's multiple islands and overall sprawl allows even the wade fisher to find good water. Brunswick to Point of Rocks is a great float that can also be waded in summer. A little farther upriver, the 8 miles from Shepherdstown to Dargan Bend is also excellent, and many spots are wadable along the way.

The East is filled with wide, shallow rivers where the Park-and-Wade method is productive and enjoyable.

24. West Virginia: Elk River

Another Elk River in West Virginia is famous for its trout, but this much longer and larger Elk is an overlooked warmwater river. This low gradient waterway loops through Braxton and Clay counties. Hwy. 4 closely parallels the stream, and floating is possible in the 60 miles from Frometown to Clendenin. While the Elk doesn't offer the spectacular beauty of higher gradient rivers or the quietness of more remote waterways, its smallmouth fishing is better now than years ago. Wood deposited generously in outside bends is the prime place for both smallies and spotted bass. Snagless topwaters like the Foam Roundhead (described in Part 2) can be good fished slow and tight to the cover. A less conventional way to fish log jams is the Float-and-Fly technique. By suspending a horizontal-riding fly, like the Winter Minnow, below an extra-large strike indicator, you can work a subsurface fly near the wood without undue snagging.

25. West Virginia: New River

The Water: Nowadays, smallmouth fans across the East speak of the New River in reverential tones. Spectacular scenery, awe-inspiring rapids and equally awesome smallmouthing are the New's allures. Lightly fished in the past due to its whitewater and inaccessibility, the New now has numerous guides using large rafts to ply even its most rugged stretches. A 53-mile section of the river (from Hinton to Fayetteville) flows through the New River Gorge and is federally protected. The New is the oldest river in North America, and has had time to carve an impressive gorge over 1,000 feet deep.

The Fish: Few, if any, other rivers in the East annually yield as many 20-inchers as the New. The river's large size, deep pools, warm temperatures and low harvest allow fish to reach heavyweight proportions. Twelve miles of the river has catch-and-release regs, but any stretch of the New below Hinton offers a good shot at a lunker. Numbers of smallies can be even more impressive. A pair of early summer float anglers sometimes land over 80 fish a day.

Seasons, Flies, Special Tips: The pre-spawn months of March and April seldom produce high numbers of fish, but average sizes are excellent for anglers who meet the early-season challenges of cold water and heavy flows. Many guides regard June as the easiest and best fly fishing month. Topwater fishing is consistent during much of the summer. October is also prime; topwatering can still be productive early in the month, with subsurface methods better as the water cools.

Access and Use: There are over a dozen access sites, primarily used as landings for rafts and kayaks, scattered through the New River Gorge. Wade fishing is limited due to the New's large size and innumerable rapids, some rated Class IV. Because of the whitewater, employing a guide is the best way to fish the river. Fly-fishing-friendly guide services include: **Canyon Rim Ranch (304-574-3111) and Mountain State Anglers (877-359-8463).** Whitewater rafting is very popular during summer weekends, making off-times the best for fishing.

26. West Virginia: Greenbrier River

The Water: Though it doesn't carry as much flow as some bigger rivers, the picturesque Greenbrier is the longest undammed river in the eastern US. It offers 158 miles of free-flowing smallmouth water. In fact, nearly the entire river from Durbin down to Hinton is classic bronzeback habitat with a continuous series of short pools and riffles. The only significant rapids are a few that crop up during the high flows of April; the rest of the year the Greenbrier is very float-fishing-friendly. The river also runs very clear and clean due to the lack of industry and agriculture along its banks.

The Fish: This is a popular river where angler harvest is still significant, so most Greenbrier bronze are under 15 inches. However, larger fish are also caught, especially by more experienced anglers. One stretch that will up your odds is the 8 miles from Roncevete to Fort Spring. It's more isolated than most of the river, with little bank fishing, hence it holds larger smallmouth.

Seasons, Flies, Special Tips: Many anglers consider April and May the best time for big fish, but stronger spring flows make wading and craft control more challenging. Summer is probably the easier time to score on the Greenbrier. High clarity means "subtle simulation" flies (like small bushy woolly buggers) are effective. Quiet topwaters like Sneaky Petes also do well, and Buzz Bombs can be terrific, too. "Buzzing" the prop fly quickly past weed beds or over subsurface rock ledges can generate heart-stopping strikes.

Access and Use: The West Virginia DNR lists 9 major float trips on the Greenbrier. A stretch noted for great scenery and high numbers of fish is the 10 miles from Renick down to Anthony in Greenbrier County. During the low flows of late summer, the 6 miles of lower river from Barger Springs to Willow Wood Bridge (Hwy. 12) is good if the upper river becomes too shallow. Bridges, canoe launches and parallel roads offer dozens of access points along the river. Float fishing is most productive, but many head-of-pool areas also offer good wade fishing opportunities.

27. West Virginia: South Branch Potomac River

The Water: When I first tried the South Branch 20 years ago, I was impressed with its productivity and how easy it was to fish. It's much the same today. This modest-sized river offers over 75 miles of good-to-excellent water in Grant, Hardy and Hampshire counties. With 18 different accesses and few major obstacles, the river offers plenty of good floats. On-foot fishing is also effective, especially above Petersburg.

The Fish: Famous for its 10- to 14-inchers, the South Branch also has some bigger fish, protected by two catch-and-release sections that have been in place 15 years. Perhaps the best place to hook a heavyweight is in the lower catch-and-release section, 9 miles of deeper pools from Rommey to Blue's Beach Bridge.

Seasons, Flies, Special Tips: Floating and wading the upper river is most popular during late spring through mid-summer. Early in the season, water levels are too high for some anglers, and late-summer levels are often too low for easy floating. During low water periods, finesse fishing with small subtle patterns can still be productive. And the morning and evening bites are excellent even during August.

Access and Use: The 14 miles from Big Bend to Petersburg, with its narrow canyons, high cliffs and heavily forested banks is a favorite of those seeking spectacular settings. A less wild, but still very fishy float is the 8-mile C&R stretch from Welton Park to Fisher Bridge in Hardy County. The South Branch has less gradient downstream of Morefield, which means fewer shallow riffles, more pools and more floating pressure. Use can be heavy on weekends, but with such high fish populations even weekenders can score.

28. West Virginia: Cacapon River

This is the go-to spot when other rivers are too roily. I once fished the Cacapon after a 5-inch rain. Most area waterways were muddy messes, but the Cacapon had excellent visibility. In fact, after a couple weeks without rain the clarity on this mid-sized Hampshire and Morgan County stream becomes so high you can almost see its hefty bronze sneering at you. This is the time to employ finesse techniques. Sneak into position, make longer casts and use light leaders. Also try subtle patterns like smaller Murray's Hellgrammites or Geibe's Damsel Flies.

There's lots of wading water upstream of Hwy 127. The uppermost section between Capon Spring and Capon Bridge also has numerous road access points. Downstream of Hwy 127 the stream is larger, floatable and not as clear. There are at least 4 different day floats from Hwy 127 to the river's junction with the Potomac.

29. Virginia: South Fork Shenandoah River

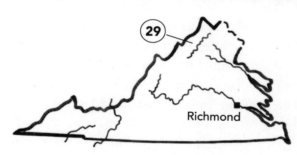

Richmond

The Water: The South Fork is made for fishing. It is an older river where most whitewater rapids have been worn away, leaving an abundance of easy-to-fish eddies, boulders, current breaks, logs and grassbeds. From the northern Virginia town of Elkton down to Front Royal, the river has at least 15 canoe launches, making it easy to do float trips ranging from half day to week long.

The Fish: As of this writing, the portion of the South Fork from the Shenandoah dam to the Luray dam has a 14- to 20-inch protected slot regulation. This special protection and more anglers releasing even "legal" fish is improving smallmouth sizes. The South Fork is still known for numbers rather than lunkers, but big fish are possible. The special regs water is the best for quality fish, but 15-inchers are becoming more numerous all through the Shenandoah watershed.

Seasons, Flies, Special Tips: Like on so many clear eastern rivers, late spring and early summer is often the easiest time to fool the bigger bronzebacks on the

South Fork. Later in the summer anglers do well with finesse techniques and subtle simulations. Surface fishing is excellent and Skipping Minnows and Micro Poppers are great producers.

Access and Use: Weekend use of the South Fork is substantial, but weekdays are relatively quiet. The 6 miles from Simpson (Karo) to Front Royal is an excellent float. A nice 2- or 3-day trip is the 18 miles from Foster's to Bentonville. During late summer, the river below Bentonville often becomes too shallow for easy floating, but perfect for wade fishing. Summer waders will also find fishy, uncrowded water on the upper reaches around Port Republic.

30. Virginia: Rappahannock River

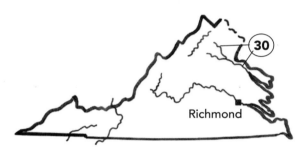

The Water: Though this northern Virginia river is near Washington DC and popular with paddlers, it isn't fished nearly as much as many other rivers in Virginia. On weekdays anglers will find lots of scenic, uncrowded water. The "Rap" upstream of Fredericksburg all the way to its headwaters at Chester Gap is undammed and completely natural.

The Fish: The Rap is best known for its excellent numbers of 10-to 14-inchers, though it yields an occasional lunker. Competent anglers will enjoy consistent fishing all season long. Multi-dozen fish days are common. Those wanting to up their odds for an 18-incher should focus on the lower reaches around Fredericksburg.

Seasons, Flies, Special Tips: A cool flow means the Rappahannock fishes best from June on. In its clear water, small topwaters can be productive in mornings and evenings, but a wide variety of bugger and rabbit-strip variations do better during midday. The river's relatively shallow depths make it easy to get the fly down to the fish with a floating or slow sink-tip line.

A thoroughly enjoyable way to experience this river is to float a 5- to 8-mile section of river and stop to wade-fish below the Rap's numerous mild rapids. During calm mornings a 5-wt rod is perfect; a 6-wt stick is better if an afternoon breeze kicks up.

Access and Use: Several easy day trips are possible above Kelly's Ford. You can launch small craft at road bridges and other access points. These accesses also provide the on-foot angler with good wading sites, all the way upstream to Hwy. 211. A 25-mile stretch from Kelly's Ford down to Motts Run Landing offers a multi-day float through a remote, pristine section of the river.

31. Virginia: Rapidan River

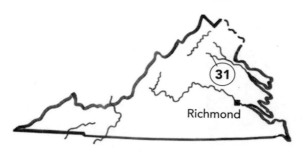

Though not quite as famous as larger rivers like the James, the Rapidan is nevertheless a favorite of some Old Dominion anglers. A tributary of the Rappahannock River in the central part of the state, the Rapidan is fortunate not to have single town of note on its banks and few bridges. This gives the river a quiet, pastoral feel.

Prime fishing water starts at Hwy. 29 and continues to the Rapidan's junction with the Rappahannock. Like on many Virginia rivers, the park-and-wade method of stopping to fish head-of-pool areas on foot is a fun and productive way to fly fish. However, anchoring and fishing deeper water will produce larger fish. An easy float is from Hwy. 3 (Germanna Ford) to Ely Ford. A slightly more challenging route is from Ely Ford to the mouth.

The East has many famous large rivers, but it is also home to dozens of tiny streams where cautious approaches are in order.

32. Virginia: James River

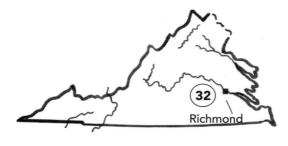

The Water: The James is one of Virginia's premier smallmouth destinations. From its headwaters near Clifton Forge all the way to Richmond, this central Virginia river offers over 200 miles of good to excellent water.

The Fish: The James certainly has plenty of 14-inchers, but it is most notable for large fish. The number of smallmouth over 20 inches annually reported from the James is the highest in the state. To help maintain this quality fishery, the upper river from Lick Run to Arcadia has reduced-harvest regs.

Seasons, Flies, Special Tips: Smallmouthing starts early on the James; April produces the most big fish of the year for those employing pre-spawn subsurface techniques. However, summer flows are more stable and the warmer months are better for high numbers of fish. Overcast summer days often produce excellent topwater fishing all day. Those willing to bundle up and fish deeper can also catch fish all winter.

Access and Use: The upper reaches above Buchanan are easier wading than downstream, and this stretch has several bridge and road accesses. The very popular section from Buchanan down to Scottsville sees lots of canoe traffic, but holds a multitude of fish. Deeper, slower water downstream of Scottsville reduces recreational paddling, and those willing to fish deeper will find hefty mid-river bronze.

33. Virginia: Cowpasture River

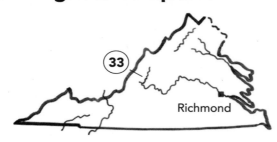

The Cowpasture is one of two streams that create the legendary James River. And while the smaller Cowpasture isn't nearly as famous as the James, it's still a fine waterway for smallmouth. The best water starts in Bath County around Williamsville and flows through Allegany County to Clifton Forge. Canoeing is possible in the lower sections, and surprisingly nice-sized fish can be caught downstream of Hwy. 39.

Some fans of the Cowpasture believe this stream is quite underrated and should be ranked as one of Virginia's top small streams. They feel it is both one of the most consistent fish producers and less crowded than many of the big-name waters.

34. Virginia: New River

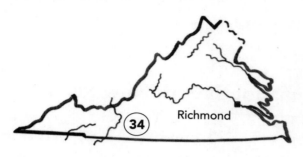

West Virginia often lays claim to the New River, but plenty of smallmouth disciples will say the river is just as good in Virginia. The New twists 160 miles through the southwest corner of the Old Dominion before it enters West Virginia. This beautiful river offers both challenging whitewater sections and Class I riffle water.

The 6 miles from Mouth-of-Wilson to Brindle Creek (Route 601) in Grayson County is an easy and productive float. In Montgomery County the 11 miles From Claytor Dam to Peppers Ferry (Hwy. 114) is another fish-filled stretch. Perhaps the most scenic float is the 6 miles in Giles County from Eggleston to Pembroke, with 400-foot cliffs and hordes of smallies below them.

These and numerous other stretches all offer good canoe fishing as well as park-and-wade opportunities. The New's superb habitat supports high densities of fish along with bona fide 20-inchers. Best of all, summer topwater fishing is excellent. Bruce Ingram's **"New River Guide" (Ecopress: 800-326-9272)** covers the entire New River.

35. Virginia: North Fork Holston River

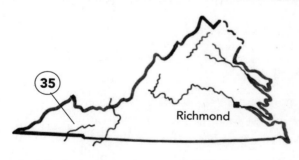

Tucked in the extreme southwest corner of the state along the Clinch Mountains is a modest-sized stream with outsized fish. The North Fork Holston has some of the best average smallmouth sizes in Virginia and recently received a 20-inch-minimum regulation from Saltville all the way down to the Tennessee line, so it will hopefully stay that way. Fourteen- to 18-inchers are common in both Scott and Washington County and even larger ones possible, especially in the fall. The North Fork Holston can floated and wade fished in many areas.

For most Virginians and other smallmouth anglers who live near the coast, the North Fork is extremely remote and requires hours of mountain driving. This has made the stream tough to get to, but it has also protected the fishery. Hopefully, as more people discover remote waterways like this Holston River trib, they will work to protect these fragile waters with strong environmental laws and protective angling regulations.

36. North Carolina: South Fork New River

This medium-sized New River tributary is one of North Carolina's best smallmouth rivers. In the mountainous northwest corner of the state, the South Fork offers over 60 miles of scenic and fishy water. There is 50 miles of water upstream of where the North and South Fork merge and another 10 miles of excellent habitat between the forks and the Virginia border. Numbers of smallmouth are high, though fish over 16 inches are limited.

The South Fork has a dozen landings and offers several different day floats. One especially good trip is from Elk Shoals Methodist Campground down to the North and South Fork junction. Wading requires particular caution due to under-tows from the high-gradient areas of the river. The South Fork is turbid in the spring, so summer and fall are prime times.

37. North Carolina: Little Tennessee River

Deep in the Nantahala Mountains of western North Carolina, the scenic Little Tennessee River is a delight. It starts as a slower flowing farmland stream, but quickly becomes a boulder-strewn mountain river tumbling from the Georgia border down to Lake Fontana. Some of best water is midway down, around the town of Franklin. Numerous canoe floats are possible in this section and smallmouth sizes are excellent for a cool, fast-flowing mountain stream. Good numbers of sleek 15- to 17-inchers are possible.

Working bank eddies and wood cover with subsurface flies is the most consistent fishing technique, but when the water is slightly off-color topwaters are also excellent. Floating several miles of stream in a day is a good idea, but canoe anglers often fish too quickly on fast-flowing streams like the Little Tennessee. One way to fish slower is to have a stern anchor that can be easily and quickly raised and lowered, so you regularly use it.

24

The Upper Midwest

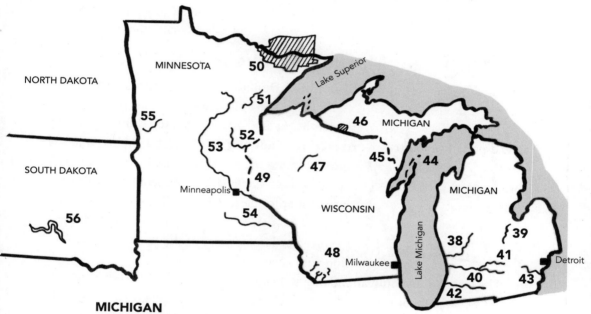

MICHIGAN
38. Muskegon River
39. Shiawassee River
40. Grand River
41. Flat River
42. Kalamazoo River
43. Huron River

WISCONSIN
44. Lake Michigan's Door Peninsula
45. Menominee River
46. Wisconsin/Upper Peninsula:
    Sylvania Wilderness Area
47. North Fork Flambeau River
48. Southwest Creeks
49. St. Croix River

MINNESOTA
50. Boundary Waters Canoe Area
    Wilderness
51. Cloquet River
52. SnakeRiver
53. Upper Mississippi River
54. Root River
55. Otter Tail River

SOUTH DAKOTA
56. Lake Sharpe

The Upper Midwest

Lake-rich Minnesota, Michigan and Wisconsin are famous for their walleye, muskie and Great Lakes salmon and trout fishing. Historically, this has meant exceptionally low angling pressure on smallmouth, especially riverine populations. So amazingly large smallies swim here. While catch rates are seldom as high as on more-fertile eastern rivers, many Upper Midwest waterways routinely yield fish over 4 pounds. Even the region's smallest creeks are big-fish producers, with 17-inchers regular catches. And of course, many of the region's lakes, including those in the famed Boundary Waters Canoe Area, also hold unusually high percentages of 4-pound-plus smallmouth. Low angling pressure and big fish—what a combination!

38. Michigan: Muskegon River

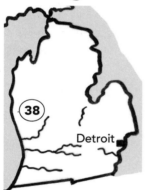

The Water: Despite its fame as a trout and salmon destination, the Muskegon is actually a warmwater river—a very fine one. During the summer months the exotic coldwater species (and their pursuers) mostly vacate the river, so the native smallmouth and their fans have it largely to themselves. And it's a lot of water for us and the smallies—over 135 miles of good habitat. It starts at the Osceola and Clare County border and goes nearly to the river's junction with Lake Michigan.

The Fish: Smallmouth abundance is high on much of the river. And areas with adequate pool habitat support fine fish over 18 inches. The upper reaches around Evart are very good for high numbers of fish, while the lower reaches around Newaygo hold larger smallies. Walleyes are also common in the river, and even during the warmest periods you can still find a few trout, especially at the mouths of tributaries.

Seasons, Flies, Special Tips: June through August is a fine time to connect with the smallies and avoid crowds on the Muskegon. Working bank eddies and cover will consistently pay off. For great numbers of fish in a beautiful setting, try wading between Evart and Hersey.

Access and Use: The lower 45 miles of river below the Croton Dam is popular steelhead water, but also supports many fine smallmouth. This section can be waded down to Newaygo, while a boat is required for the remaining river. Upstream of the Croton, Hardy and Rogers dams there is 60 miles of largely unimpeded river. Various roadways provide canoe launch sites and wading access on this lightly used section.

39. Michigan: Shiawassee River

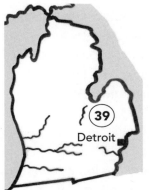

Another overlooked smallmouth fishery in trout-oriented Michigan, the Shiawassee in central Michigan has 50 miles of fine smallmouth fishing. The good water starts at Byron in Shiawasse County and flows to Chesaning in Saginaw County. This relatively clear stream is slow to muddy up after rains. About 50 feet wide in the upper reaches and only about 100 feet near Chesaning, the Shiawassee is an easy-to-wade shallow waterway with gravel/rubble bottom.

One reason for the low angling pressure is a fish consumption advisory from old sediment contaminants. With numerous shallow riffles, summer fish are heavily concentrated in deeper pools and outside bends. Smaller bottom-bouncing patterns are best. Henderson Park between Owosso and Chesaning is a good place to stop and fish. Fifteen bridges also offer access to other parts of the river. When early summer levels are normal, floating is also possible downstream of Owosso.

40. Michigan: Grand River

The Water: At 250 miles, the Grand is Michigan's longest river and it holds copious smallies along with other warmwater species. But because the state is so trout-centric, the mighty Grand gets far less attention than many smaller coldwater streams. While the river has a series of low-head dams over its course, much of the water between these obstructions is good to excellent smallmouth habitat. The best water is the 130 miles from Eaton Rapids down to Grand Rapids.

The Fish: Smallmouth numbers are high in the best stretches of the Grand, and heavyweights are possible, too. Walleyes and power-packed channel cats are also common catches, especially downstream of Ionia. Fish ladders allow 5 different coldwater species to ascend the river, and these runs usually start in early September.

Seasons, Flies, Special Tips: June through August is the best time to fish the Grand. The bronze are biting, but fishing pressure is low. Wade fishing is productive and the topwater bite is consistent. Bottom-hoping chartreuse rabbit-strip patterns will catch smallies, walleyes and cats. If you want to fish smallmouth in the fall, avoid the dams. The Grand's dams draw spawning trout and salmon, plus hordes of anglers.

Access and Use: The Grand passes through some of southern Michigan's larger towns, but much of its banks are wooded, scenic and accessible, with a variety of walk-in and launch sites. One fine wade fishing stretch is the 15 miles between the Eaton Rapids Dam and Dimondale Dam. One great float with high catch rates is through the Portland State Game Area upstream of the town of Portland.

41. Michigan: Flat River

A Grand River tributary in Ionia County near Lowell, the clear-running Flat River is the place to go when other streams are too muddy. And when heavy rains roil the Flat, it generally clears quicker than other streams in the area. The prime water is from Greenville down to the dam at Lowell. Don't expect giants, but smallmouth numbers are excellent in many areas of the Flat.

A couple of small dams block the stream, but most of this 30-mile stretch of the lower Flat is rocky, free-flowing and wadable. Float fishing is also possible when water levels are good, and a number of bridges can serve as launch sites. The upper river above Greenville also holds bronzebacks, and in the spring big brookies coming from coldwater tributaries can be caught there, too.

42. Michigan: Kalamazoo River

This southern Michigan river offers high quality, close-to-home smallmouthing yet receives only low angling pressure. The Kalamazoo has high numbers of smallmouth from its North Branch at Concord in Jackson County down to Allegon. This 120 miles of good water is only marred by a few impoundments. The shallow, hard-bottomed North Branch is especially conducive to wading, and both smallies and pike can be caught there. Downstream of Abion, wading is still possible in many areas, but you can cover more water with a small watercraft. A scenic and high-numbers stretch is through Fort Custer State Park. Below Morrow Lake and right through the town of

Kalamazoo, 20-inch smallmouth have been caught, along with the occasional lunker pike.

Kalamazoo smallmouthing is consistent summer through fall if heavy rains don't roil the water. My blockhead poppers made their debut on the K'zoo several years ago and quickly became popular with local guides. Float fishers targeting wood downstream of Otsego will connect with excellent-sized fish. **Little Rivers Guide Service (219-848-4762)** offers trips on the 'Zoo and other area rivers.

Because the Upper Midwest is a lake-rich region, angling pressure is low on its smallmouth rivers, and fish like this are common.

43. Michigan: Huron River

The Water: Some call this Michigan's blue-ribbon smallmouth river, and it's hard to argue with that assessment. This southeast Michigan stream is near millions of people, yet much of its banks are protected by parks and smallmouth are numerous. Better yet, the best water is wadable.

The Fish: The upper Huron (from Portage Lake to Strawberry Lake) is mostly impounded, but a free-flowing stretch above Strawberry up to Kent Lake is good water. Perhaps the best fishing is the 15 miles between Portage Lake and Ann Arbor. Good habitat, plus a portion of this section protected by special regs, means high numbers of fish, including some over 18 inches. A third good section is the 16 miles from Belleville Dam down to Flat Rock.

Seasons, Flies, Special Tips: Because the Huron doesn't have runs of trout and salmon, it doesn't get inundated with cold water anglers in the spring or fall. This means uncrowded smallmouthing from May through October. Topwater fishing is consistent in the summer, and late evening hatches of the giant Hexagenia mayfly can produce spectacular fishing. Wood cover is common and is a magnet for fish.

Access and Use: As already mentioned, the Huron can be divided into three distinct sections, all of which are wadable during normal summer flow levels. Public park land borders much of the river, offering numerous access points. Small craft floats are also possible. Naturally, being so near Detroit and Ann Arbor, the river isn't undiscovered wilderness, but the use rate isn't excessive.

44. Wisconsin: Lake Michigan's Door Peninsula

"The Door" has become one of North America's hottest smallmouth destinations. Wisconsin's Door Peninsula, jutting out into Lake Michigan, has numerous shallow rocky bays that are smallmouth filled. Multi-dozen catches of 16-inch-plus fish are common there among spin fishers, and fly anglers can do almost as well. Boats allow you to reach the most water, but some shorelines can even be productively wade-fished or float-tubed.

Midway up the Peninsula is the prime water: Little Sturgeon Bay, Rileys Bay, Sand Bay, Sawyer Harbor and Sturgeon Bay. Each has several public accesses.

Washington Island (at the end of the peninsula) also has good fishing. Clarity is high because of the water-filtering zebra mussel, but mid-sized fish can be caught in 4 feet of water. A sink-tip line will reach the bigger boys at 8 feet. Late May through June is the spawn, but July also has potential. Morning topwatering is great, but sleek-profiled subsurface patterns are the best for midday.

45. Wisconsin: Menominee River

Milwaukee

It was a blessing in disguise: Decades ago, paper mill pollution caused consumptive anglers to abandon the Menominee, thereby allowing its smallies to prosper. Today, this Wisconsin/UP border river continues to offer fine fishing. A large river over 90 miles long, the Menominee is impounded at 9 locations, but its surviving moving water is prime habitat.

One productive free-flowing section is the 26 miles from the White Rapids Dam down to the Grand Rapids Dam. Smallies over 20 inches swim there along with fair numbers of pike and muskies. Even sandy stretches have some smallmouth around the river's numerous sunken logs. A few places can be waded, primarily the area known as Sixty Islands. Most other water is best floated. The 2 miles below the final dam in Marinette is open to Lake Michigan and has smallies, pike, walleye, steelhead, brown trout and chinooks.

46. Wisconsin/Upper Peninsula: Sylvania Wilderness Area

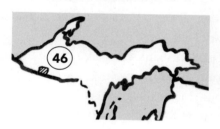

The Water: Though it borders Wisconsin, technically Sylvania lies in Michigan's Upper Peninsula and requires a Michigan license. A 20,000-acre federally designated wilderness, the Sylvania Tract is magnificent old-growth forest dotted with over 2 dozen crystalline lakes and ponds. Twenty miles north of Eagle River, Wisconsin, and part of the Ottawa National Forest, Sylvania offers a unique, non-motorized, "artificials-only," "no-kill" angling experience. Canoes and float tubes are the mode of water transportation.

The Fish: Sylvania's no-harvest laws maintains a climax fishery—a high percentage of the smallmouth population is over 15 inches. A dozen lakes up to 850 acres hold smallies and another dozen ponds have quality-sized largemouth. The 3 largest lakes (connected by short portages) are Clark, Loon and Deer Island, and all 3 have hefty smallmouth over 20 inches. Even small lakes such as Mountain and High have good numbers of 15- to 17-inchers.

Seasons, Flies, Special Tips: Fishing season opens in late May and many fish Sylvania from the opener through mid-June. Sight fishing for nesting fish during this period is very popular. Others prefer not to target spawning bass and focus on the early summer period (late June through mid-July). Many Sylvania lakes are extremely clear, but working downed trees during mornings, evenings and cloudy days invariably pays off even in July. Small divers and Sneaky Petes produce, as do black Shenks Streamers and brown woolly buggers fished on a sink-tip.

Access and Use: There are several entry points into Sylvania and the small size of the area make day trips practical. Ease of entry and the popularity of canoe-in campsites leads to moderate use. Several Wisconsin and Illinois fly clubs hold group outings at Sylvania. Tuesday through Thursday sees the lightest use. The **Watersmeet Forest Service Office (906-358-4551)** can fill you in on Sylvania's wilderness regulations.

47. Wisconsin: North Fork Flambeau River

Milwaukee

The Water: A beautiful Northwoods stream, the mid-sized North Flambeau has long been a popular canoeing destination and muskie haunt. Its fine smallmouth population receives less attention. From Turtle Flambeau Flowage to its junction with the South Branch in Sawyer County, the North Branch offers 70 miles of smallmouth and muskie water. Except for a few places, like the town of Park Falls, most of the banks are forested. Dozens of stream-bank campsites on state forest land are scattered along river.

The Fish: The average size of Flambeau smallies is good and 14-inchers are common. Late-summer fish can become fat as footballs, making a 19-incher a bona fide four-pounder. Muskies are also numerous for a river this size. Forty-five-inch giants are possible, but 28- to 35-inchers are more common.

Seasons, Flies, Special Tips: May through July is prime time for Flambeau bronze. August is also good, but beds of long, thin vegetation make weedless top-waters the way to go during late summer. When fishing the Flambeau, a small diameter wire leader should be used, both to save your fly and to land the muskies, which relate to the largest pools and eddies. Multi-species fans on the Flambeau employ a 7-wt for smallies and rig a 9-wt outfit with a large Deceiver for muskie.

Access and Use: The most popular section of river for canoeing and fishing is from the Crowley Dam to Co. Rd W. Half a dozen canoe landings are available. Downstream of Co. Rd W is also beautiful and fishy, but several Class II rapids require care. The 20 miles above Park Falls is also a good float and less used. Upper river floats can start at the Turtle Flambeau Dam when river levels are normal or above.

48. Wisconsin: Southwest Creeks

Milwaukee

The Water: Fly rodders who flock to southwest Wisconsin's trout streams are missing some of the nicest smallmouth creeks anywhere. There are 15 productive warmwater streams clustered in Grant, Iowa and Lafayette counties. In the heart of Wisconsin's scenic coulee country, these wading-size creeks twist past timbered ridgelines, limestone bluffs and through pastured valleys. There are 4 main streams: the Grant, Platte, Galena and Pecatonica, each with several fish-holding tributaries.

The Fish: Small water, big fish! Those words don't often go together, but southwest Wisconsin creeks produce some outstanding specimens. I've released plenty of 17-inch and larger bronze there over the years. The Grant, Galena and Platte most consistently yield fish over 15 inches. The lower 10 miles of the Grant and Platte are silty, so the middle reaches are best for both sizes and numbers of fish. Tributaries like Ames Branch, Shullsburg Branch, Little Platte, and Rattlesnake and Pigeon creeks often hold high numbers of 10- to 14-inchers.

Seasons, Flies, Special Tips: Agricultural runoff can keep these streams murky in May and June, so prime time is after mid-July or anytime significant rain hasn't hit the watershed for at least a week. The Crayfish Hop using a Holschlag Hackle Fly can be exceedingly productive in the creeks' shallow pools. Topwatering is mostly an evening affair and because of low oxygen levels early in the morning, smallies don't get active before 8:00 AM.

Access and Use: Few streams in the southwest are large enough to float, so use is low. Bridges are the primary access points. Wading is through private land, but Wisconsin's enlightened trespass laws allow wade fishing on many waterways. Stay in or near the stream and avoid cattle, cropland and any land with "keep out" signs.

49. Wisconsin: St. Croix River

Milwaukee

The Water: One of the prettiest waterways in the upper Midwest, this Minnesota/Wisconsin border river was one of the first waters to be federally protected by the Wild and Scenic Rivers Act in the early 1970s. The 90 miles above the St. Croix Falls impoundment is quiet, shallow, small craft water. The lower 50 miles of the St. Croix has spectacular bluffs, but it's deep water and is a big-boat playground on weekends.

The Fish: I'm not exaggerating, St. Croix smallmouthing really is better than it was 40 years ago. Today's strong catch-and-release ethic in the region has made 16- and 17-inchers regular catches. Even the lower river (heavily fished due to its proximity to Minneapolis) produces 20-inchers. The upper river receives much less pressure and holds strong numbers of various-sized fish.

Seasons, Flies, Special Tips: The upper 'Croix often carries a heavy flow during May and early June, so the most consistent fishing is in late June through early September. Summer topwatering is outstanding, like it is on most Upper Midwest rivers. However, upper river fishing often ends abruptly in late September when smallies vacate their summer locations and migrate downstream to deep water.

Access and Use: Some of the best fishing is from Hwy 70 upstream to the mouth of the Namekagon River. Ten landings are distributed over this 45-mile section and recreational canoeing is light during weekdays and only moderate on weekends. The 30 miles above the Namekagon is shallow and rocky. This section is better for wading than floating, and has an abundance of fish to 15 inches.

50. Minnesota: Boundary Waters Canoe Area Wilderness

Minneapolis

The Water: It's no mystery why this destination is world-famous among outdoor enthusiasts. Two million acres of officially designated wilderness and over 1,000 interconnected pristine lakes makes the "Boundary Waters" a canoe and camping paradise. Straddling the Minnesota/ Ontario border, this famed area also offers fabulous lake smallmouthing in a spectacular setting. A myriad of islands, points, protected bays and rubble-laden shorelines make it fly-fishing-friendly.

The Fish: Including the Ontario portion (Quetico Park) and Minnesota's half of the Boundary Waters, over 400 of the lakes contain smallmouth. These range from 40-acre "ponds" to massive 10,000-acre bodies of water. Angler kill depresses fish sizes in entry-point lakes, but more-remote interior waters have smallmouth exceeding 5 pounds, along with big pike, walleye and lake trout.

Seasons, Flies, Special Tips: Late-May through mid-June is the most popular time with Boundary Waters smallmouthers. I also like the early July period, but to be successful in summer requires a willingness to fish hard during mornings and evenings. Poppers are often unbeatable then. But the bright light of midday and high water clarity also make a selection of subsurface flies essential. Large lakes such as Brule, Basswood, Crooked, Knife, Saganagons, Agnes, Sturgeon and Quetico all have high quantities of smallmouth. Base-camping on a large lake is a way to maximize your fishing time.

Access and Use: Thankfully, both Minnesota's BWCAW and Ontario's Quetico Park diligently preserve their wilderness character by restricting the number of entry permits issued. Although many Boundary Waters canoeists don't fish, they book up the popular dates and entry points months in advance. So plan early and consider less popular entry points. And remember, a Boundary Waters trip is more than just fishing. Moose, dramatic scenery, starlit nights and the call of the loon make the experience awe-inspiring no matter how many fish you catch.

51. Minnesota: Cloquet River

This beauty is unknown to even most Minnesota smallmouth aficionados. The mid-sized Cloquet tumbles quietly through the forests of St. Louis County, noticed by only a few Duluth area fly fishers seeking big brown trout. However, the river's smallies are much more numerous. Nearly 30 miles of the lower river, from the Island Lake Dam down to the St. Louis River, are boulder-strewn and smallmouth-laden. Low alkalinity keeps the numbers of lunkers low, but good numbers along with the occasional trout, pike, walleye and channel cat makes the Cloquet a great destination.

Wading fishing with felt-soled footwear is possible around Hwy 53, but floating is the way to reach the Cloquet's more-remote sections. The 10 river miles below Hwy 53 may be the fishiest float. Upstream, a nice 8-mile trip is from Co. Rd. 48 to Co. Rd 15. Hitting head-of-pool areas with black or chartreuse Ice Buggers is a consistent technique.

52. Minnesota: Snake River

Though it's an easy drive from the Twin Cities, this east-central Minnesota stream is seldom too crowded. One reason is that the Snake during dry spells often gets too low to easily canoe. This doesn't prevent the stream from being good bronzeback water.

The 30 miles of upper river from the Snake River Forest (east of Woodland) down to Co. Rd 11 (south of Mora) has moderate numbers of mid-sized smallmouth along with many pike. It's also floatable during normal early and mid-summer flow levels. The middle reaches of the Snake are sandy, but the lower 12 miles below Cross Lake (near Pine City) is extremely rocky and fish-filled. Due to numerous shallow Class I rapids, this lower section down to the St. Croix also becomes difficult to float by late July. However, waders with felt soles can have high-number days below Cross Lake by targeting boulders and head-of-pool areas.

53. Minnesota: Upper Mississippi River

The Water: Boulder-laden and just 600 feet wide, the Mississippi upstream of Minneapolis bears no resemblance to the congested commercial river below the Twin Cities. The upper Mississippi is large enough for jonboats and other shallow-draft craft, but a heavy algae stain keeps visibility low year-round, requiring cautious boating to avoid the river's innumerable rocks.

The Fish: The 50-plus miles from St. Cloud to Anoka is protected by catch-and-release regulations. Because of the special regs, 17- and 18-inchers are common, and every year many over 20 inches are caught and released. There are also good numbers of 10- to 15-inchers, so 50-fish days are possible, particularly in early fall.

Seasons, Flies, Special Tips: From the late-May season opener through June, flows can be quite high, making craft control challenging. Wade fishing opportunities are limited due to the river's size and substantial flows, but those with good boat handling skills can catch fish.

I've fished and guided on the Mississippi for decades, and most of my clients' biggest fish have been caught after the 1st of July. The hot-water season is especially good for lunkers. Because of the limited clarity, topwater action is consistent during mid-summer. In early fall, white Ice Buggers or Whitetail Hares are hard to beat for high numbers of fish.

Access and Use: While popular with a growing number of Twin Cities smallmouth fans, angling pressure on the upper Mississippi is still less than one-third what it is on popular eastern waterways. Ten concrete or gravel boat landings are scattered along the river allowing for floats of varying lengths.

Various guides ply the upper Miss'; the pros from Smallmouth Angler are the best.

54. Minnesota: Root River

The Water: A mid-sized stream in southeast Minnesota's scenic bluff country, the limestone-laden Root offers good fishing for 55 miles from Chatfield down to Rushford. The Root is almost always floatable by canoe, but during late-summer and early-fall dry spells, you'll have to drag over some shallow riffles. Too much water is a more common challenge; heavy rains on the stream's agricultural watershed cause the stream to run extremely turbid. Periods of low rainfall offer the best fishing.

The Fish: Fishing the Root for years, I've long regarded it as a great "numbers" destination. Lots of 10- to 14-inch smallmouth are likely, either by canoe or on-foot angling. However, 18-inch-plus dandies are also possible, especially in its lower reaches downstream of Lanesboro.

Seasons, Flies, Special Tips: Early-season fishing (late May and June) is good if water visibility is at least 18 inches. During July and August bottom-bouncing flies are best, especially the golden Clouser Minnow and Hare Leech. September and October are the best "big fish" months. My biggest Root smallmouth, nearly 21 inches, came in late October on a yellow Hare Leech.

Besides smallies, large brown trout over 14 inches swim the Root in springtime. Dark-colored woolly buggers are excellent for both species, until water temperatures climb into the 70s and most trout leave the Root for its numerous cold-water tributaries.

Access and Use: Angling pressure is only light on the Root, and weekend recreational canoe use is seldom more than moderate. A dozen bridges span the Root, offering on-foot or canoe access. Canoe rental services are available in both Chatfield and Lanesboro.

55. Minnesota: Otter Tail River

It's still a secret. The Fisheries Department introduced smallmouth into this small western Minnesota river a decade ago with great success. Today, the Otter Tail has high numbers of smallies wherever there are rocky substrates. Four dams block the stream around Fergus Falls, but the short floats between the impoundments offer fast and furious action. Fish up to 19 inches are also abundant for 6 miles downstream of the Orwell Dam.

Catch-and-release smallmouth regs protect the Otter Tail, plus the DNR has done some habitat work on the stream to improve the smallmouth fisheries.

I'm not the type that automatically supports smallmouth stocking, but I think introducing the species into the Otter Tail has been an unqualified success. The smallie has prospered in a stream degraded by agriculture and the Army Corps of Engineers, creating a high-quality self-sustaining fishery where there were previously few gamefish.

56. South Dakota: Lake Sharpe

The Dakota prairie isn't often thought of as smallmouth country, but several Missouri River impoundments in South Dakota are steadily becoming prime

bronzeback destinations. The best is Lake Sharpe in the middle of the state. With recently enacted 12- to 18-inch protected slot regulation and good habitat, Sharpe smallies are increasing in both size and number. Smallmouth can be found in the entire lake, but the best water is in the lower half of Sharpe from Fort Thompson up to the West Bend Recreation Area.

Shoreline action is good during May and June; riprapped banks and Sharpe's innumerable small bays hold spring fish. The prime summer locations are shallow flats, some only 5 to 8 feet deep. With miles of shoreline between landings, a full-sized lake boat with at least 20 horsepower is best. Midday winds are also an issue, making an 8-wt rod the best choice.

25

The Lower Midwest

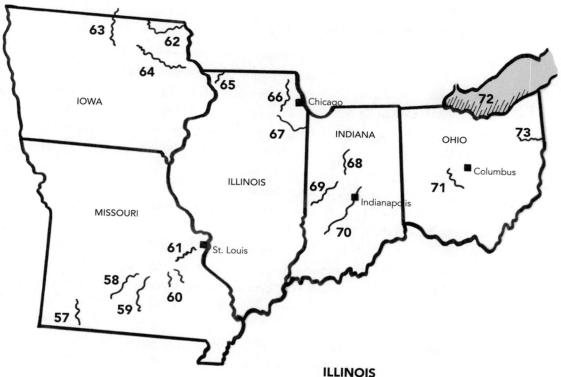

MISSOURI
57. James River
58. Osage Fork
59. Big Piney River
60. Courtois and Huzzah Creeks
61. Bourbeuse River
IOWA
62. Upper Iowa River
63. Cedar River
64. Turkey River

ILLINOIS
65. Apple River
66. Fox River
67. Kankakee River
INDIANA
68. Tippecanoe River
69. Sugar Creek
70. West Fork White River
OHIO
71. Big Darby Creek
72. Lake Erie
73. Little Beaver Creek

The Lower Midwest

The rivers in the agricultural states of Ohio, Indiana, Illinois and Iowa certainly aren't pristine, but tucked away in this farmbelt are some surprisingly good waters. High alkalinity keeps fertility high and the streams least impacted by agriculture or angler harvest produce both large sized and good numbers of fish. Missouri is the one hilly state of the region. Its rugged Ozark Plateau in the southern half of the state is laced with beautiful fast-flowing limestone streams that hold high numbers of mid-sized bronzebacks.

57. Missouri: James River

The Water: Formerly one of the finest fisheries in the region, this southwest Missouri river is now somewhat overlooked. When the lower James was impounded to create Table Rock Lake many believed the entire river was lost. Fortunately, over 60 miles of productive upper river survived. During moderate flows, the river can still be floated from Hwy 125 just east of Springfield down to Galena. Only one small impoundment (Lake Springfield) near Galloway blocks the route.

The Fish: I once did a fish "survey" of the James. Floating the middle river in late fall when the water was low and clear, I was impressed with all the 12- to 14-inchers swimming under my canoe. And there are much bigger bronze in the river near Table Rock Lake. These downstream pools also have good numbers of large-mouth, including some nice 15-inchers.

Seasons, Flies, Special Tips: Early summer is prime time, but the dog days can also be good on the James. Small topwaters sometimes pay off, though small olive rabbit buggers are more consistent.

Access and Use: The upper 10 miles of stream (above Lake Springfield) is often too shallow to float, this semi-developed stretch is good wading water. A nice 6-mile float is from the Shevlen Rock Rd down to the Hootentown Access off Hwy O. Halfway down this stretch, Finley Creek comes in from the east, and it's also a fine stream for wading. The remaining 22 miles of river below Hootentown is large enough to float with jonboats and receives considerable use. Fall may be the best time to fish this portion, both for big fish and to avoid the crowds.

58. Missouri: Osage Fork

It's true, Missouri's easy floating rivers are often crowded during summer weekends. Streams with a few blocking riffles or trees offer much better opportunities to escape the throngs. One of these is the Osage Fork of the Gasconade in Webster and Laclede counties. While 40 miles of the Osage Fork is floatable during normal years, log jams and braided channels will require a little dragging of your watercraft. Fortunately, this does a fine job of depressing use of the stream. Locals fish some of the longest pools, but canoe traffic is low.

Very good numbers of smallmouth are present and they concentrate in the head-of-pool zones. The park-and-wade method is an excellent way to fish these areas. A few largemouth or spotted bass will be caught, too. During normal years, floating can start at Hwy 5, but obstructing trees can be significant in these upper reaches. You'll find somewhat easier floating in the 23 miles from Hwy B down to Hull Ford access.

59. Missouri: Big Piney River

The Water: With towering bluffs, mild rapids and limestone pools, the Big Piney is classic Ozarks. Twisting through Mark Twain National Forest and Fort Leonard Wood Military Reservation, this central Missouri river offers over 75 miles of float fishing water in a strikingly beautiful setting. Overfished in past years, the Big Piney is once again becoming one of Missouri's best smallmouth streams, thanks to catch-and-release regulations.

The Fish: Fish numbers are especially good in the upper and middle reaches of the river from Houston down to the junction of Hwys J and M in Phelps County. There are larger fish over 14 inches in the 15-mile special regs section from Slabtown Access to Ross Bridge. Bigger fish are also turning up even outside the protected water, as local anglers slowly moderate their harvest mentality.

Seasons, Flies, Special Tips: A closed spring fishing season and cool flows mean a late start on many Missouri rivers. Late May into early July is the most popular fishing period, primarily because of the difficulty some anglers have in catching smallies during the clear water of late summer. However, summer fishing is generally first-rate during the low-light times of mornings, evenings, rainy days and even after dark.

Access and Use: Float trips, historically in wooden jonboats, have been popular on the Big Piney and other Ozark waterways for nearly a century. Nowadays, weekend canoe use by recreational paddlers can be intense, so mid-week is a better time for fishing. Overnight trips (camping on the Ozarks' famous gravel bars) are also popular, and they're a good way to fish because you're on the river in the morning and evening. There is also good wade fishing on the upper reaches around Houston.

60. Missouri: Courtois and Huzzah Creeks

These little gems run parallel to each other through Crawford County. Pronounced "Coort-a-way" and "Hoo-za," these scenic Meramec tributaries are each about 25 miles long. Much of the surrounding land is in Mark Twain National Forest. Most fish on these streams are under 15 inches, but on a 5-wt outfit they'll seem much bigger.

Floating the Courtois and Huzzah is mostly an early-season affair, and even then most often only downstream of Hwy. 8. Even when water levels are adequate, floaters need to be alert due to the narrow channel and often tight turns. Fortunately, both streams are great for wade fishing almost all the time. On the Huzzah, fish can be caught all the way up to Dillard, but the larger pools start downstream of the Hwy. V bridge. On the Courtois, anglers start wade fishing (and floating, when levels are high) near Brazil in Washington County. Even smaller, more intimate fish-holding water continues upstream another 5 miles to the hamlet of Courtois.

61. Missouri: Bourbeuse River

This is my kind of Ozark stream—even during mid-summer the Bourbeuse doesn't become exceptionally clear. This means the smallies aren't as shy and midday fishing is often excellent. This stream is also one of the crookedest in the region; it winds for nearly 100 miles and never leaves Franklin County. Although it's just west of St. Louis, the Bourbeuse isn't as crowded as some other Missouri streams. There is little whitewater to excite the thrill-seekers and not enough towering bluffs for the gawkers. But the Bourbeuse does have some surprisingly hefty smallmouth, including the occasional 20-incher.

The 25 miles of water upstream of Hwy. H is on-foot territory, and summer floating starts at the Hwy. H bridge. Several more bridges and official Missouri Dept. of Conservation landings provide access all the way to Meramec. Because the water isn't ultra-clear, larger flies work well on the Bourbeuse, especially if you're targeting big fish.

62. Iowa: Upper Iowa River

The Water: Forty years ago folks considered this the state's premier smallmouth stream, and most still feel the same way about this superb waterway. Snaking across northeast Iowa, the Upper Iowa offers 50 miles of great water. From Lime Springs in Howard County to Hwy 76 in Allamakee County, much of the stream has good habitat with limestone substrates and 3- to 5-foot-deep pools.

The Fish: This is a high numbers river, where float-fishing anglers sometimes experience 50-fish days. The no-kill section between Bluffton and Decorah is the best area to connect with lunkers up to 20 inches. Trout are also scattered through the river and are most often caught around the mouths of coldwater tributaries. The lower end near Hwy 26 is sandy, but outside bends there hold a plethora of warmwater species, including smallies, white bass, sauger, drum and channel catfish.

Seasons, Flies, Special Tips: Dry spring weather can mean fast-paced fishing, but muddy water is more often the case before mid-June. Late-summer low water levels may mean dragging over some riffles, but August fishing is hard to beat. White Shenks Streamers catch both smallies and brown trout.

Access and Use: Canoe liveries make weekend paddling popular from Kendallville to Decorah. However, the Kendallvile to Bluffton float is exceptional, with soaring bluffs and high catch rates; you can avoid the crowds by fishing midweek. Another option I like is the river downstream of Slinde Mounds Preserve; there are lower densities of fish, but also less human use, and big fish are possible there, too.

The Lower Midwest is laced with small and medium-sized small-mouth streams. This nice Illinois smallie was caught in the spring.

63. Iowa: Cedar River

The Cedar isn't nearly as well-known as the Upper Iowa River, and a core of serious small-mouth fans like it that way; they have the Cedar's numerous smallies to themselves. The upper Cedar from the Minnesota border near Otranto downstream to Floyd offers over 25 miles of good to excellent smallmouth water. Catch-and-release regs govern several miles of the upper river near St. Ansgar, so today the Cedar may have more fish over 16 inches than when I first fished it 40 years ago.

Limestone bluffs are scattered along this mid-sized river, and all of the water is easily floatable by small craft. Several low-head dams necessitate short portages, and one large dam at Mitchell impounds the river upstream to Hwy. T26. The largest, deepest pools are downstream of Osage and occasionally give up 20-inchers. Wade anglers do best on the Cedar from late July through September. Small tributaries such as Otter, Deer, Turtle and Rock creeks can also support smallmouth when water levels are elevated.

64. Iowa: Turkey River

During my formative years, I spent countless hours prowling northeast Iowa's Turkey River drainage. Fortunately for me and other smallmouth fans, plenty of bronze still swims in the Turkey. From Cresco all the way down to Elkader, the Turkey has good to excellent numbers of smallies. Some big fish are present in the lower reaches, but fish numbers are several times higher upstream of Clermont.

July through September is prime and also the best time for wading. On-foot stalking is particularly good around Fort Atkinson and a few miles south of Cresco. Floating is possible starting at the mouth of the Little Turkey (near Eldorado). Yellow and chartreuse flies are excellent for the stream's algae-stained water, and so is the Holschlag Hackle Fly with its yellow legs. While the Turkey may muddy up a little easier than some streams, it has excellent potential and doesn't receive as much canoe or angling pressure as other good Iowa rivers.

65. Illinois: Apple River

Beautiful, productive and public! You can't say this about many creeks in Land of Lincoln, but it applies to the Apple River. A northwest Illinois creek in Jo Davies County, the Apple winds past towering limestone bluffs for several miles in Apple River Canyon State Park. Plenty of anglers ply the state park waters, but reduced-harvest regs allows good numbers of 10- to 14-inchers to survive. There is enough postcard-perfect pool and riffle water in the park for a day's fishing if you include the stream's South Fork tributary. Weekday fishing sometimes produces 30-fish catches.

A much-less-pressured portion of the Apple is the difficult-to-access 15 miles downstream to Hwy 20. Landowner permission to wade is sometimes possible, and high-flow floating is another way to experience the lower Apple. During spring and early summer flow rates, use the lightest, most shallow-draft craft possible. Keep your float short, stay off the banks and be prepared to jockey around riffles and the occasional fence.

66. Illinois: Fox River

Within casting distance of 6 million people, this Chicago area waterway is, amazingly, a bona fide smallmouth fishery. Once heavily polluted, a much cleaner Fox now provides back-yard bassing to increasing numbers of fly fishers. The upper Fox in McHenry and Kane counties is very urban and has several low-head dams, but even here rocky stretches and park land provide some habitat and access. One of the better areas is from Geneva to North Aurora.

The lower Fox, in Kendall and La Salle counties down to the Dayton Dam, offers 30 miles of better water. Wading is possible here if river levels are low, but floating the lower Fox is best. The 12 miles from Sheridon to Wedron is excellent and has scenic bluffs. Wade fishing around the islands downstream of Yorkville is another possibility. Minnow forage and low visibility water means Fox bronzebacks bite on large, bright flies worked very slowly along the bottom, against-the-current and on a sink-tip line.

67. Illinois: Kankakee River

The Water: It's a welcome sight: a wooded, boulder-studded, smallmouth-rich river barely 75 miles from Chicago. While the entire 50-mile portion of the Kankakee that flows through Illinois holds smallies, its lower reaches really shine. From Bourbonnais down to the Kankakee's mouth, the river is several hundred feet wide, rocky and fast flowing. The 12-mile portion that passes through Kankakee State Park is especially scenic and is regarded by many as the most productive piece of smallmouth water in Illinois.

The Fish: Smallmouth catch rates can be impressive on the lower Kank'; even wade anglers sometimes have 30-fish days. Most fish are under 13 inches, but protective regulations have been implemented to improve sizes. These new regs seem to be paying off with increasing numbers of larger smallmouth caught.

Seasons, Flies, Special Tips: Heavy flows and turbid water often limit spring success, making mid-summer through late fall the prime time on the Kankakee. Bright-colored patterns, including those in white and chartreuse, are consistent.

Access and Use: The Kankakee is large enough for boats, and numerous launches are available, especially on the upper river. Downstream of Bourbonnais, the state park offers many on-foot access points, and when water levels are low this section is shallow enough to wade. However, summer use can be heavy in the park, making weekdays the best time to fish. Around the I-55 bridge is a more overlooked area that's shallow, rocky and fishy.

68. Indiana: Tippecanoe River

Once one of the state's top smallmouth rivers, the Tippecanoe still holds plenty of bronze in some parts. While intensive agriculture has diminished the fisheries on the upper reaches of this northwest Indiana river, smallmouth numbers are strong downstream of Monticello. From the Lake Freeman Dam all the way to the Wabash, the "Tippy" offers high numbers of fish, plus real shots at 18-inchers.

With the Freeman Dam to mitigate flows, moderate rain doesn't roil the lower Tippy like most farmbelt streams. From Lake Freeman to Hwy 18, floating is possible all season long and catch rates can be outstanding in this section even for the on-foot angler. Once I released 40 fish in just 6 hours of wading. Another bridge access is Pretty Prairie Rd a few miles upstream from the Wabash. Though sandier, there are still smallies around every bit of gravel, rock and stick in this section. The Tippecanoe offers consistent fishing spring through fall, and all the standard techniques pay off.

69. Indiana: Sugar Creek

The Water: The Hoosier state's smallie fishing is a well-kept secret. Few nonresidents consider Indiana a smallmouth Mecca, but the state has several first-rate waterways. One of the very best is Sugar Creek. A Wabash River tributary in Parke and Montgomery counties, Sugar is a beautiful small to mid-sized stream with over 50 miles of prime smallmouth habitat.

The Fish: Though the stream is relatively shallow and only 50 feet wide in places, it holds some 19-inch-plus fish. These larger specimens are most prevalent downstream of Hwy 32. Both the fish and the stream lose size above Crawfordville, but some smaller bronzebacks can still be had in these lightly fished upper reaches, all the way to Thorntown.

Seasons, Flies, Special Tips: Rains can quickly muddy this farmbelt stream, so fishing is better when the watershed hasn't received hard rain for at least a week. Spring, summer and fall angling are all productive. The Crayfish Hop is a particularly deadly summer technique, and the Holschlag Hackle Fly and various other "weight forward" patterns are consistent producers. An unusually scenic area is the dramatic limestone bluff stretch in Shades State Park.

Access and Use: Canoe fishing is possible starting at Crawfordville. A half-dozen bridges and several other adjacent roadways provide plenty of access between Crawfordville and Turkey Run State Park. During normal flows, a core of Indiana fly fishers also effectively wade-fish this 30-mile section.

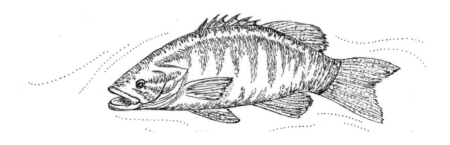

70. Indiana: West Fork White River

Often just called the White, this mid-sized river is an urban and agricultural waterway that holds small-mouth. For nearly 15 miles, the White flows right through Indianapolis. In this urban setting, smallies can be found in bank eddies, along riprapped shores and at the mouths of feeder creeks. Considerable amounts of park land allows on-foot access, and float anglers can also easily fish the metro river.

Downstream of Indianapolis, smallmouth fishing on the White significantly improves, especially in the 20 miles between Martinsville and Spencer. Rocky substrates are limited, so fish are concentrated around wood or hard-bottom areas. Smallmouth over 20 inches are available, as are white bass and other warmwater species. The lower White is a big enough river that float fishing is the preferred method.

71. Ohio: Big Darby Creek

The Water: In a state where too many streams suffer from heavy abuse, the Big Darby is a wonderful exception. A fertile, mid-sized stream just west of Columbus, the Big Darby still holds fine small-mouth, thanks in part to groups like The Nature Conservancy and The Smallmouth Alliance. Plenty of people live close to the stream, but many of its banks are still tree-lined. Smallmouth are present for over 50 miles, from Union County to the Big Darby's merger with the Scioto River.

The Fish: Smallies over 18 inches are caught regularly in the Big Darby. Some of the best "big fish" water is in Franklin County where a 15-mile stretch is protected by special regs, from Hwy 40 down to Orient.

Seasons, Flies, Special Tips: Pre-spawn fishing can be excellent in April and May if spring rains aren't heavy. More consistent summer activity starts in June and both surface and bottom-bouncing techniques are effective then. Late-season fishing can also be excellent right through November. Due to the stream's only moderate clarity, larger flies are often best.

Access and Use: Two dozen bridges provide generous access to most of the stream. Upstream of Plain City is largely the domain of waders; below this town floating is possible. With so many bridge accesses, floats of various distances are easy to organize. Naturally, plenty of people fish or paddle the Big Darby during the summer. The less-accessible lower reaches around Darbyville see less activity, and weekday use is reasonably light on most of the stream.

72. Ohio: Lake Erie

I couldn't leave it out. Sure, it's a huge body of water that requires a serious-size boat, but Erie's eye-popping bronze warrants attention from serious small-mouthers. The Bass Islands off of Port Clinton have long been famous smallmouth water, and this area still offers thousands of acres of fish-holding shoals and shorelines. Some of the Ohio shore's productive shoals are Ruggles, Crib, Round, Niagara, Gull and West. The Michigan and New York shorelines also have dozens of honey holes.

Lake Erie bronze can be caught all season long, but early through mid-fall is particularly good. Often large schools of big fish will be on relatively shallow humps or shoals (sometimes only 6 to 10 feet deep). Erie bait slingers are notorious for their soft-shelled craws, but try different fly patterns and you'll likely find one that will pay off that day. Sometimes flies that resemble bottom-hugging Gobies (such as the Woolhead Goby) work well. Smallies love this small odd-shaped non-native species that's now widespread in Lake Erie.

73. Ohio: Little Beaver Creek

This may be the prettiest stream in Ohio. It's also one of the best small stream fisheries in the state. In Columbiana County near the Pennsylvania border, the Little Beaver holds state Wild River status and plenty of smallies, too, for 36 miles. Reduced-harvest regs also protect 17 miles of the stream below Hwy 7. The most accessible portion is the 4 miles in Beaver Creek State Park, but there is also excellent fishing in the less-pressured water downstream and upstream of the park. Little Beaver's modest size makes wade fishing easy, but the park-and-wade method using a canoe or pontoon boat is also practical downstream of the state park. Fishing is good from early April into November, with fish up to 20 inches possible. On-the-bottom fall fishing produces the biggest bronze, but summer topwatering with poppers and small divers has its own charm and effectiveness.

26

The Mid-South

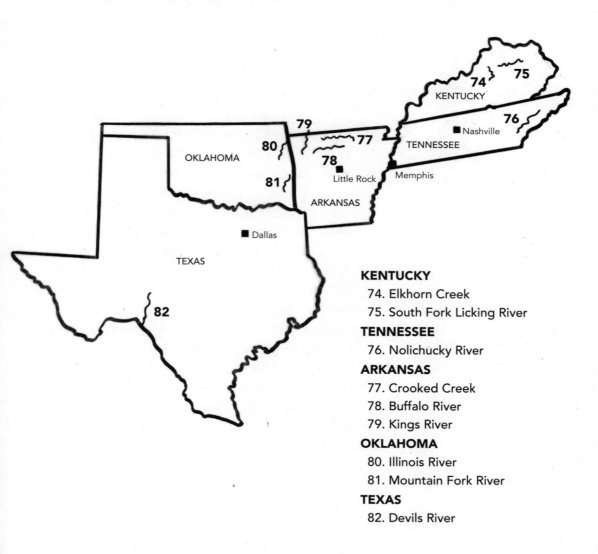

KENTUCKY
74. Elkhorn Creek
75. South Fork Licking River

TENNESSEE
76. Nolichucky River

ARKANSAS
77. Crooked Creek
78. Buffalo River
79. Kings River

OKLAHOMA
80. Illinois River
81. Mountain Fork River

TEXAS
82. Devils River

The Mid-South

Those who don't live in this region generally assume Mid-South smallies mostly reside in huge, sprawling reservoirs. But moving water fans will be surprised and impressed that so many scenic smallmouth rivers remain in the region. Much of this hilly and mountainous region is part of the species' native range, so hundreds of waterways were once smallmouth-laden. Previous eras of dam building inundated some good water and on other streams a pervasive harvest mentality continues to limit smallmouth sizes. Fortunately, dam building has declined and better angling regulations and attitudes are starting to restore fish sizes. And many Mid-South waterways also offer great scenic beauty and exemplary floating or wading experiences.

74. Kentucky: Elkhorn Creek

Years ago, anglers in the know regarded the Elkhorn as one of the top 5 mid-sized smallmouth streams in North America. That might have been an exaggeration, but this Frankfort County stream is certainly one of Kentucky's top smallmouth waters. Excellent habitat, great scenery and easy floating as well as wading all make the Elkhorn a favorite. Sporadic reproduction can cause the population to fluctuate, but a 12- to 16-inch protected slot and supplemental stocking is the Fisheries Division's attempt to stabilize and improve the Elkhorn's fisheries.

The most popular fishing and canoeing section is the 19 miles from Forks of Elkhorn (near Frankfort) down to Peaks Mill. The first 7 miles has some enjoyable Class II and III rapids, while the remaining 12 miles is all Class I. The lower 10 miles of both the North and South Forks of the Elkhorn are also fine smallmouth water and can also be floated much of the year.

A favorite local fishing technique is a two-fly rig using a small woolly bugger attached to a popper by a 10-inch dropper. The best fishing occurs before October, since many Elkhorn smallies migrate to the Kentucky River in the fall.

75. Kentucky: South Fork Licking River

Kentucky has an unusually large number of mid-sized streams. Unfortunately, many no longer produce quality smallmouthing like they used to, due to degradation and over-harvest. One stream the Fisheries Division and knowledgeable anglers both still rate as "excellent" is the South Fork Licking River. Starting in Bourbon County and looping its way north through Harrison and Pendleton counties to Falmouth, the South Fork holds serious numbers of bronzebacks.

Low-height dams limit the fishery in Harrison County, but everywhere the stream runs free, both on-foot and float fishing will produce from spring through fall. Small hellgrammite and woolly bugger patterns in olive or black are good during the summer.

76. Tennessee: Nolichucky River

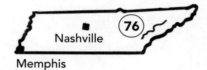

The Water: Indigenous people once called the Nolichucky the "river of death." Nowadays bronzeback addicts call the river "awesome." The 'Chucky is over 100 miles of superb smallmouth water winding through the mountains of extreme eastern Tennessee. Although this waterway is next door to Kentucky, Virginia and North Carolina, limited access keeps the crowds at bay.

The Fish: While too much harvest hurts smallmouth sizes on many mid-south waters, fortunately the Nolichucky's limited accessibility allows the fish to grow larger. This river is a consistent producer of 15-inchers. Much larger fish are also possible, including dandies exceeding 20 inches. Some of the best big fish action is between Greeneville and Jonesborough.

Seasons, Flies, Special Tips: Though it's a southern river, cool mountain drainage means spring activity doesn't start until early to mid-April. But good fishing holds up through most of the summer. Woolly buggers and rabbit strip patterns in brown, yellow and olive are season-long producers. During the low flows and high clarity of mid-summer, targeting shaded banks with quiet topwaters is another action-packed technique.

Access and Use: While the Nolichucky isn't as accessible as some Tennessee rivers, numerous easy canoe floats are still possible. Two great trips are the 6 miles from the Hwy. 81 bridge down to Hwy. 81/107 and the 8 miles from that bridge down to Bailey Road. Below the Davy Crocket Dam there is another excellent 8-mile stretch from the Route 70 bridge to Route 321. Six miles of the upper river from the Chestoah to Embreevile has numerous Class II rapids and makes an exciting and productive trip for experienced paddlers.

Beautiful boulder-strewn (and smallmouth-laden) rivers such as this one are typical in the mountainous Mid-South region.

77. Arkansas: Crooked Creek

Crooked Creek is the most famous stream in the state. It's both a premier smallmouth destination and a battleground over Arkansas' destructive gravel mining laws. (Arkansas law allows landowners to excavate a river's gravel substrates.) While some areas of the river have been hurt by gravel mining operations and angler harvest, this mid-sized river still hold lots of smallies. Canoe and wading anglers will find over 50 miles of good water in Boone and Marion counties. The river around Yellville has long harbored good numbers of 12- to 15-inchers. Summer fishing pressure can be substantial, and when the water is clear the fish can play hard-to-get. Finessing them by working a small Tube Fly or Spider Fly along the bottom is one possibility. Fishing in the fall, when few other anglers are around, is another way to score on the Crooked.

78. Arkansas: Buffalo River

The Water: Plenty of fly fishers view Arkansas' Ozark mountains purely as a trout destination. But, of course, long before rainbows and browns were introduced, native smallies swam in almost every northern Arkansas stream. One of the best remaining spots is the Buffalo River, in Newton, Searcy and Marion counties. Undammed and federally protected, the Buffalo still offers 130 miles of prime smallmouth water and beautiful Ozarks scenery.

The Fish: Buffalo smallies aren't as large as they were 60 years ago, but better regs and better ethics are improving average sizes. Twelve- to 15-inchers are common on the more remote sections of the river, and some 20-inchers are caught every year.

Seasons, Flies, Special Tips: Naturally, the warm and slow flows of summer are prime time. But Arkansas' mild climate also means comfortable late and early season fishing, while weather farther north is too cold. Because the Buffalo is a tributary of the trout-rich White River, a smallmouth and trout combo is a possibility for those planning multi-day trips to the area.

Access and Use: The lower 102 miles of river below Pruitt (Hwy. 7) is floatable year-round by canoe, with only occasional mild rapids to contend with. Upriver of

Pruitt is the domain of whitewater paddlers and wading anglers. The entire river is a popular paddling destination, and fishing is good in both the upper and lower reaches. One of the most remote areas holding some of the biggest fish is the 25 miles through the Lower Buffalo Wilderness Area, from Rush off Hwy. 26 down to Buffalo City. A 3-day trip through this section is extraordinary. For more river info try the **Buffalo National River website: (www.nps.gov/buff)**.

79. Arkansas: Kings River

Still one of the nicest streams in the Ozarks, the Kings River flows across Madison and Carroll counties, twisting through gorgeous hills. Besides 50 miles of rugged bluffs, forested hills and clean gravel bars, there are some unusually fine small-mouth swimming in the Kings' fertile flow. Though most are less than 14 inches, some heavy bronze also lurks in this rather smallish river. Nineteen-inchers are most often caught in the spring and early summer. Plugging shoreline cover with olive or brown woolly buggers is a tried-and-true technique.

Spring and early summer is also the prime time for floating. Trips on the Kings of from 1 to 5 days are possible from the town of Marble to Table Rock Lake. And below Hwy. 62, water levels are sometimes sufficient for canoeing well into July. Sturdy-legged wade fishers can also get in on the action if they stay upstream of Hwy. 412 (Marble).

80. Oklahoma: Illinois River

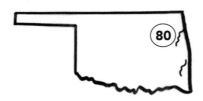

The Water: This beautiful river is popular with Oklahomans, but few outside the state have heard of it. The Illinois originates in Arkansas' Ozark foothills and flows into northeast Oklahoma near Watts. From Watts to Tenkiller Lake, the scenic Illinois is undammed for 70 miles, offering excellent floats past steep bluffs and forested banks. The Illinois' numerous, yet safe, Class II rapids make recreational canoeing popular.

The Fish: A great mixed-bass stream, the Illinois has good numbers of small-ies, along with spotted, largemouth and white bass. The Neosho strain smallies here don't grow large, so the Illinois is a numbers river, rather than a lunker hotspot. Stocking also maintains a fair trout fishery, especially below the Tenkiller Dam where the state record trout was caught.

Seasons, Flies, Special Tips: Because summer weekends are busy with youthful canoeists, spring and fall fishing is best. Early-season angling can start in April and the late season can extend through November. September is a particularly prime period. Targeting trout around fast water in the morning and smallies in eddies during late afternoon is a popular and productive strategy. Small poppers are consistent bronze producers well into fall. The upper river near the Arkansas line has the most scenic bluff land.

Access and Use: Over a dozen public accesses allow float fishers to plan trips ranging from half a day to a week long. Canoes, pontoon boats, jonboats and driftboats are all employed on the Illinois. During lower flow periods wade fishing is also productive. As Oklahoma's longest free-flowing scenic river, the Illinois sees considerable paddling and camping use during the summer, but much less during the "off" seasons. Larry Clark's **"On-the-Fly" guide service (onthefly@tah-usa.net)** offers Illinois River floats.

So much limestone, so many great streams. The Mid-South is full of limestone laden waterways, including creeks like this one.

81. Oklahoma: Mountain Fork River

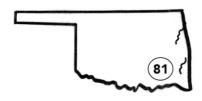

A small, beautiful stream in southeast Oklahoma's forested hill country, the upper reaches of the Mountain Fork River offers Ozark float fishing with fewer people. Upstream of Broken Bow Reservoir in McCurtain County, the Mountain Fork has over 20 miles of remote water.

Spring comes early this far south; April and May offer active smallies and enough flow to float a canoe. Low flows makes mid-summer canoeing very difficult, but water levels are often sufficient again in September and October. High catch rates plus 19-inchers are possible on the Mountain Fork, but clear water calls for longer casts and cautious approaches. Larger tributaries like Eagle Fork Creek also hold lots of fish, especially in the spring.

82. Texas: Devils River

Smallmouthing in the dessert! This southwest Texas stream may be the most southerly on the continent, and one of the few that flows through ruggedly beautiful dessert. Looping through Val Verde County to its terminus at Amistad Reservoir, the Devils is remote and access is limited due to few roads and most surrounding land being privately owned ranches. But its clear waters hold smallmouth up to 20 inches.

Slippery rocks and Class II and III rapids require good wading skills and may necessitate lining your canoe through some of the river's whitewater chutes. Trips should be carefully planned and organized, preferably with a guide service. Fishing the Devils River has its challenges, but hardy anglers will be rewarded with nice smallies, plus the experience of floating a wild and unique southern river during the winter, far from civilization.

27

The West

CALIFORNIA
83. Russian River
84. Feather River
85. North Fork American River

OREGON
86. Umpqua River
87. John Day River

WASHINGTON
88. Columbia River
89. Yakima River
90. Grande Ronde River

IDAHO
91. Snake River/Hells Canyon

ARIZONA
92. Black River

The West

Though it's far from the species' native range, the West now has some stunningly good smallmouth water. Numerous lower-elevation rivers are large, warm and slow enough to offer excellent smallmouth habitat. And as many of these rivers continue to warm due to human impacts such as damming, irrigation, development and global climate change, they'll likely become even more favorable for smallmouth.

In some of these watersheds smallies have been present for over a century, in others they are more recent arrivals. Old-timer or newbie, bronzebacks are prospering in many western rivers and lakes. Besides favorable habitat, being ignored by locals fixated on coldwater species has helped smallies grow large. For the traveling angler, the West now presents the opportunity for high quality smallmouth and trout combination trips.

83. California: Russian River

The Water: Some Californians still regard the smallmouth as a new immigrant, but in reality the species has been well-established in northern California for over a century. One smallie stronghold is the Russian River in the Napa Valley just north of San Francisco. The middle reaches of the river, flowing through what's often called Alexander Valley, is especially noteworthy. This 25-plus miles from Cloverdale down to Healdsburg is very bronzeback-friendly, with warm temperatures, a mild gradient, gravel bars, nice pools and wood cover.

The Fish: While the Russian isn't known for giant smallmouths, the numbers of feisty footers is good and 17-inchers are occasionally caught. The highest numbers are in the middle reaches, but smallies can also be found upstream of Cloverdale along Hwy. 101. Below the Healdsburg dam it's bigmouth and smallie combo water.

Seasons, Flies, Special Tips: June through September is the most consistent time on the Russian. Subsurface patterns worked around bank cover, such as overhanging bushes, is a consistent technique.

Access and Use: Fortunately, the Russian isn't nearly as crowded as more popular northern California steelhead rivers, and this is especially true during the summer months. However, private land limits bank access, so floating is the easiest way to fish the river. The river is easy to canoe and several launch sites are available between Cloverdale and Healdsburg.

84. California: Feather River

Due north of Sacramento, the Feather is regarded by some as the Golden State's top smallmouth river. The river has smallies from Lake Oroville all the way to its merger with the Sacramento River. Naturally, some areas are better than others. One prime stretch on the upper river is the Gridley Rd access down to the Live Oak Rd access. Other choice water is around the Verona Access near the Sacramento River. Floating is the best way to fish the Feather, but wading is also possible around the Gridley and Live Oak accesses.

Shifting sands annually alter the Feather's channel, so riprapped banks are the permanent hotspots. Summer topwatering is excellent, and standard subsurface techniques extend the smallmouth season into late fall. While lunkers are limited on the Feather, catch rates can be in the multi-dozen range during the prime summer period.

85. California: North Fork American River

This beauty runs along I-80 northeast of Auburn. Though fast-flowing, the river has numerous smallie-holding pools and eddies. While fly rodders can hook plenty of fish on the North Fork American, it would be a mistake to expect legions of lunkers. Smallmouth over 17 inches seem to be unusual specimens.

On-foot angling is excellent on the North Fork. A handy way to access the water upstream of Auburn is from a trail that runs along the river.

Public access points include Yankee Jim Rd and Ponderosa Way. Like other northern California smallmouth rivers, the summer months offer the easiest fishing. But those wishing to extend their smallmouth season can also score during colder months by employing the spring, fall or winter techniques described in Part 1 of this book.

86. Oregon: Umpqua River

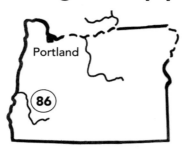

The Water: Smallmouth fishing is becoming so good in the Pacific Northwest that even trout purists are starting to see the light. The Umpqua River is a big reason for these conversions. From a stocking three decades ago, Micropterus dolomieui now inhabits 100 miles of the main stem, plus the lower reaches of the South Umpqua. The river offers stellar fishing from the junction of the north and south branches (near Roseburg) to the coast (near Reedsport). Beautiful rocky pools divided by short rapids, set in spectacular western scenery, makes the Umpqua a visual and piscatorial feast.

The Fish: The Umpqua is known for numbers, sometimes phenomenal numbers. Forty-fish days are common and even triple-digit catches can happen. Most of the smallmouth are under 13 inches, but the nonstop action will make you forget about the lack of lunkers.

Seasons, Flies, Special Tips: The fastest action occurs from mid-May through September. The warm water period of July and August is especially prime. The Umpqua's clear water generally means smaller flies do best. On-foot sight fishing is also possible in late summer. Try a Girdle Bug; its highly visible legs help you to see the strike when you drift/twitch the fly through a run.

Access and Use: The Umpqua has long been famous for its steelhead and salmon runs. However, summer isn't prime time for those species, so warm weather smallmouth fans won't have to contend with bank-to-bank drift boats. The lower 30 miles (below Elkton) is some of the best water and is accessible off Hwy. 38. Various boat landings are available along the river, and several guide services float the Umpqua for both smallies and cold water species.

87. Oregon: John Day River

Here's some superb fishing in the middle of nowhere. This north-central Oregon river is remote, but spectacular scenery and unbelievable smallmouthing make it well worth the pilgrimage. A high dessert tributary of the Columbia River, the John Day is protected by state "Wild and Scenic Rivers" status and has enormous numbers of smallmouth.

The river is undammed, and over 150 miles of it in Gilliam, Wheeler and Grant counties offers excellent fishing. Thirty- to 50-fish days are common, and while most fish are under 13 inches, the occasional 18-incher adds big fish excitement. The late May through July period offers the heaviest bite, with topwaters providing consistent action.

Numerous guide services using rafts or driftboats offer both overnight trips and single-day floats on the John Day. Multi-day floats are most popular on the more-isolated lower river. Do-it-yourself floats are also possible, if you have the proper watercraft and good boat handling skills. Upstream of Spray, highways 19 and 26 parallel the river and offer much easier access.

88. Washington: Columbia River

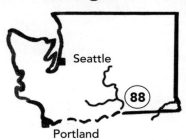

The Water: The Columbia is the second-largest river in the U.S. and the most famous in the West. Once the main artery for migrating trout and salmon, the Columbia now holds far fewer coldwater species, but many more of the warmwater variety, because of 9 blocking dams on the lower river. Smallmouth are especially abundant in the 275 miles from the Priest Rapids Dam down to the Bonneville dam near Portland.

The Fish: Many knowledgeable smallmouthers believe the Columbia offers some of the best "big bass" angling on the continent. Five-pound fish are regularly caught by jig and crankbait chuckers. A growing troop of fly anglers who have learned to handle the Columbia's size and winds are also hooking hefty fish.

Seasons, Flies, Special Tips: Pre-spawn action starts in early April, and good fishing continues into July. By late summer most large fish have moved deep. Slowly working a black rabbit-strip pattern is a tried-and-true technique. Sinking lines help to both cut the wind and reach deeper fish. Naturally, a larger motorized craft is best for fishing the wide (and often windy) main river. But during the early season, even float tubers and canoeists can catch smallies on this huge waterway by fishing the more-sheltered sloughs and backwaters off the main channel and targetting the riprap.

Access and Use: Numerous boat landings have been built on the lower Columbia. Some easy-access areas experience significant angling and boating use during summer. The most remote free-flowing section is the "Hanford Reach," downstream of Priest Rapids Dam. Numerous backwaters can be accessed off Hwy. 14 between Portland and McMary Dam. One helpful map is the **"River Cruising Atlas"** showing landings, depths, etc.

Expanding smallmouth populations and increasing sizes are making the West a prime destination for quality smallmouth fishing.

89. Washington: Yakima River

The Yak' is a seasonal sensation. During the spring and early summer the number of smallmouth in the lower Yakima swells to over 3,000 fish per mile. Beginning in early April, thousands of adult smallmouth leave the Columbia and move into the Yakima to spawn. The river's best fishing is from its confluence with the Columbia near Richland upstream 28 miles to the Wanawish Dam. Prime time is May, but April and June also offer excellent fishing. Thirty- and 40-fish days are common, with many smallies from 12 to 16 inches, but 20-inchers are also possible.

As a mid-sized river with no real rapids, the Yakima is easily floatable by canoe or drift boat. Accesses off Snively Rd, Twin Bridges and Duportail Rd are all undeveloped, making lightweight craft preferred. On-foot angling is also possible, especially between the Wanawish Dam and Benton City. A significant smallmouth fishery is also established in the 20 miles upstream of the Wanawish Dam to the Prosser Dam.

90. Washington: Grande Ronde River

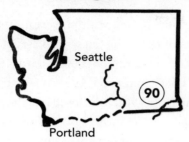

Here's some great smallie water that's little known. The Grande Ronde is a medium-sized tributary of the Snake River along the Washington/Oregon border. Once water warms in July, the river holds good numbers of smallmouth, especially in the 26 miles of river downstream of Hwy. 129. During warmer summers, smallmouth move upstream all the way to Troy, Oregon, offering a total of 60 miles of fishing. Fifteen-inchers are common in the lower Grande Ronde, and 18-inchers aren't rare. Rainbows and bull trout, as well as fall steelhead are also present, making combination trips a possibility.

Some Grand Ronde guides are now including smallies as one of the species they guide for. Non-guided floating is possible, too, though there is one major rapids 4 miles upstream of the mouth. One good 9-mile day-trip is from Hwy. 129 down to Shumaker Creek Access. The Shumaker access also gives on-foot anglers several miles of unposted river to fish. Mac Huff of **Eagle Cap Guide Service (machuff@oregontrail.net)** guides for smallies as well as coldwater species on the river.

91. Idaho: Snake River/Hells Canyon

The Water: It has an ominous name and is tough to get to, but Hell's Canyon is worth the effort. This rugged section of the mighty Snake is in Hell's Canyon National Recreation Area along the Oregon/Idaho border south of Lewiston. Besides tremendous fishing, a 2,000-foot-deep canyon, massive rapids and plentiful big game all make a trip to this portion of the Snake River a never-to-be-forgotten experience.

The Fish: Smallmouth fishing in the Snake has been notable for decades, and it remains so. Substantial numbers of smallies of all sizes, along with hefty trout, are the primary allure. There's great fishing from the Hells Canyon Dam downstream through the entire canyon. The Snake also has lots of smallies upstream to Payette, Idaho.

Seasons, Flies, Special Tips: Summer and early fall is the time for Snake smallmouth. However, river levels can vary widely from year to year based on snow and rainfall amounts. Most years, water temps have reached the 60s by June and smallies will take a variety of both subsurface and topwater patterns. Where currents are swift, quick-to-reach-bottom flies are best. In slack eddies and pockets, small poppers and divers produce well.

Access and Use: Because Hell's Canyon is interspersed with powerful rapids, guide services with huge jet-drive boats or rafts offer the easiest way to access the most remote reaches. However, limited on-foot access is also possible, such as from several small roads off Hwy. 95. Adventurous hikers can reach the river and will find good fishing. Walking the banks and casting from shoreline boulders is a good fishing method used by even some boat-equipped anglers who stop to fish. Many fly fishers annually travel to the mountain West in pursuit of trout; why not add a Snake River adventure to your next western trip?

92. Arizona: Black River

Some of Arizona may be dry desert, but the White Mountains just 2 hours east of Phoenix are practically a verdant paradise, with clear streams flowing through forests and steep canyons. One of the most noteworthy of these waters is the Black River, where smallmouth have swam for 60 years. In fact, the Black's abundant smallies, combined with a beautiful setting, makes it perhaps the best wading stream in the entire West.

The Black River offers nearly 70 miles of high-quality smallmouth water that is well off the beaten path. The stream is the boundary between the White Mountain and San Carlos Apache Reservations. Access to it requires a tribal fishing permit and a substantial drive with a high-clearance vehicle.

The stream can be accessed from Fort Apache south on Y10, Y20 or Y22. May through July period is the best time. Day trips are possible, but getting a camping permit and staying a night or two is a much easier and more enjoyable way to fish the river. Globe and Fort Apache are the two closest towns where lodging is available and permits may be obtained. **White Mountain Apache Reservation (520-338-4385).**

28

Canada

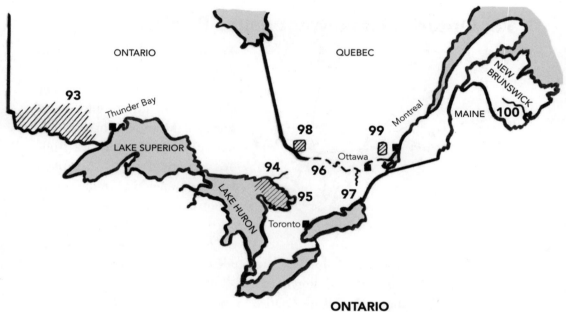

ONTARIO
93. Northwest Lakes Region
94. French River
95. Georgian Bay, Lake Huron
96. Ottawa River
97. Mississippi River

QUEBEC
98. Beauchene Reserve
99. Kenauk Preserve

NEW BRUNSWICK
100. St. John River

Canada

While much of Canada's vast northern reaches are too cold to support smallies, a sizable portion of southern Ontario, Quebec and New Brunswick has small-mouths. Much of this water is less than 150 miles from the US border, close to many Americans. Though Canadian smallmouth are very slow-growing, histori-cally low angling pressure allows the fish to reach excellent size. Hundreds of pris-tine Canadian lakes and rivers hold 18-inch-plus smallies, and most of these waters are lightly fished. Beautiful, uncrowded northwoods settings and high-jumping bronze—it's time to pack your bags, eh?

93. Ontario: Northwest Lakes Region

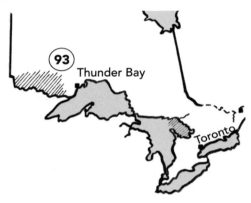

The Water: Until you see this area from the air, it's hard to imagine how many lakes there are. The chunk of northwest Ontario just north of Minnesota has literally hundreds of pristine, rock-stud-ded, forest-fringed, fish-filled bodies of water in a 5-million-acre region between Lake of the Woods on the west and Quetico Park on the east. The lakes range from 80 to 25,000 acres, and virtually all have a multitude of islands, bays and points—offering miles of wind-protected shorelines.

The Fish: Smallmouth, while not native to most of northwest Ontario, have been expanding in the area for decades; they now prosper in hundreds of lakes. Because of a focus on other species, plus lodges promoting catch-and-release there are many 17 inchers and increasing numbers of 20s. Some lakes also have a multi-tude of other species. In select places, you can even score a "Super Slam"—catching smallmouth, largemouth, pike, muskies, lake trout and walleyes on a fly, all in a single trip.

Seasons, Flies, Special Tips: Late May to late June and September are the times to find the smallies and the other species shallow and easy to reach with flies. Sight fishing spawning bass is possible in the spring. Pike over 20 pounds are also possi-ble and even lake trout can be caught shallow in the early spring. Topwater fishing is often excellent, and working streamers around downed trees will produce an assortment of species.

Access and Use: Numerous northwest Ontario lakes have drive-in access, but others are only accessible by float plane or boat. Naturally, the more remote waters have the least angling pressure. On many lakes there are well-run lodges, which often offer fishing on several small nearby lakes, as well as the lodge lake. These are truly wilderness angling experiences with all the comforts of home. A favorite of mine is Slippery Winds Resort on Yoke Lake. With hefty smallies, plus largemouth, muskies, pike, lake trout and walleyes, beautiful Yoke Lake is hard to beat. The **Smallmouth Angler.com** website describes these northwest Ontario fly fishing trips in more detail.

94. Ontario: French River

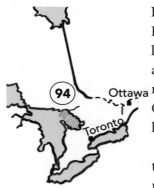

It's sort of a local secret. The 75-mile-long French River is actually a series of beautiful island-studded lakes that is relatively easy to access, yet it's uncrowded and holds a diverse fish population. The French drains mighty Lake Nipissing and flows into Lake Huron's Georgian Bay. Much of the river and its connected lakes are in French River Provincial Park.

Most of the lakes, and the flowing water between them, hold sizable smallmouth along with big pike, muskies, lake trout and walleyes. As in much of Ontario, the smallies are overlooked by local anglers in favor of species they regard as better eating. The system is best fished with small motor boats, which can be rented in the area. Accesses include the town of French River off Hwy. 69 and Wolseley Bay off Hwy. 528.

95. Ontario: Georgian Bay, Lake Huron

Of all the hot Great Lakes smallmouth hotspots, this may be the most overlooked. While Georgian Bay has long been regarded as a prime destination for other warm and coldwater species, nowadays smallmouth numbers and sizes have both improved there. Good numbers of thick-shouldered fish can be found on many of the points and shoals of the bay. Some of the best water is from Midland (on Seven Sound) north to Parry Sound. While only a slice of Lake Huron, this area includes thousands of acres of small bays, islands, points and channels. A boat is required, but with so much protected water, careful anglers can get by with standard-sized lake craft.

Much of the shoreline is protected by provincial or national park designation. Shallow-water angling is possible during the spawn, but full-sink lines are best during most of the season. Those willing to explore and work the 20-foot depths can find concentrations of big fish. A floating fly (like a Foam Diver or Balsa Minnow) on a sinking line can be very effective for offshore smallmouth.

96. Ontario: Ottawa River

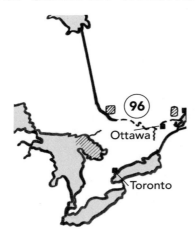

One of eastern Canada's most historic rivers, the Ottawa nowadays serves as the Ontario/Quebec border. A large waterway, it is also the site of the country's capital city bearing the same name. In fact, few other major metropolitan areas offer such good river fishing as the city of Ottawa does. Smallmouth are numerous between parliament and the prime minister's residence, brown trout are common at the Des Chenes rapids area, and big pike are regular catches at the west end of the city in weedy Shirley's Bay.

Outside of the capital, the Ottawa River offers even better fishing, with excellent largemouth populations in the 75 miles of lily pads and wood downstream to the Carillion Dam. Husky smallmouth haunt the faster-flowing sections of river. The Rockland to Hawesbury area has good potential, and on the upper river the section from Mattawa down to Point Alexander is worth trying. Mid- and late-summer fishing is the prime time.

97. Ontario: Mississippi River

No, not that river. This Mississippi is an Ottawa River tributary in southeast Ontario. Though it's accessible by road in many places, this 50-mile-long river still offers wooded beauty, uncrowded conditions and excellent angling for smallmouth, largemouth and pike.

The upper river near Hwy. 509 is actually a series of fishy lakes. These lakes, including 9-mile-long Crotch Lake, have plenty of smallies, as well as lodges, boats and other facilities. The lower Mississippi from Appleton to Galetta is a big river, best fished by watercraft. It contains lots of wood, lily pads and other fish cover that is excellent habitat for both bronzebacks and bigmouths.

And don't scoff at Ontario largemouth before you catch a few. Although in many American waters largemouth fight noticeably less than the mighty smallmouth, it seems that Canadian bucketmouths fight nearly as hard as smallies. I've caught hundreds of chunky 17- to 20-inch largemouth from Canadian waters, and often their spirited battle rivals the smallie's.

98. Quebec: Beauchene Reserve

Though La Reserve Beauchene (as it's called in French) is a little smaller than Kenauk Preserve, it has just as much smallmouth water. There are 14 smallmouth lakes nestled in its 50,000 acres along with 2 dozen other lakes supporting huge brook trout, pike, splake and lake trout. Beauchene is a northwoods fishing reserve along the Quebec/Ontario border, an hour east of North Bay, Ontario. Massive smallies over 5 pounds are caught annually, and early-summer anglers regularly release quantities of fish over 17 inches. With all the other species also available, it's easy to plan a successful combination trip. Spring trips targeting brookies over 3 pounds are especially popular.

The main lake (Lac Beauchene) is over 12 miles long and offers huge smallies along with other species. Some of the smallest and most remote lakes are reserved for fly fishing only. Boats are available for all waters. Beauchene is a private concession that offers complete services, including American Plan lodging and housekeeping cabins. The Reserve is also committed to maintaining its high quality fishing with catch-and-release and barbless-only rules. **Beauchene Reserve info: 888-627-3865.**

Wilderness lakes and rivers, where outsized bronzebacks like this roam, are common in Canada.

99. Quebec: Kenauk Preserve

This 65,000-acre parcel in southern Quebec is an angler's dream. Kenauk, just north of the Ottawa River and near the town of Montebello, is a private preserve that offers excellent fishing and accommodations at very reasonable prices. It contains over 70 lakes and one river. Trout are regularly stocked in many lakes to cater to the majority of anglers who are coldwater-oriented, but the native smallies swim unmolested in numerous lakes. Some of these smallmouth waters are just 100-acre gems, while the largest, Lake Papineau, is several thousand acres.

Montebello Lodge serves the Preserve, and several lakes also have rental cottages. Small boats are placed on many of the smaller lakes, and the number of anglers per lake is carefully regulated to prevent crowding. Fishing for both smallies and largemouth is good all season. If the Kinonge River and the lakes inside Kenauk aren't enough, the bass-filled Ottawa River is adjacent and easily accessible. **Kenauk Preserve info: 800-567-6845.**

100. New Brunswick: St. John River

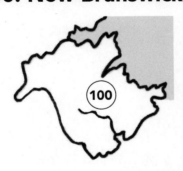

Bordering Maine, southern New Brunswick seems more like New England rather than the Canadian northwoods. Flowing through this bucolic setting is the St. John River, one of eastern Canada's best waterways for smallmouth. Originating in Maine, the St. John is more fertile than many northern rivers, hence it supports more smallies. It is also impounded in places, offering excellent lake habitat, especially for larger smallmouth.

Early summer is especially good on the lake stretches, but fine fish can also be caught all summer long on the riverine portions of the St. John. The river passes through Fredericton on it way to the Bay of Fundy. The Bay warrants a side trip to see its 30-foot tides, some of the highest in the world.

Those with their own lake boats can effectively fish the St. John's impoundments or hire someone to shuttle them for the riverine portions. Guides are also available, and though they may not be fly-fishing-savvy, they can put you on fish.

Appendix A: Resources and Contacts

Arkansas
Game & Fish Commission
(agfc.state.ar.us)

California
Dept of Fish & Game (dfg.ca.gov)

Connecticut
Bureau of Natural Resources
(dep.ct.us)

Idaho
Dept of Fish & Game
(fishandgame.idaho.gov)

Illinois
Dept of Natural Resources
(dnr.state.il.us)

Indiana
Dept. of Natural Resources
(in.gov/dnr)

Iowa
Dept. of Natural Resources
(iowadnr.com)

Kentucky
Dept. of Fish & Wildlife (fw.ky.gov)

Maine
Dept. of Inland Fisheries
(state.me.us/ifw)

Maryland
Department of Natural Resources
(dnr.state.md.us)

Massachusetts
Dept of Fish & Game (mass.gov/dfele)

Michigan
Dept of Natural Resources
(michigan.gov/dnr)

Minnesota
Dept. of Natural Resources
(dnr.state.mn.us)

Missouri
Dept. of Conservation
(conservation.state.mo.us)

New Brunswick
Dept of Natural Resources—Fish &
Wildlife (gnb.ca/0078/fw)

New Hampshire
Fish and Game Dept.
(wildlife.state.nh.us)

New Jersey
Division of Fish & Wildlife
(state.nj.us/dep/fgw)

New York
Bureau of Fisheries (dec.state.ny.us)

North Carolina
Inland Fisheries Division
(nc.wildlife.org/fs)

Ohio
Division of Wildlife (dnr.state.oh.us)

Oklahoma
Dept. of Wildlife Conservation
(wildlifedepartment.com/fishing)

Ontario
Ministry of Nat. Resources—Fish &
Wildlife (mnr.gov.on.ca/MNR)

Oregon
Dept of Fish & Wildlife
(dfw.state.or.us/ODFW)

Pennsylvania
Fish & Boat Commission
(sites.state.pa.us/fish)

Quebec
Ministry of Natural Resources
(mrn.gouv.qc.ca/english)

South Dakota
Game, Fish & Parks Dept
(sdgfp.info/Wildlife/Fishing)

Tennessee
Wildlife Resources Agency
(state.tn.twra)

Texas
Parks and Wildlife Dept.
(tpwd.state.tx.us)

Vermont
Agency of Natural Resources
(anr.state.vt.us/fs)

Virginia
Dept of Game & Inland Fisheries
(dgif.virginia.gov/fishing)

Washington
Division of Aquatic Resources
(dnr.wa.gov)

West Virginia
Division of Natural Resources
(wvdnr.gov/fishing)

Wisconsin
Bureau of Fisheries (dnr.state.wi.us)

NATIONAL RESOURCES

US Chamber of Commerce
Member Directory (uschamber.com)

United States Geological Survey
Real-Time Water Data
(waterdata.gov/nwis/rt)

Smallmouth Angler
Smallmouth Fishing Information
(smallmouthangler.com)

The Smallmouth Alliance
(smallmouth.org)

Trout Unlimited
(tu.org)

Federation of Fly Fishers
(fedflyfishers.org)

Appendix B: List of Contributors

A great many people contributed in various ways to this book, and I want to offer each a hardy and heartfelt "thank you." Here are some of the individuals who helped me . . . (sorry if I left some out).

Eric Altena
Midwestern Biologist

Tom Andersen
Umpqua Fly Co. Rep

Greg Breining
Writer & Editor

Jay Bunke
Smallmouth Angler
Fly Tier

Larry Clark
Oklahoma guide

Greg Coffey
Illinois Fly Tier

Dennis Dauble
Fisheries Biologist

Jerry Darkes
Ohio Writer

Pat Ehlers
Fly Shop Owner
and Guide

Ken Faver
Indiana Angler

Steve Flint
New York Guide

Mike Furtman
Minnesota Writer

Mike Griffith
Guiding Client

Bob Geibe
Pennsylvania Fly Tier

Jim Hauer
Wisconsin Boat Builder

Tom Helgeson
Midwest Fly Fishing
Publisher

Mark Hoffmeyer
Smallmouth Alliance
Officer

Mac Huff
Oregon Guide

Bruce Ingram
Virginia Writer

Dan Johnson
Smallmouth Angler
Fly Tier

Mike Kelly
New York Writer

Roger LaPentar
Wisconsin Guide

Bob Long Jr.
Illinois Fly Tier

Frank McKane
Outdoor Writer

Geoffrey McMichael
Fisheries Biologist

Bruce Miller
Wildlife Artist

Ross Mueller
Book Author

Bob Nasby
Minnesota Casting
Instructor

Curt Nordrum
Fly Tier

Bill Olexa
Connecticut Writer

Ron Nelson
Artist and Illustrator

Ray Ottulich
New York Guide

Craig Reindeau
Georgia Fly Tier

Arlin Schlekamp
Fisheries Biologist

Dennis Schmidt
Magazine Editor

Jim Swenson
Guiding Client

Ed Vaughn
Kentucky Angler

Martin Wood
Texas Book Publisher

Index

More Praise for *Smallmouth Fly Fishing*

"I own numerous fishing books. This excellent volume should be listed in the same sentence as many classics, including books by Lefty Kreh."
　　　—Kenneth Hartmann, Chicago, IL

I'm a trout fly fishing guide, with an addiction for smallmouth that will never be satisfied. This book is filled with colossal amounts of useful information that will help me. It's just what I'm looking for."
　　　—Ramsey Romanin, Edwards, CO

"Fantastic book—lively, well written, hugely informative. Superb."
　　　—Ray Cox, Roanoke, VA

"Just wanted to let you know how much I enjoyed and learned from your book. It's been a big help in my success at catching smallies."
　　　—Dave Rosset, Des Moines, IA

"Amazing! One of the most informative books I've ever read for any species"
　　　—Tryg Sarsland, Springfield, NJ

"Wow! What a fabulous book, the best fishing book I have ever seen. Needless to say, I need a five more copies as gifts."
　　　—Dr. Karl Glander, Greenwood, IN

"Great job! I just wish you had left a few secrets for us dedicated bass buggers."
　　　—Colby Sorrells, Mansfield, TX

"It's classic Holschlag writing—very comprehensive, fun to read, full of facts and no BS."
　　　—Kurt Sleighter, Minnetonka, MN

"Being new to fly fishing, this book is the best investment I have made."
　　　—Brad Himes, Crawfordsville, IN

"A great book for those of us addicted to fly fishing for smallmouth bass."
　　　—Bob Baily, Irmo, SC

"I have several smallmouth books, some by famous authors. Yours is far better than any of them."
　　　—Jim Simons, Louisville, KY

"I read your book cover to cover and really enjoyed it. Your debunking old wisdom on smallmouths is very well done."
　　　—Warren Phillips, Woodbine, MD

"I have seen the few books that have been written on fly fishing for smallmouth bass. For my money, Tim's new book is the best of the lot."
　　　—Dan Kreher, Ellisville, MO

"I counted the fly fishing books in my library at over 100, yet your this book is the one I would keep if forced to choose one."
　　　—Jay Bunke, Rochester, MN

"Splendid book! Amazingly comprehensive, Bravo! I had paged through a copy a friend-of-a-friend had, and just that alone got me onto some fish—I scored an 18"—my best flyrod smallmouth ever. A week later it came into my local flyshop and I snapped it up! Now that I've re-read the book, with certain passages literally dozens of times (fun to read!) I feel really confidant with the new retrieves and the terrific fly patterns."
　　　—Rob Hoffhines, Wilmette, IL

"Excellent book! I wish more writers would show the reverence and passion and details of technique that you show, rather than speaking about some new piece of equipment all of the time."
　　　—Nathan Johnson, Stewartville, MN

More Praise for *Smallmouth Fly Fishing*

"My wife gave me the book for Christmas. It was my best present, and I can hardly put it down."
 —Danny Schieffler, Fort Smith, AK

"Here is a photo of a fish from the Shiawasse—20+ inches of pure river smallmouth—that I caught doing the Hop you teach in the book. This is a killer technique. Accounts for probably 90% of my smallmouths. I have been using the HHF (from the book) with some great success. I love the fly."
 —John Biehn

"I live in Maryland and fish the Susquehanna River. The book really hit home with me and I found it meshed with a lot of the observations I have had while pursuing smallmouth with spin fishing gear."
 —Dave Stine, Conowingo, MD

"I read the book, applied some of your suggestions, and landed a really nice 18- to 19-inch pre-spawn smallie."
 —John Callaci, Westchester, IL

"I'm impressed. I'm half way through it the second time and I fully intend to read it a third time too! For the last 10 years I've done all of my bass fishing with a fly rod."
 —Steve Root, St. Paul, MN

"Wow! What a great book. I'm really impressed with the color pages, the thorough discussion of gear, the fishing techniques, and the great smallie destinations."
 —Greg Kozak, Lansing, MI

"Thanks for the lovely book."
 —Glenda Zalunardo, Winchester, OR

"Tim, your new book is GREAT! Just finished reading it. Everything about it is perfect."
 —Chris Reynolds, Clarkesville, IN

"Thank you for sharing your knowledge and passion about smallmouths. The book has definitely made me a much better smallie fisherman in a very short order of time.
 —Robin Hill, Alaska fishing guide, NY

"Wonderful book! "
 —Nelson Ham, Green Bay, WI

"It's the best book yet written on the subject. I've been fly fishing for 50 years".
 —Bob Goldfarb, Rutgers Univerity, NJ

"Fantastic book; I have given it as a gift to several friends who've been equally pleased."
 —Mitch Faddis, St. Louis, MO

"I just finished the book and really loved it. I can't wait to get out on a stream and try some of the new techniques."
 —James Lord, Minneapolis, MN

"Wonderful book. You can really tell that you have a true passion for this wonderful gamefish!" —Steve Delisi, Marine on St. Croix, MN

"Your knowledge on smallmouth fly fishing surpasses any other author I have read."
 —Kevin Lunde, Coeur d' Alene, ID

"I love your book, *Smallmouth Fly Fishing.*"
 —John Morresi, Fairfield, CT

"This book is chocked full of useful information and delivered in a gorgeously pleasing format. In fact, reading it was like wading or floating a river with Tim . . . surprises and experimentation around every bend (turn of the page) yet all the while down to earth and fun to read. Well done!!!"
 —Jay Bunke

More Praise for *Smallmouth Fly Fishing*

"I Love it !!!"
—Kelly Chambers, Muncie, IN

"Wonderfully written. It is a great educational tool for an avid fly fisher like me".
—Constance Whiston,
fly-fishing guide, Springfield, MO

"Beyond impressive. Tremendous!"
—Joe Bednar, Battle Creek, MI

"Thanks for your superb book!"
—Richard Berke, Columbia, MD

"Your book is the only thing my husband wants for Christmas"
—Kerry Franke, Cincinnati, OH

"A great new book by Tim Holschlag. I recommend you buy it before it sells out and you have to pay premium prices to out of print booksellers, like with his first book."
—Clyde Drury, editor,
The Smallmouth Bookshelf

"Never have I read a more put-together book than yours. I have fished and hunted my whole life and just picked up a flyrod last year. I'm 44 and love it. I have read a lot of fishing books, but yours is the best bar none. I fished smallies a long time and your book broke a lot of myths."
—Scott Meier, Springfield, MO

"*Smallmouth Fly Fishing* is wonderful. I have been sooooo deeply hooked on fly fishing for bass since I was 12 years old that, at 43, I know I will never be released from this addiction."
—David Pickering, Toronto, Ontario

"Excellent compendium of the smallmouth species. I have recommended this book to many of my friends."
—Robert Bays, Little Rock, AK

"Great book! I had been reading Harry Murray's book and the *In-Fisherman* smallmouth book. Your book is dramatically more informative."
—Dan Anderson, Eagle River, WI

"I am impressed."
—Dr. P.V. Hakes, McCall, ID

"Thanks so much for writing this book! It's great. I live near the Susquehanna River in NE Pennsylvania, and have been fishing for smallmouth on the fly rod for 7 or 8 years."
—Dave Shane, Shickshinny, PA

"Thanks for your book, I'm enjoying all of it."
—Claude Hammersmith, Kay Largo, FL

"Very nice. Great content, laid out well, good pictures. I'm sure it will do well."
—Jerry Darkes, author,
Guide Patterns for Smallmouth Bass

"Imagine my surprise! I didn't know you were writing a new book, much less an encyclopedia! For a whole hour, I sat without moving, just reading through all the different categories and looking at the pictures. I can't believe how valuable it is. I am terribly impressed. This is a "must-acquire.""
—Marianne Michael, Hills, IA

"Tim Holschlag put his heart and soul into this book, and it clearly shows. I will cherish and enjoy it."
—Mark Hoffmeyer, Marion, MN

"Great work. A seasoned smallie angler like me learned a few new tricks."
—Craig Amacker, owner, Fontana Sports

"Very nice smallmouth book. The float and fly technique really works in the fall on deep slow pool tailouts. I also like the hi-tail crawfish pattern."
—David Hansen

Book Order Form

Get *Smallmouth Fly Fishing* for a Friend !

SPECIAL 10% DISCOUNT — ONLY **$26.95** (RETAIL $29.95)

> • Order by phone: 612-781-3912
> • Order online: **www.smallmouthangler.com**

SHIP TO:

Name _____

Address _____

City_____ State_____

Zip _____

E-mail_____

Phone_____

AUTHOR AUTOGRAPH:

_____

PAYMENT: ❑ Check enclosed

❑ MasterCard   ❑ VISA   ❑ Discover

Card #_____

Exp. date: _____ Signature: _____

PLEASE SEND:

_____ Books x $26.95 each: $_____

Shipping and handling:

first book, $4.95: $_____

_____ add'l books $2.00 ea.: $_____

SUBTOTAL: $_____

Minnesota Res add 6.5% tax: $ _____

($2.07 for 1 book)

($1.88 each add'l book)

TOTAL: $_____

SMALLMOUTH ANGLER

2309 Grand St. NE

Minneapolis, MN 55418